An OPUS book

Hinduism

OPUS General Editors

Walter Bodmer
Christopher Butler
Robert Evans
John Skorupski

OPUS books provide concise, original, and authoritative introductions to a wide range of subjects in the humanities and sciences. They are written by experts for the general reader as well as for students.

R. C. ZAEHNER

Hinduism

Oxford   New York

OXFORD UNIVERSITY PRESS

Oxford University Press, Walton Street, Oxford OX2 6DP

Oxford New York Toronto
Delhi Bombay Calcutta Madras Karachi
Petaling Jaya Singapore Hong Kong Tokyo
Nairobi Dar es Salaam Cape Town
Melbourne Auckland

and associated companies in
Berlin Ibadan

Oxford is a trade mark of Oxford University Press

ISBN 0–19–888012–X

© *Oxford University Press 1962, 1966*

First published 1962
Second edition published as an Oxford University Press paperback 1966
Reprinted 1984, 1985 (twice), 1987, 1988, 1990, 1992

Printed in Great Britain by
Biddles Ltd
Guildford and King's Lynn

Contents

Note on Transliteration and Pronunciation   vi

Introduction   1

1 Veda   14

2 Brahman   36

3 Moksha   57

4 God   80

5 Dharma   102

6 Bhakti   125

7 Encounter   147

8 Yudhishthira returns   170

Bibliography   193

Index   201

Note on Transliteration and Pronunciation

So far as possible diacritical marks except the long sign (⁻) have been avoided and the latter has been omitted in such well-known names as Gandhi (for Gāndhī). There remain only ṁ, ṛ, and ś. ṁ represents the nasalization of the preceding vowel, ṛ was originally a vowel but now approximates to *ri*, while ś is a sibilant half-way between English *s* and *sh*, being rather nearer to the latter. No distinction has been made between the different *l*s in Tamil (*l*, *ḷ*, and *ḻ*), nor has the series of 'cerebrals' in Sanskrit (*ṭ*, *ḍ*, *ṭh*, *ḍh*, *ṇ*) been differentiated from the pure dentals (*t*, *d*, *th*, *dh*, *n*).

C is pronounced as English *ch* in 'church', the remaining consonants as in English. The vowels are similar to those of Italian. Apart from *sh* pronounced as in English the *h* of the aspirated consonants proper (*kh*, *gh*, *ch*, *jh*, *th*, *dh*, *ph*, *bh*) is clearly heard as in such English words as 'dog-house', 'pothole', 'mad-house', and 'top-heavy'. *Th* is never pronounced as in English.

To Charles Monteith

Introduction

'HINDU' is a Persian word: it means simply 'Indian'. Hinduism is thus the '-ism' of the Indian people. The suffix '-ism' is rarely affixed to the name of a people, and the only examples that readily come to mind are 'Hellenism' and 'Judaism', the first denoting a way of life and the second a national religion. Which is the more apposite and the more true in the case of Hinduism? Sir Sarvepalli Radhakrishnan who has devoted much of his life to interpreting his country's religion and culture to the Anglo-Saxon world entitled one of his books *The Hindu Way of Life*, not *The Hindu Religion*, and this would imply that to him at least Hinduism was a 'Hellenism' rather than a 'Judaism', a way of life characteristic of a whole people, an intangible though none the less real national ethos rather than a religion in the Western sense of the word, that is, obedience to a revelation believed to be God-given and the worship of God in accordance with the content of that revelation. Judaism is, in addition, also a rigorous and refined system of God-given *law*.

Hinduism is, in fact, both a Hellenism and a Judaism: it is both a way of life and a highly organized social and religious system, but unlike Judaism, the essence of which is submission to the One God who is personal, transcendent, and holy, who reveals himself in history and acts in history, Hinduism is quite free from any dogmatic affirmations concerning the nature of God, and the core of religion is never felt to depend on the existence or non-existence of God, or on whether there is one God or many; for it is perfectly possible to be a good Hindu whether one's personal views incline towards monism, monotheism, polytheism, or even atheism. This is not what ultimately matters. If, then, God or the gods are not central to this strange complex of beliefs, what is?

The Hindus themselves call their religion the *sanātana dharma*, 'eternal *dharma*'. And here, at the very outset of our inquiry, we are faced with the difficulty of finding an adequate translation for words embodying concepts that elude precise definition. No word is more important or more omnipresent in the sacred texts, yet these very texts warn us time and time again that this *dharma* is 'subtle' and 'very difficult to know'. Indeed it is the very ambivalence of this key concept that both gives to Hinduism its distinctive flavour and sets up within it a tension that is never wholly resolved.

The word *dharma* is used in two distinct general senses in the great Hindu texts. It means first what is set down in the sacred texts themselves, and particularly in the texts dealing with Hindu customary law. In this usage it corresponds approximately to what we call 'canon law', a 'law' that is clearly defined, refined, and ever more minutely explained in the legal treatises themselves. By extension it is used to represent the religious assumptions on which these laws are based. *Dharma* in this sense is not at all 'difficult to know', for it is formulated at enormous length throughout the huge corpus of Hindu sacred literature, and is therefore, in its broadest connotation, best translated as 'religion'. It is, then, both 'law' and 'religion'.

'Law' and 'religion' are, however, only expressions of something far more fundamental, and that is the eternal law that governs all human and non-human existence, what we would understand by 'natural law': and it is this law that is 'subtle' and almost impossible to know. In the natural order there is no difficulty, for it means no more than the laws that operate in nature and are nowadays the subject-matter of the natural sciences. But how do things stand in the moral order?

Etymologically the word *dharma* derives from a root *dhṛ-* meaning 'to hold, have, or maintain'—the same root from which are derived the Latin *firmus*, 'firm', and *forma*, 'form'. *Dharma* is, then, the 'form' of things as they are and the power that keeps them as they are and not otherwise. And just as it maintains the whole universe in being in accordance with eternal law (*sanātana dharma*), so, in the moral sphere, does it maintain the human race by eternal moral law. But here a dilemma creeps in, for law exists on two levels: on the one hand it is written down in the sacred texts, on the other it is inscribed in the hearts and consciences of men. Sometimes the two exist side by side in harmony, sometimes there is tension and conflict.

Hinduism is a vast and apparently incoherent religious complex, and any writer on Hinduism who accepts the Hindus' own definition of their religion as *sanātana dharma*, 'eternal *dharma*', must make up his mind which of the two aspects of *dharma* he considers important to emphasize. And here he too is in a dilemma, for if he tries to compress the whole of Hinduism's 4,000 odd years of history into some 200 pages, the reader will be utterly confused by a mass of apparently self-contradictory detail and will fail to descry that which is eternal and un-changing in this *dharma* he is studying. If, however, he picks out and etches in high relief what seems to him to be the essence of this subtle something so 'difficult to know', he may well be —and rightly—accused of presenting a picture of Hinduism that is neither scholarly nor objective. He must choose between producing a catalogue or school textbook which will give the student the maximum number of facts within a very limited compass, or he will attempt, at his peril, to distil from the whole mass of his material the fine essence that he considers to be the changeless ground from which the proliferating jungle that seems to be Hinduism grows. This is the course the present writer proposes to follow for reasons that will very soon become apparent.

Hindus sometimes pride themselves, with some truth, that their religion is free from dogmatic assumptions, and that, this being so, their record in the matter of religious persecution is relatively clear. They do not think of religious truth in dogmatic terms: dogmas cannot be eternal but only the transitory, dis-torting, and distorted images of a truth that transcends not only them but all verbal definition. For the passion for dogmatic certainty that has racked the religions of Semitic origin from Judaism itself, through Christianity and Islam, to the Marxism of our day, they feel nothing but shocked incomprehension. This large tolerance and this antipathy to 'creedal' religion as such was noticed by the first Muslim to make a thorough study of the phenomenon of Hinduism at a time when Islam was making its first sanguinary incursions into India. Writing in the eleventh century A.D., Al-Bīrūnī, the great Muslim encyclopaedist wrote:

They [the Hindus] totally differ from us in religion, as we believe in nothing in which they believe, and vice versa. On the whole there is very little disputing about theological topics among themselves; at the utmost, they fight with words, but they will never stake their soul or body or their property on religious controversy.

This is broadly speaking true, but the absence of dogma in Hinduism can be over-emphasized; for there are certain presuppositions in post-Vedic Hinduism which are rarely, if ever, disputed. The chief of these is the doctrine of the transmigration of souls or rebirth which all sects and all philosophical schools accept as not so much a revealed dogma as a self-evident fact of existence. This doctrine itself presupposes the further doctrine that the condition into which the individual soul is reborn is itself the result of good or bad actions performed in former lives; and these actions and the modifications they produce in the myriad sum-total of ever-reincarnating souls from eternity without beginning to eternity without end themselves constitute the stuff of the moral as distinct from the natural universe. Yet no hard and fast distinction can be made between the two, for the same ineluctable law of cause and effect rules both. This is the law of *karma* ('action'), the law according to which any action whatsoever is the effect of a cause and is in its turn the cause of an effect. The whole process goes by the name of *saṁsāra*, the 'course' or 'revolution' to which all phenomenal existence is subject, and which is itself subject to and conditioned by an endless causal past, the *dharma* of the universe.

To this *dharma* there is neither beginning nor end, neither for the sum-total of existence (the macrocosm) nor for the individual soul (the microcosm): everything is in bondage to the fetters of Time and the fetters of desire—the desire above all to live and the desire to do (*karma* = doing). Time itself is a revolving wheel returning ever again to the point from which it started, and in it there can be neither purpose nor salvation. So much is taken for granted by very nearly all the Hindu sects and philosophical schools, and all of them find their common presuppositions profoundly unsatisfactory and disquieting.

This being so, it is the aim of each and all of them to escape from the wheel of Time and of action which is itself conditioned by Time, but that such an escape is possible is affirmed by all: it is called *moksha* or *mukti*, and is variously translated as 'escape, release, liberation, or emancipation'. It is not unlike what we in the West call the freedom of the Spirit. The manner in which this blessed state can be achieved—whether it can be achieved by the individual's own unaided efforts, or whether he must rely on the grace and assistance of a higher power—and the nature of the condition of the soul that has fought itself free from the fetters of Time and the desire to live on in time, these are matters about which the Hindus differed profoundly among themselves, however much some of them may try to blur the distinctions now. On three basic assumptions, however, they are all at one, namely (i) that the universe is governed by cyclic Time, (ii) that the individual soul as microcosm is governed by the same law of cause and effect as is the macrocosm, and (iii) that release from this constantly changing form of existence is ultimately possible for all.

The reader will now be familiar with four technical terms that will be constantly recurring throughout this book—*dharma*, *moksha*, *samsāra*, and *karma*. There is one more which it may be convenient to introduce at this point: and that is *brahman*.

This term will form the subject-matter of our second chapter, and a proper understanding of it will lead to a proper understanding of Hinduism as a whole, for 'classical' Hinduism, the basic presuppositions of which we have baldly outlined above, is also called 'Brahmanism', the religion of *brahman*: and *brahman* can either mean the eternal substrate of the universe from which the 'eternal' *dharma* proceeds, or it can mean the spiritual prerogative of the Brāhman caste which is the cornerstone on which the whole Hindu social edifice was built. There is, then, a causal link between the eternal *brahman* which is the ground of all existence and the Brāhman caste, and it is for this reason that the Brāhmans were regarded as gods upon earth. We shall have to return to this relationship in a later chapter: for the moment we must confine ourselves to the term *brahman* alone.

In the earliest texts *brahman* can be roughly equated with 'the sacred'—sacred formula, sacred chant, sacred action. Later, since the 'sacred' as manifested in ritual was felt to be the bond that linked temporal man with what is eternal, it came to be used to represent both the eternal as it is in itself beyond space and time and as it manifests itself in the phenomenal world. It is, therefore, in the terminology of classical Hinduism, both the *state* that is natural to the liberated soul (*moksha*) and the source from which all phenomenal existence derives its being; it is the link between the world of *samsāra* which is conditioned by space and time, cause and effect, and *moksha* which transcends all four: it is both eternal Being and the unchanging source of all change. It is *moksha* and it is the 'eternal' *dharma* too, for this *dharma* is the law which both has its roots in the eternal and governs the world of *samsāra* made up, as it is, of the numberless individual *karmas* or actions of individual men.

Brahman—dharma—moksha—samsāra—karma: these are the key concepts of classical Hinduism. None of them corresponds at all to what we call God, and it was not without reason, then, that Al-Bīrūnī, the great Muslim polymath who had made a thorough study of Hinduism in the original Sanskrit, declared that the Hindus 'differ totally from us in religion, as we believe in nothing in which they believe and vice versa'; for Islam, against the background of which Al-Bīrūnī wrote, was itself a branch sprung from the Judaic stem for which the whole of religion was summed up in awed obedience to One holy and transcendent God who was totally other than all he had created. For the Hinduism with which Al-Bīrūnī made contact the nature of God and even his very existence were matters of secondary importance.

Historically Hinduism may be divided conventionally and conveniently into four distinct periods. The earliest of these, of which the principal literary monument is the Rig-Veda, is frankly polytheist and clearly akin to the religions of other Indo-European nations. This then develops into a pantheistic monism in which the All is seen to be centred on the One or is wholly identified with the One: in its extreme form the individual human soul is identified with the Absolute. In effect this means that the gods are dethroned and the human soul is set up in their place. This is the form of Hinduism recently revived both in India itself and far beyond her borders in the Western world which lays all its stress on *moksha*, the liberation of the human soul from time, space, and matter. This, for many, constitutes the highest religious truth of which all forms of religion, both Hindu and otherwise, are but imperfect and impermanent manifestations.

The third phase, which is perhaps the most important, is the development within Hinduism of strong monotheistic trends on the one hand and the crystallization and ossification of the caste system on the other. Preoccupation with the liberation of the soul from the bondage of time and matter gives way to a rapt adoration of God, that is to say, of the great traditional gods, Vishnu and Śiva, now regarded by their devotees as the supreme Reality and absolute Lord. This religion of loving devotion or *bhakti* became the real religion of the mass of the people and has remained so ever since. It was not easy to fit into the general scheme of classical Hinduism with its almost deterministic view of the phenomenal world and its stress on *moksha* as the final end of man. How it was done we shall see in the sequel.

It has too often been said that Hinduism as such regards the world as an illusion. This has never been true of Hinduism as a whole but only of one (though at present predominant) school of Vedānta philosophy which is itself only one among six philosophical schools: it has never been true of the sacred writings themselves nor of popular religion. Nevertheless it is true to say that there is and, except in the very earliest period, always has been a double tension within the Hindu religion— the striving after liberation from this world which all admit to be the final goal of man on the one hand and man's obligation to do what is right *in* this world on the other, the tension between *moksha* and *dharma*—and in the second instance the tension of two types of *dharma*, the *sanātana dharma* or absolute moral order which can never be precisely defined yet is felt to have absolute validity, and the *dharma* of caste and canon law as laid down in the various law-books. These tensions are most plainly exhibited in India's Great Epic, the *Mahābhārata*, which sums up within its vast bulk every shade and nuance of classical Hinduism, both its orthodox formulations and the outraged protests that these evoked.

Hinduism is, or was, as much a social system as a religion. Its primary presuppositions of transmigration, the wheel of birth, death, and rebirth, and the hope of liberation from this bondage have already been touched upon. This is the ideological framework in which it moves. Its social framework has from very early times been the caste system, and this has, until very recently, become increasingly rigid, increasingly complicated, and increasingly identified with Hinduism as such. Indeed until a century or so ago the acceptance of the caste system was considered by the orthodox to be the sole effective criterion of whether one was or was not a Hindu. In matters of belief it mattered not at all whether one believed in one god or many or in none at all, nor did it much matter on how one interpreted 'liberation' or whether one rejected it outright so long as one fulfilled the duties prescribed for one's caste. This was one of the hallmarks of the Hindu; the other, much less rigid because much less detectable, was that one should recognize the Veda as revealed truth. To ignore caste or to reject the Veda was to put oneself outside the pale of Hinduism. This it was, and not his philosophical views, that excluded the Buddha and the *dharma* he founded from the Hindu fold.

The fourth phase of Hinduism we are living through today: it is the denial of its formal self and the reassertion of its spiritual essence. This revaluation of Hinduism was prepared by the reform movements of the nineteenth century, but only reached and touched the hearts of the entire Indian people with the advent of a saint who seemed to incarnate all that was best in Hinduism, Mahātma Gandhi. For it was he who lent his enormous prestige to the onslaught on what all that was finest in India had for centuries felt to be a canker in the very heart of their religion, the caste system itself and its ugly corollary, the creation of a disfranchised religious proletariat, the out-castes or untouchables. Gandhi exposed the glaring discrepancy between the two *dharmas*, the 'eternal law' that is so 'difficult to know' but which was inscribed on India's social conscience and what was now seen to be a man-made *dharma* which gave its sanction to a social system which had developed into some-thing monstrously unjust. The tension that through the centuries had existed between the two *dharmas* was brutally exposed to the light of day; and it is no accident that Gandhi met his death at the hand of an orthodox Hindu.

Thus while it was once possible to define a Hindu as one who performs his caste duties and accepts the Veda as revealed truth, this simple formula can no longer satisfy, for Hinduism is today, more than any other religion, in the melting-pot: what were once considered to be essentials are in the process of being discarded, but the hard core remains, and it is with this core that this book is principally concerned.

The corpus of sacred literature in Hinduism is enormous. It is divided into two distinct categories of greater and lesser sanctity—*śruti* and *smṛti*. The first of these words means literally 'hearing', the second 'memory'. *Śruti* comprises the Veda itself, and this is considered to be eternal, the eternal 'word' heard by the *Ṛshis* or 'sages' of immemorial antiquity: it is eternal truth, eternal 'wisdom' or 'knowledge', for that is what the word *veda* means. The Veda as we have it is historic-ally divisible into three strata—the *Saṁhitās* or 'collections' of hymns and formulas, the *Brāhmanas* or sacrificial texts, and the *Āraṇyakas* or 'forest treatises' which culminate in the *Upan-ishads*, esoteric treatises which seek to interiorize the symbolism of the sacrificial ritual.

The Veda as a whole reflects the first two phases of Hinduism we distinguished above. Of these the first is now of historical interest only, for the *Rig-Veda*, the oldest of the Saṁhitās or 'collections', represents an extraverted and life-accepting type of religion which was very soon to be submerged in an in-troverted and esoteric form of religion which constitutes one of the essential ingredients in all the subsequent developments of this many-sided religion. The turning-point is reached with the Upanishads and their dual search for the eternal 'self' (*ātman*)

within man and the eternal ground of the universe outside him
(*brahman*). This aspect of Hinduism, its 'pantheistic monism',
has perhaps been over-stressed in modern times, for, though
certainly important, it is only one strand among many that go
to make up the rich tapestry that is Hinduism; for with the
Upanishads *śruti* ends and *smṛti* begins.

Smṛti, 'memory', does not in theory rank with *śruti* as
eternal truth: it is what is 'remembered' by the race and transmitted down from generation to generation. What exactly
ranks as *smṛti* has never been defined with the same rigour as
has been done in the case of *śruti* which comprises the Veda and
nothing else. *Smṛti*, on the other hand, is generally understood
to comprise the *Sūtras* (aphorisms, usually philosophic in
content), the Law Books (books on *dharma* in the narrower
sense), the *Purānas* (long mythological works in verse extolling
one or other of the great gods), and last but not least the two
epics, the Mahābhārata and the *Rāmāyana*.

Tucked away in the middle of the Mahābhārata is the most
important, the most influential, and the most luminous of all
the Hindu scriptures, the *Bhagavad-Gītā* or 'Song of the
Lord'. This marks a turning-point in Hinduism, for here for
the first time a totally new element in Hindu spirituality makes
itself felt—the love of God for man and of man for God. The
Rig-Veda had known many gods, but none of them attained
to undisputed pre-eminence as did, for instance, Zeus in
Greece and Jupiter in Rome. On the contrary, the old myths
lost their savour, and in their place appeared impersonal
concepts like *brahman* which came to mean both the ground
of the universe and what is immortal in the human soul. True,
in the Upanishads the first glimmerings of a theistic interpretation of the universe begin to appear, but it is only in the
Mahābhārata, and more particularly in the Bhagavad-Gītā,
that God slowly disengages himself from the universe of which
he is still the material as well as the efficient cause, and confronts
man as person to person. The Bhagavad-Gītā is thus the water-
shed that separates the pantheistic monism of the Upanishads
from the fervent theism of the later popular cults. Though not
ranking as *śruti* it is nonetheless the focal point around which all
later Hinduism was to revolve, and so all-embracing is its

appeal that it has commanded not only the allegiance of the
orthodox but also that of modern and modernist Hindus, and
not least of Mahatma Gandhi himself. It is the sacred fount
from which the popular cults of rapt devotion to God (whether
it be Vishnu or Śiva) naturally flow. From the time of the
Gītā on, Hinduism becomes increasingly monotheistic, though
the pantheistic flavour remains and is still very much alive in
modern times.

Quite apart from the Gītā, however, the Mahābhārata,
India's gigantic Epic, of which the Gītā is but a tiny part,
comprises within itself the whole of Hinduism as no other book
can hope to not only because whole slices of it are devoted to
purely religious discussion but also because its hero, Yudhishthira, incarnates the Hindu's dilemma between the two
dharmas that we have sketched out above. His dilemma is all
the more poignant in that he is himself the son and embodiment
of the god Dharma who presides over righteousness and truth.
Yet ever again he is forced against his will and his better
judgement to do things he knows to be wrong because either
they form part and parcel of his religious duty (*dharma*)
as a warrior or because he is bidden to do so by Krishna who is
himself the Supreme Lord incarnate and whose commands it
would be blasphemous to set aside.

It is often said that Hinduism is so obsessed by its quest for
'liberation' that it has very little to say in the matter of day-to-
day morality and of man's relations to his fellow. This is partly
due to what appears to be a lack of proper perspective among
many modern Hindu apologists themselves as well as to an over-
emphasis on the philosophical side of Hinduism which, though
important, does not touch the heart of or evoke a religious
response from the average Hindu. It is due, too, to a tendency to
stress the Upanishadic element in Hinduism at the expense of
the more mundane and this-worldly side we find in the Epics.
For whereas, in the Mahābhārata, we have the whole of
Hinduism in all its myriad aspects *in parvo*, in the Rāmāyana
we are shown what the Hindus conceive to be a perfect life—
the life lived by the God Vishnu in his incarnation as Rāma.
Thus it is to the Epics that we must turn if we would understand
the Hindu concept of *dharma*—'righteousness', 'morality', or

'virtuous conduct' as applied to this world. The tension between
dharma and *moksha* is perhaps never resolved, but at least in the
Great Epic we sense that the two concepts were felt to be two
facets of the same thing, that *dharma* in the sense of 'right
action' was the corollary and the prelude to participation in the
infinite.

The Epics and the Purāṇas are the great store-houses of
devotional Hinduism, and they mark the end of the 'classical'
period in which Sanskrit remained the language of holy writ.
Official Hinduism, with the Veda as its sacred book and sole
source of infallible wisdom, had become increasingly identified
with the caste system, itself originated and buttressed by the
highest caste, the Brāhmans, and it was only the three 'twice-
born' classes that had access to this saving wisdom. The lowest
class, the Śūdras, were forbidden all access to the Veda, as were
also women and, of course, outcastes. It was, then, largely to
satisfy the needs of these religiously disfranchised persons that
purely devotional religion developed in the *smṛti* literature, for
this, since it did not share the absolute sanctity of the Veda,
was open to all and, together with it, the message of God's love
for all men irrespective of caste differences.

Because this new type of religion addressed itself to all men
and was not confined to the superior castes alone, an extensive
literature began to develop in the various vernacular languages
of India much as vernacular hymn-writing developed in
Protestant Europe after the Reformation. Sanskrit, indeed,
retained its special position as the sacred tongue *par excellence*,
but what was most vital in Hinduism now found expression
in languages that all could understand. This, the triumph of
bhakti, the loving adoration of a personal God, constitutes the
third phase of Hinduism, and it is reflected too in the theologies
of the later Vedāntin philosophers who rejected out of hand the
classical monist ontology elaborated by the great Śankara in
the ninth century A.D.

The last phase dates from the British occupation and culminates in a determined attack on the whole system of caste
to which Gandhi, in his later period, lent the whole weight of
his immense moral authority. Thanks largely to the activities
of Christian missions Hinduism became increasingly interested

in the right ordering of society—in social *dharma*—and therefore in social service and the redress of gross social inequalities based on immemorial taboo and sanctioned by the authority of religion. The struggle between the old and the new in which it seems the new must in the end triumph, however protracted and bitter the struggle, is still going on. Hinduism is living through a time of crisis which threatens the very presuppositions on which it has hitherto been built, and it is too early yet to see how and in what direction it will transform itself; but transform itself it must since in the highly industrialized society which is already beginning to engulf India, the taboos associated with caste cannot survive, nor would many today, except the most rigidly orthodox, wish to retain them. This will not mean that the *sanātana dharma*, the eternal *dharma* that is the especial property of the Indian people, will disappear; for this *dharma*, though it may be 'subtle' and 'difficult to know' is what gives Hinduism in all its phases its peculiar bitter-sweet flavour—the flavour of self-forgetfulness and renunciation certainly, but the flavour too of a thirst for righteousness in an unrighteous world and a constant yearning for truth wherever it may be found. This flavour is embodied as nowhere else in the legendary figure of Yudhishthira, the gentle and compassionate 'King of Righteousness' and in the historical figure of Mahātma Gandhi who declared that Truth was God.

1
Veda

THE SACRED LANGUAGE OF the Hindus is Sanskrit, and
Sanskrit is itself a development and formalization of the more
ancient 'Vedic' in which the Vedas were composed. It is an
Indo-European language with very close links with the Iranian
group of languages spoken throughout the first Persian Empire.
The Indo-Iranians formed the most easterly group of the Indo-
European people, and both Indians and Iranians spoke of
themselves as *āryas* ('Aryans'), a term that later came to mean
'nobleman' or 'gentleman' in contradistinction to the conquered populations. Just when these Aryans invaded India is
anyone's guess, and scholars have dated this event anywhere
between 4000 and 1000 B.C., though the consensus of opinion
would now appear to be settling on the second half of the second
millennium B.C.

The only datable inscription concerning these remote times
comes not from India or even from Iran, but from a Turkish
village in Eastern Anatolia called Boghaz Köy. Here was discovered the text of a treaty between the Hittite king Shuppiluliumash and the king of Mitanni, Mattiwaza. The name of the
latter is Indo-Iranian, and he was a worshipper of Indo-
Iranian gods. This treaty dates from the earlier half of the
fourteenth century and in it are mentioned four gods (in a
slightly differing form) prominent in the Vedas—Varuna,
Mitra, Indra, and the Nāsatyas. The presence of this Indo-
Iranian people in Eastern Anatolia who spoke a dialect apparently rather more Indic than Iranian has been thought by some
to prove that the Indo-Iranian tribes were still on the move

towards their final destinations in the fourteenth century B.C. If this were so, the Aryan irruption into India could scarcely have taken place earlier than the twelfth century B.C. It seems, however, more likely that the Mitanni were a separate branch of the Indo-Iranian group which had split itself off from the main body at an early date; and if this is so we are still reduced to guesswork as to when the Aryans entered India.

Until quite recently our only source for the pre-Aryan civilization in India was the Veda itself, and the Vedic poets were not likely to speak in flattering terms of the peoples they were in the process of subduing. They were, so they tell us, dark-skinned, snub-nosed, and ugly, and their religion included the worship of the phallus (RV, 7.21.5: 10.99.3). With the excavation of the sites of Mohenjo-Dāro and Harappā in the Indus valley, however, our knowledge of the pre-Aryan peoples of northern India has been considerably enlarged. These were certainly no barbarians, as readers of the Veda might be led to suppose, but enjoyed a highly developed urban civilization comparable to that of contemporary Mesopotamia. Unlike their conquerors they were literate, but all attempts to decipher their script have so far proved unavailing, and what we can learn of their religion is therefore strictly limited to what can be deduced from their iconographical remains.

Students of Indian religion have long been struck by the sharp difference that distinguishes the this-worldly religion of the Rig-Veda, whose kinship with the sister religions of the other Indo-European peoples makes itself immediately felt, both from the inwardness of the Upanishads and the extravagances of the later theistic cults in which the position of the Supreme Being has been usurped by minor Vedic gods whose position in the sacred canon itself gives no indication of the future greatness that was to fall to their lot. There seemed to be no explanation of this phenomenon except that the religion of the conquered peoples had once again emerged into the light of day and, as so frequently happens, transformed the religion of the conqueror into something that was not recognizably his at all.

Phallus-worship, for instance, is a clear case in point. This played no part in the religion of the Vedic Aryans, yet in the later religion not only is the ithyphallic god, Śiva, worshipped throughout the land, but his symbol, the phallus, is widely worshipped and cherished as the emblem of deity. This at least could be explained with near-certainty as being a reversion to a pre-Aryan religious practice because the Veda itself mentions phallus-worship as being characteristic of the enemies of the Aryans. This very natural inference has now been proved by the discovery at Harappā of seals representing precisely such an ithyphallic god. This god is seated with his legs drawn up to the body and with the heels touching: his head is surmounted by a pair of horns, and on one of the seals he is attended by an elephant, a tiger, a rhinoceros, and a buffalo. All this seems to prefigure the Rudra-Śiva of later times, for the posture in which he is sitting is one of those favoured by Yogins to this day, and Śiva, despite-the erect phallus, is himself the great Yogin and patron of ascetics. So too, as early as the *Atharva-Veda* he is known as *paśupati*, 'the Lord of Beasts', and has the closest association with the bull whose horns adorn him on the Harappā seal.

Conspicuous among the Harappā finds are figurines of women, usually naked or half-naked, and scholars have seen in these representations of a mother-goddess. Such a goddess is typical of the religion of Mesopotamia, but is conspicuously absent from the pantheon of the Vedas. In the later literature, however, such a goddess reappears in the form of the terrible goddess Durgā or Kālī, the consort of Śiva, who to this day enjoys a widespread cult particularly in Bengal. So, too, numerous cone-shaped objects have turned up which can scarcely represent anything but a phallus, and this, as we have seen, is the emblem *par excellence* of Śiva. Thus we find that the intelligent guesswork of earlier scholars has been confirmed by the new evidence supplied by archaeology. Much that is typical of 'classical' Hinduism derives not from the invading Aryans, but from the indigenous populations they conquered.

It is customary to say of the religion of the Rig-Veda that, in contradistinction to the later religion, it is life-affirming, this-worldly, and dynamic, and there is much truth in this; but the Rig-Veda can hardly be separated from the rest of the Vedas, for it is no more than a collection (*saṁhitā*) of strophes (*ṛks*) compiled for the use of the *Hotṛ* who was only one among the many priests that officiated at the sacrifice—the priest who is in charge of the 'invocation' of the gods. Along with the *Hotṛ* functioned the *Udgātṛ*, the 'priest who chants aloud', and the *Adhvaryu*, the priest in charge of the sacred action or sacrifice itself. The former used a collection (*saṁhitā*) of 'chants' (*sāman*) known as the *Sāma-Veda* ('the Veda of Chants'), the contents of which are almost entirely drawn from the Rig-Veda, whereas the latter used the *Yajur-Veda* ('the Veda of Sacrifice') several recensions of which exist, but these are of considerably later date and probably do not reflect the sacrifice as it was practised in Rig-Vedic times.

It is probably impossible for a modern scholar to reconstruct the significance of a 'primitive' religion, particularly that of the Vedas which seem to take for granted much material the nature of which we can only surmise. The attempt to explain Vedic religion as 'nature-worship' as was commonly done in the hey-day of Vedic studies in the nineteenth century, failed because so much of the evidence obstinately refused to fit into this narrow frame. Similarly the philological method (now revived by Thieme and others) which would explain the nature of any given deity *solely* by the etymology of his name, failed in its turn not only because the etymology itself is often doubtful, but also because a god, like a man, grows and develops into something very much more than his name. More recently attention has been focussed on the ethnological approach which tends to emphasize social trends existing in given societies and to explain the divine society portrayed in myth by analogy with the social structure of the human society of the god's devotees.

All these methods are legitimate and valuable, but necessarily incomplete in themselves: only when they are combined are they likely to give even an approximately correct picture of the religious world in which the Vedic Indian moved. Thus, for example, the naturalist school saw that the Vedic pantheon could be roughly divided into three classes of gods—heavenly gods, gods of the atmosphere, and gods of the earth. The tripartite classification is accepted by the ethnological school, but it sees the distinction not so much as between heaven, atmosphere, and earth as between the three great classes into which Vedic society seems to have been divided—Brāhmans (priests), *Kshatriyas* (warriors among whom were included the 'kings' or tribal chieftains), and *Vaiśyas* (the mass of the common people, peasantry, and artisans). Unfortunately the principal exponent of this school, M. Dumézil, has confused this legitimate distinction by substituting a separate function of 'sovereignty' for that of the Brāhman-priests. This is unnecessary and vitiates all his arguments. The threefold partition of the divine society is none the less valid, but here, as so often in religion, it is not a case of 'either/or' but of correspondence, analogy, and interconnexion. Thus the Vedic Indians themselves declared that the three great classes of priests, warriors, and peasants were identical with the fire-god Agni, the warrior-god Indra, and the *viśve devāḥ* or 'all-gods', the divine 'people' corresponding to the common people of the tribes.

Vedic mythology is concerned not only with nature-myths, or with functional deities whose 'original' function can be deduced from the etymology of their names, or with the social structure of a tribal society, but also with a combination and integration of all these into an orderly whole, what the Veda calls *ṛta*, 'right order' and 'truth' and the later texts were to call *dharma*. Professor Renou is therefore surely right when he says that the great nineteenth-century French scholar Bergaigne 'has shown us the right method, the method of seeking correspondences between the world of men, the performers of the sacrifice, the microcosm on the one hand, and the "aerial" world of the gods [the recipients of the sacrifice], the macrocosm on the other. The duty of the *Ṛshis* [those ancient sages who were thought to have "heard" the Veda] was to ensure the ordered functioning of the world and of religious ceremonial by reproducing the succession of cosmic events, the *ordo rerum* in their acts and in the imagery they conceived. The term *ṛta* is a designation of the cosmic order on which human order, ethics and social behaviour depend,' and this human order, in Indo-Iranian society, seems to have been based on a more or less rigid distinction between priest, warrior, and peasantry. To these three original classes were later added a fourth, the *Śūdras*, 'servants' or 'slaves'. The raw material of this great class or 'caste' was almost certainly drawn from the ranks of the conquered pre-Aryan peoples, and this fourfold division of society was thus seen to correspond to a similar division among the gods.

Nothing, however, either in the Veda or in later Hinduism is nicely cut-and-dried, and no statement can safely be made without qualification, for these ancient sages, in extolling their gods, tended to attribute to them qualities borrowed from other deities; in the particular god they addressed they tended to see the greatest of them all, and this in turn led to an outright identification of one with another or with all. 'What is but one the wise call [by] manifolds [names]. They call it Agni, Yama, Mātariśvan' (RV, 1.164.46). Yet insidious though this tendency is, certain gods nevertheless retain characteristics distinctive to themselves which look out of place when transferred to other deities.

Of the Vedic gods only six need detain us here, Varuna, Indra, Agni, Soma, Rudra, and Vishnu; Rudra and Vishnu because they were later to develop, each in his own way, into the Supreme Being, Varuna both because he is generally regarded as the highest ethical creation of the Vedic Indians and because he seems to be the celestial Brāhman *par excellence*, Indra both because he is the most popular of the gods and the most frequently invoked and because he is the warrior-king among the gods as well as being, on the naturalistic interpretation of his activity, a god of the storm. Agni and Soma, for their part, are terrestrial gods in that the one *is* fire and the other *is* the plant sacrificially slain in the ritual: in their case there is no difference between the divinized cult object and the god whose outward and visible sign the cult object is. The naturalistic basis of both is undeniable.

It is in Agni that the divine and human worlds most nearly coalesce, for Agni is the god who, as fire, consumes the sacrifice and, as priest, presents it to the gods above: he is the mediator between gods and men. Just as his 'birth' on earth is produced by the friction of the two fire-sticks, the upper being the male and the lower the female, so is he, on the macrocosmic scale, the son of Heaven (*Dyaus* cf. Greek *Zeus*) and Earth. He is not only the priest who brings gods and men together in the oblation, he is also the element that binds together the three worlds: in heaven he is born ever again as the sun, in the

atmosphere he is kindled in the waters, that is, in the storm-
cloud and comes down to the earth in the form of lightning,
while on earth he is kindled by the hands of men. His threefold
birth corresponds to the threefold structure of the universe, and
this threefold pattern of existence will meet us again and again
in later times. Again he is omnipresent—in heaven, atmosphere,
and earth—and he is eternal—he is the first to conduct the
sacrifice and no sacrificer is older than he, yet old though he is,
he remains always 'very young'. He is the symbol both of the
renewal of all things and of the interrelatedness of all things.
Though he is greater than heaven and earth and all the worlds
and a mighty king, he is also a humble householder—he is the
household fire which even today is the centre of the domestic
ritual, or again he is a guest in the houses of men. On the
macrocosmic scale he surpasses all things in greatness, on the
microcosmic he is the friend and kinsman of men: he is both
very great and very small, very old and very young, uniting
within himself the opposites in a manner that was later to
become utterly characteristic of Hindu thought. Born in heaven
he descends on to earth; born again on earth he, as the mouth
of the gods, devours the oblation and, as priest, brings down
the gods to share in the sacrificial feast. He is the meeting-
place of gods and men and the bond of union between them:
pervading everything in heaven and atmosphere and earth
as sun and lightning and fire he is none the less the 'navel of
the earth' (RV, 1.59.2), the sacral 'centre' of the family, the
tribe, and ultimately of the whole universe.

The figure of Agni is instructive from the mythological point
of view, for it shows how the physical element of fire can give
rise to a whole nexus of mythology, the object of which is to
unfold a whole scheme of interconnexions between the human
world of family and tribe on the one hand and the great world
outside so often hostile to man on the other, and to knit them
together in a coherent unity. The point of meeting is the sacrificial altar on which the fire, as priest, consumes the oblation in
the name of the gods, thereby transmitting their virtue to the
world of men whose representative he is.

So too with Soma. He is a deity with an indisputably naturalistic basis. Both in India and in Iran the plant Soma (Iranian

'Haoma') and fire were the indispensable ingredients of the
sacrifice. From the texts it appears that the plant was of a
yellowish colour and that it was to be found in the mountains:
from its juice an intoxicating liquid was prepared which was
believed to give strength and long life to gods and men: it was
the drink of immortality. In the hymns to Soma the pressing of
the sacred juice through a woollen filter into a vat containing
milk and water is likened to all manner of celestial phenomena
with which it would appear to have nothing to do. These com-
parisons which sometimes amount to identification are repeated
and intensified in the later Vedic literature (the Brāhmanas and
earlier Upanishads) and pave the way for that greatest identification of all—that of the human soul with the Absolute itself—
which, despite violent and recurring reaction against it, was to
cling to Hinduism throughout the ages. Thus the woollen
sieve through which the juice of the divine plant is filtered is
identified with the sky, and the filtering and pouring of the
juice into the water and milk that awaits it is made to represent
all manner of cosmic processes. Because the juice is liquid it is
compared to and identified with the rain, and Soma becomes the
Lord of streams and son of the waters. Because the plant is
golden in colour it is compared to the lightning and the noise
made by the pressing is compared to the thunderstorm. Assimilated to the sun it fills heaven and earth with its rays. More
surprisingly, perhaps, it is not only assimilated to a bull but
itself becomes a bull, and the descent into the milky waters of
the vat is likened to the fertilization of a herd of cows. Rain,
storm, sun, and fertility, then, all fall within the province of
this strange being who is both plant and god, and the whole
cosmos is thus seen to be contained in this single act of the
pressing of the Soma plant.

The sieve which filters the juice, as we have seen, is likened
to the sky; indeed it *is* the sky. Soma is 'in the navel of heaven
in the woollen filter' (RV, 9.12.4), it 'traverses the lights of
heaven, the woollen filter' (ibid., 9.37.3), or 'purifying himself
in heaven . . . he walks with the sun in the filter' (ibid., 9.27.5).
In none of this is any incongruity felt, for the cultic act creates
a magical rapport with the entire cosmos, and the woollen
filter thus becomes the centre of the universe and identical with

the sky. And so it is that the golden plant though born of the mountains on earth is also the 'child of heaven' (ibid., 9.38.5), and though 'running in the vat' it is also 'heaven's Lord who has a hundred rays' (ibid., 9.86.11).

All this and more besides derives ultimately from the ritual pressing and filtering of the Soma plant. The filtered Soma, however, was highly intoxicating and inspired the gods to great deeds against their enemies and against the enemies of the Aryan people. The god most closely associated with Soma is Indra, the warrior-god *par excellence*; and because it is the inordinate quaffing of Soma that gives him the power to overcome his enemies, Soma himself becomes a mighty warrior, and as Indra advances to a position of near-supremacy in the pantheon, Soma too is associated with his creative activity. By association and interconnexion each god shares in the activities of his fellows: each merges into the other, and ultimately each will merge into the All.

By the end of the Rig-Vedic period Indra had become the greatest of the gods. Like Agni and Soma he is ambivalent. For long he was regarded as being primarily the god of the storm; later his character of warrior-god of the Aryans was emphasized; later still his positive power in recreating order in a disordered world has been pushed into the foreground. Or again the latent tension that exists between him and the other great god of the Veda, Varuna, is thought by some to reflect a real tension between the Brāhman priests and the Kshatriya warriors in their social relations on earth. Of mythology in the Greek sense of the word there is little in the Rig-Veda, but Indra is the exception to the rule, for he is constantly involved in mythological battle. His adversary in battle is usually called *Vrtra*, and Indra's own stock epithet is *vrtra-han*, 'slayer of Vrtra'. But *Vrtra* (in the neuter) is also used in a more general sense meaning 'obstruction, defence' or according to Gershevitch 'vigour'. And so Indra is essentially the 'destroyer of [his enemies'] power to resist', the 'destroyer of their vigour'. Vrtra, the 'encompasser' is the demon who imprisons the waters, and as such he may be considered to be the demon of drought: but he is also the lord of ninety-nine fortresses, which suggests that he may be a human foe. Be that as it may, the salient episodes of the myth are that Indra smashes the fortresses and slays Vṛtra: the waters are released, the sun is made to shine, and Vṛtra's wealth in cattle is liberated.

This myth may be interpreted in three ways. Either Indra is simply the warrior-god of the Aryans, and Vṛtra (who also appears in the neuter plural) is simply the enemy's power to resist that must be overcome. In this case the mountains which Indra smashes will be the enemy fortresses, and the rivers he releases will be the rivers of the Indus valley which the Aryans overran, whereas the cattle he sets free will not be mythological representations either of the waters or the rays of the sun, as some would have it, but quite literally enemy cattle 'liberated' by the conquering Aryans. Or else this is a myth of the thunder-storm, Vṛtra being the demon of drought, and Indra's mace the thunderbolt that releases the waters, scatters the darkness, and enables the sun to shine. Or again it is the violent restoration of the cosmic order which has been temporarily disturbed. The cosmos reduced to a chaos by Vṛtra's imprisonment of the waters is once again set free, and Indra can recreate and refashion the world. None of these interpretations fit the myth perfectly, nor should we expect them to. For the invading Aryans the conquest of new and fertile lands and the fighting that this involved may well have seemed to 'imitate' both the cosmic recreation of new life out of a universe that had run down and the violence of the thunderstorm which is the harbinger of life renewed. Sometimes again Indra who, with his fair hair and beard, is more fully anthropomorphized than any of the other gods, is simply the supreme warlord of the Aryans who crushes and lays low the Dasyus or Dāsas, the pre-Aryan population of the Indus valley: in this capacity he is spoken of as a 'man' (nara) rather than a god. At other times he is very much more than this, for his slaying of Vṛtra results not only in the release of the waters and the liberation of the kine, but also in the re-establishment of order in the world. In this capacity he is already on the way to becoming a creator god.

In some ways Indra prefigures Krishna, the incarnate god of the Great Epic, for though he was to rise to the rank of king of the gods (in classical Sanskrit the word *Indra* means simply 'lord' or 'king'), his beginnings are humble and his character is

recognizably human: to the end he remains a hero though a
hero endowed with all the attributes of godhead: he is the
Heracles of Vedic mythology. Like Heracles, and like Krishna
for that matter, Indra's childhood is beset with difficulties.
He is not born in the ordinary way but emerges from his
mother's side. Once born he is wanted by none but feared by
all; his mother attempts to hide him and leave him to his own
devices 'like an unlicked calf' (RV, 4.18.12). 'Among the gods he
found none to have mercy on him', for Indra was a hero of
fearful might who threatened to upset the older order of things.
At his birth mountains, heaven, and earth were seized with
trembling, and all the gods were afraid. No sooner is he born
than he robs Tvashtṛ, his father, of the Soma and quaffs an
enormous draft of it 'worth a hundred cows'. Thus fortified his
stature expands to such an extent that it fills the two worlds;
immediately he slays Vṛtra, that is, destroys all that obstructs
him, and gives the waters free course. Thereupon he turns
upon his father, 'seizes him by the foot and smashes him to
pieces' (ibid., 4.18.12).

On the cosmic scale this myth can only mean that Indra
destroys an older cosmic order that is running down. This is a
process that takes place in eternity, for Indra's birth, his quaffing
of the Soma, the slaughter of Vṛtra, and the freeing of the
waters take place simultaneously. This cosmic struggle is
reflected and re-enacted in the struggle of the Aryan invaders
with the Dāsas, which is itself a form of sacrifice. There may,
however, be a third interpretation of the myth, for Tvashtṛ,
Indra's father, is elsewhere identified with Varuna, the universal
king who rules by magic power, and between the two throughout the Rig-Veda, there is palpable tension. Varuna's characteristics are, as we shall see, those of a Brāhman-priest whose
power derives from the sacred word, while Indra is plainly,
among other things, the personification of the warrior class.
This myth, and the rivalry that undoubtedly exists between
Indra and Varuna, may well represent the struggle (never wholly
resolved) between the two higher 'twice-born' castes, the
Brāhmans and the Kshatriyas.

Indra is the hero, *vīra* (cf. Latin *vir*), the 'most manly of men';
and however swift his rise to supremacy in the Vedic pantheon

may have been, he remains a hero, a man-god, not just a man or just a god, to the end. In a very real sense he is the Vedic precursor of the Krishna of the Great Epic. His relationship with men is very close: he is their 'friend', their 'brother', and their 'father and mother'. He is vastly generous and quick to wrath—the typical warrior king—and his favourites are not the priestly families so often mentioned in the Rig-Veda, but fighting men. His thirst for the Soma is wellnigh unquenchable as is his appetite for the flesh of bulls. His might is immeasurable and his generosity knows no bounds for it is he who distributes the spoils of war.

Indra's constant companions are the Maruts. Like him they are youthful warriors, but they are also the geniuses of the thunderstorm. For whereas the interpretation of Indra as god of the storm is frequently very forced, the close connexion of the Maruts with thunder and lightning, wind and rain, cannot be denied, so often are they mentioned in connexion with these phenomena or actually are them. They hold the lightning in their hands and the lightning is their spear. Their golden-wheeled chariots gleam in the lightning as they rush forth like boisterous winds. They pour down rain in torrents, create darkness thereby, and cover the eye of the sun. Unmistakably they are gods of the thunderstorm. It has, however, been suggested that the Maruts are the heavenly counterparts of a young men's tribal confederation or what we would call a commando-group specially attached to the person of the warrior king. Certainly they are almost as completely anthropomorphized as is Indra himself, and their habits are very strange. They love to deck themselves with golden ornaments, to scrub each other clean, and to lick each other's backs. They are irresponsible and gay, yet wrathful as serpents. They are always present at the slaying of Vṛtra and they egg great Indra on with their songs.

Thus while there can be no doubt at all that the Maruts are storm-gods, playful and fearful at the same time like the lightning, singing with the voice of wind and thunder, and pouring forth torrential rain, there is no reason to deny that the phenomena of the storm may have called to mind the behaviour of the Aryan *corps d'élite* here below. Cosmologically too they may represent the forces of renewal and regeneration which follow on the destruction of the old order, for the Maruts, too, like Indra, are ever young.

Indra and the Maruts, then, represent both the eternal renewal of the cosmos by the violent destruction of the old constricting order, the annual renewal of the earth's life at the advent of the rainy season, and the subjugation of the human and divine enemies of the Aryans. Indra himself is also the apotheosis of the fighting hero, the Kshatriya.

Unlike Varuna who is king by divine right Indra is king by right of conquest: he is king because he has conquered Vṛtra: he is 'leader of the human peoples and the generations of the gods', because 'he warded off Vṛtra *by his strength*' (RV, 3.34.2-3). And it is through his heroic valour that he, irresistible, surpasses all the gods (ibid., 3.46.3). The older gods are subdued to his divine glory and royal dignity (ibid., 7.21.7), and none can frustrate his deeds and counsels. The Maruts themselves confess: 'not one is there known among the gods who can compare with thee, neither among those who are born already or are yet to be born' (ibid., 1.165.9). He is now both universal monarch (*samrāj*) as is Varuna and monarch in his own right (*svarāj*): he is king of gods and men, the 'lord of all that lives and breathes' (ibid., 1.101.5) and the 'eye of the eye of the whole world' (ibid., 10.102.12). He is the personification of the triumph of elemental force, the warrior who owes his kingship to the strength of his own arm.

Indra is an upstart king. Varuna, on the other hand, the great *Asura*, the guardian of the cosmic law, was universal monarch from the beginning. Even in Indo-European times the gods were divided into two classes, the *devas* and the *asuras* (*daēvas* and *ahuras* in Iranian). In Iran the distinction became absolute, the *ahuras* coalescing into the one figure of Ahura Mazdāh, the Wise Lord, the creator of heaven and earth, and the *daēvas* sinking to the rank of demons. In India exactly the reverse happened. In the Rig-Veda no hard and fast distinction is made, but the term *asura* is pre-eminently applied to the group of sovereign gods called *Ādityas*, principal of whom is Varuna, the *asura par excellence* and universal lord, whereas Indra, Agni, Soma, and most of the other gods are predominantly *devas*. The rise of Indra is part of a more general process in which the *devas* gradually come to oust the *asuras* as the ruling power of the universe. Thus already in the latest stratum of the Rig-Veda and in the Atharva-Veda the word *asura* has come to mean 'demon', and 'demon' it has meant ever since.

Signs of this conflict are already apparent in the Rig-Veda. Between the two great gods, Indra and Varuna, there is co-operation at first, but co-operation soon turns to rivalry, and rivalry to the discomfiture of the Asura king. In RV, 7.82–85 the two gods work together, but their functions are contrasted. Together they are invoked to smite the Dāsas, but each in his different way. Indra lays low the enemy in battle, Varuna does this by watching over the cosmic law. To Varuna all guilty men owe honour, while Indra is content to ride in pomp with the Maruts. Varuna, as guardian of the law and truth, is quick to anger, while Indra gives his friends spacious dwellings. Varuna is universal monarch, Indra a monarch of his own making (*svarāj*). So far there is only contrast, not contest. In another hymn (RV, 4.42), however, the rivalry between the *deva* and the *asura* comes to the surface: Varuna addresses Indra and asserts his absolute sovereignty:

'I, Varuna, am king,' he says, 'To me was the dignity of *asura* first assigned. . . . I, Varuna, am Indra [too]. I, knowing the two wide, deep firmly established areas of space in all their grandeur, [knowing] all creatures as their fashioner, I have set in motion both worlds and maintain them. I made the dripping waters swell forth; in the seat of the law did I establish the heavens. By virtue of the law is the son of Aditi (Varuna) possessed of the law, and threefold has he extended the earth.'

Varuna stakes his claim to sovereignty on law (*ṛta*, the Vedic counterpart of the later *dharma*): Indra appeals only to naked force:

'It is I whom heroes (*naraḥ*), rivalling each other in riding their goodly horses, invoke when they are surrounded in battle. I, Indra, the widely generous, stir up the battle. I, Indra, raise up the dust, I whose might is overwhelming. All this have I done; no power of the gods can restrain me, for I am invincible. Once the Soma and the hymns have made me drunk, then are both immeasurable worlds struck with terror.'

All this Varuna concedes, but he does not abdicate: he is still the universal sovereign who rules by law.

As we read the hymns of the Rig-Veda Indra's victory is seen to resemble nothing so much as a takeover bid. Attributes that had formerly been proper to Varuna now pass over to Indra. Varuna is the guardian of the law, cosmic order, and truth (*rta*), the sworn enemy of falsehood: he is the punisher of sin. So Indra too arrogates to himself the administration of the law (RV, 1.133.1). Free from falsehood (ibid., 3.32.9) he 'burns out all spirits of untruth' (ibid., 1.133.1), sharpens his arrows against the lie and drives our sins away (ibid., 4.23.7). Even the 'craftiness' or 'guile' (*māyā*) which typifies Varuna passes over into him, and to crown all the gods bestow on him the dignity of *asura* of which his destruction of Vṛtra has made him worthy.

As an *asura* he becomes the creator and sustainer of the universe which he yet transcends, for the two worlds are equal to but half of him; or again heaven and earth are his girdle. This is already typical of later cosmological thinking: the supreme God pervades the whole universe, yet transcends it, the universe being but a fraction of himself. Creation, however, in India never means creation *ex nihilo*, it means the ordering of an already existing matter into intelligible form. In this sense Indra creates heaven and earth, but heaven and earth can in no wise encompass or contain him.

Indra's promotion to the dignity of an *asura*, however, did not save that class of deity from degradation. Their eclipse in the shape of Varuna himself is movingly described in RV, 10.124 where Agni, the divine priest, deserts Varuna for Indra.

Indra speaks: 'O Agni, come to our sacrifice with its five paths, three layers, and seven strands. Thou shalt be our sacrificial priest and leader. Too long hast thou dwelt in darkness.'

And Agni replies: 'Secretly and hidden do I, a god, depart from him who is no longer a god, foreseeing immortality. If I, [now] inauspicious [to him], leave him who was auspicious, so do I go from an old comradeship to a strange stock. . . . To the father Asura I say a kindly word: from having no part in the sacrifice I go to enjoy my share in the sacrifice. Many years did I pass with him. Choosing Indra I leave the father.'

Indra speaks: 'The *asuras* have lost their uncanny power (*māyā*): if thou, Varuna, wilt but desire me, then accept, O king who tellest right from wrong, the overlordship of my kingdom.'

The poet then explains: 'Varuna set the waters free, for he has no more power over them. . . . These now follow Indra's highest power. He dwells with them and they rejoice each according to its measure. Since, like the clans, they chose him as their king, they rudely turned their back on Vṛtra.'

Varuna, like all the gods, has an ambivalent character, and nowhere is it more apparent than here. Though guardian of the law, which is identical with justice and truth, he none the less resorts to guile (*māyā*) as does Vṛtra and other enemies of the gods. Hence it is not perhaps surprising that in this hymn he is or seems to be identified with Vṛtra himself. Yet Varuna is important in his own right both because he has claims to being a purely moral god which Indra and the rest are certainly not, because he is the guardian of the *ṛta*, the Vedic antecedent of the later *dharma*, and because he has attributes which, after his eclipse, were taken over by Rudra-Śiva, the Great God of a later age.

Varuna is a universal monarch, and this status he usually shares with another 'sovereign' god, Mitra. We have seen that originally *Vṛtra* meant no more than 'obstacle' and that the dragon Vṛtra whom Indra slays is no more than a personification of this idea. So too *mitra* (neuter) originally means 'compact', and Mitra is thus primarily the personification of the compact. Varuna too probably derives his name from the same root as Vṛtra, *vṛ-* 'to envelop', and it has been suggested that he is the oath personified. In this connexion it is perhaps worth noting that already in the Rig-Veda there is a constant ambivalence between the personal and the impersonal. The gods are both physical phenomena like Agni and Soma or moral concepts like Mitra and Varuna, and anthropomorphic representations of these; they are both all-pervading essences and concrete beings with well-defined physical and moral characteristics. This ambivalence between the personal and the impersonal will reappear in a more acute form in the Upanishads and classical

Hinduism when the nature of the Supreme Being is considered. Should one speak of the god as 'Thou' or as 'It', to use Martin Buber's terminology?

Whatever the etymology of Varuna's name may be, however, he is a decidedly personal deity in the Rig-Veda: he is the conserver of *ṛta*, cosmic law and truth. *Ṛta* is the Vedic equivalent of the later *dharma* and is equally difficult to define in any precise terms. It is the law that governs the universe, the law that operates in ritual and sacrifice, and finally the moral law that with equal impartiality regulates the conduct of men. 'Sin' (*enas*, *agas*) is an infringement of the law, and may be either a mistake in the ritual or a 'mistake' in the moral order. In either case it is regarded as an offence against Varuna.

The purely physical traits attributed to Varuna appear to be secondary, and it is not at all clear why, even in the Rig-Veda, he is closely associated with the waters and with rain. Like Indra Varuna causes the rivers to flow and like the Maruts he rains down rain from heaven; but there is a marked contrast in the manner in which these deities perform the same function. Indra has to wage a terrific battle in order to set the waters free, Varuna does it effortlessly by his 'uncanny power' (*māyā*). The Maruts' production of rain is always accompanied by the maximum of violence, noise, and turbulence, but Varuna has only to resort to his *māyā*. Indra and the Maruts are warriors, Varuna the impassive priest-king whose power derives not from physical strength but from magic.

Varuna is universal lord: he is in every sense an oriental monarch. His thousand-columned golden mansion is situated in the sky, and there he sits surveying the deeds of men. The sun, which is his eye, is also his spy: seeing all things he reports them to the twin monarchs, Varuna and Mitra. Like the Indian monarchs of later days Varuna has a host of spies 'undeceived and wise' whose sole function is to report on the misdoings of men.

Varuna is the guardian of the law he has himself established; he brings order into a disorderly cosmos. 'The all-knowing Asura propped up the heavens and measured out the expanse of earth. All worlds did the great king take into his possession' (RV, 8.42.1). Once established the worlds are kept apart and in position by his law, and the sun, moon, and stars pursue their regular courses in accordance with his ordinances. He it is who presides over the natural law and maintains a regular rhythm in his well-ordered realm. The ordinances of Varuna are fixed and unalterable, and even the gods cannot transgress them. Both he and Mitra are the guardians of the *ṛta* (law, cosmic order, and truth), 'lords of truth and light, increasing truth by means of truth' (RV, 1.23.5).

Ṛta of which Varuna is the guardian can be translated as 'cosmic order', 'law', 'truth', or 'reality': it is both the ordered universe as it is in itself and the order that pervades it; and this order is as applicable to the moral conduct of men as it is to the macrocosm of heaven and earth and to the sacrifice that mirrors the macrocosm *in parvo*. But there is a difference. The order of heaven and earth and of the times and seasons which pursue their regular courses under Varuna's guidance, are observable and fixed, whereas the moral code by which men should be guided is imperfectly known, for 'the gods love the obscure and hate the obvious', and Varuna is no exception to the rule.

Varuna is 'crafty'—*māyin*, that is, possessed of *māyā* or uncanny power, and for this reason he must be approached with fear and extreme circumspection. Men know that Varuna's unalterable ordinances exist, but they do not know what they are. Varuna is a 'moral' god as European scholars do not tire of telling us, but the nature of his moral law remains undisclosed. Men, then, sin in the dark, and as they sin Varuna ensnares them in his 'fetters' and visits them with his wrath. Sin is the fetter with which Varuna binds men, and as he binds in his wrath, so can he loose in his loving-kindness. 'O Varuna, untie the upper fetter, untie the middle, untie the lower' (RV, 1.24.15), the sinner cries, 'for we would be sinless in [carrying out thine] ordinances.' This binding and loosing of the fetters of sin is the prerogative of Varuna and Mitra alone in the Rig-Veda; and the awe and *Angst* and God-fearing humility that these 'fetters' inspire is unique in the whole corpus of Vedic literature. This sense of guilt and feeling of awe in the face of a just but inscrutable God we will not meet with again until we come to the devotional hymns of the Tamil saints who flourished from the sixth to the tenth century in South India. In the case of Varuna, however, the awe is not tempered by love; it is only mitigated by the hope of forgiveness. This unquiet sense of wrong unwittingly done and the hope of forgiveness and deliverance from impalpable bonds comes out most strongly in the hymn RV, 7.86.

Wise are the generations of him who established the two broad worlds apart, who thrust the heavens up on high, impelled the great luminary on his double course, and spread out the earth. I ponder within myself: 'When shall I again be at peace with Varuna? Will he, unangered, take pleasure in my oblation? When will I behold his mercy, my mind at rest? I meditate on my sin, O Varuna, desiring to see what it is. I turn to men of discernment, asking them, and the wise all say the same: "Varuna is angered against thee." What was this most grievous sin, O Varuna, for which thou wouldst slay me, the friend who praises thee? Speak out to me, O thou sovereign who art hard to deceive. Freed from sin I would approach thee forthwith to do obeisance. Forgive the sins committed by our fathers, forgive those too that we have ourselves committed. Release, O king, Vasishtha, [as thou wouldst] a cattle-thief, let him go free [as thou wouldst] a calf caught in a trap. This transgression is not of our own free will; wine, anger, dicing, or thoughtlessness [did it]. The elder pays for the fault of the younger, and even sleep cannot hold unrighteousness in check. As a slave makes amends to his master, so would I make amends to the impatient god.

Like the *dharma* of later times Varuna's *ṛta* is 'subtle' and difficult to understand. Man is bound by sin, bound by Varuna's fetters, and only Varuna can release him, but the nature of his bondage he does not understand. In just the same way we will find that in the classical age men will be bound by the 'fetters' of *dharma* itself or Time or the Great God Śiva. Varuna was dethroned by Indra and forced into an obscure retirement, but his ordinances and his *ṛta*, his cosmic order, truth, righteousness, and law were to live on in the 'subtle' *dharma* of later times, his *māyā*, the 'uncanny power' by which he creates and acts, was to be transformed into the creative power of Rudra-Śiva and later still into the illusion that makes us believe that the phenomenal world is real, while his 'fetters' were to live on not so much as the embodiment of sin as the symbol of our temporal existence itself: they become the fetters that bind man

to rebirth and re-death in a transient and miserable world—
fetters which an inscrutable God binds on and which he alone
can untie. Varuna passed very early out of the centre of the
stage, but what was most essential in him was to pass on into
the Great God Rudra-Śiva, the most numinous and disturbing
representation of deity that Hinduism was to produce.

Rudra, of whom 'Śiva', the 'mild' or 'auspicious', was at
first but an epithet, was himself a Vedic deity. In a sense he is
an exaggerated version of Varuna. Varuna inspires both dread
and the hope of being delivered from the dreadful; Rudra
inspires terror and most paradoxically, a fascinated tenderness
for the terrible. 'He kills and he makes alive; he wounds, and
he heals; neither is there any that can deliver out of his hand.'
The words of Deuteronomy are as applicable to Rudra as they
are to Yahweh. Rudra seems ill at ease in the setting of the Rig-
Veda; he is rarely associated with other gods except the Maruts,
also called 'Rudras', who are his sons. He, the divine archer,
pursues a solitary course, seeking whom he may devour. He,
the 'great Asura of heaven' (RV, 2.1.6) and universal lord,
shoots his arrow at whom he will, and his arrows bring death
and disease, 'fever, cough, and poison' (AV, 11.2.22). Even the
gods fear that he may destroy them, for there is nothing stronger
than he. So wrathful and unpredictable is he that even the
prostrations of his devotees may move him to anger as may a
hymn inexpertly composed. The anger of such a god can never
be fully appeased, and the best that can be hoped for is that his
shafts will be directed elsewhere, preferably against one's
enemies. If in the Rig-Veda Rudra is terrible, 'spitting like a
wild beast' (RV, 2.33.11), in the later Vedas and the Brāhmanas he is far more so. Here he is 'black, swarthy, murderous
and fearful' (AV, 11.2.18), a 'robber, cheat, and deceiver, the
lord of thieves and robbers' (VS, 16.20–21).

But there is another side to Rudra: he smites that he may
heal: he is wrathful yet he is mild. 'As a boy bows down to his
father as he blesses him, so have I bowed down to thee, O
Rudra, when thou drawest nigh' (RV, 2.33.12). For he is not
only the great destroyer, he is also the divine physician with a
thousand remedies at his disposal. His hand is 'soothing,
healing, and cool' (RV, 2.33.7), and it takes away the ailments

sent by other gods. In Rudra the opposites meet, but are not yet reconciled; and this is one of the reasons that this terror-inspiring god was able to develop to his full stature as Rudra-Śiva, for in Śiva all opposites were to meet only to be transcended and reconciled.

In the Atharva-Veda Rudra has already received the title of *paśupati*, the 'lord of cattle'; and it is in this guise that his devotees loved to worship him in later times, for they saw themselves as Rudra's flock and the god as the lord of the flock. Rudra is, however, not only the lord of cattle but of all wild life too, and this trait he may have borrowed from the religion of the pre-Aryans, for such a god surrounded by all manner of wild animals already appears on the Harappā seals. However that may be, it seems clear that the Rudra of the Vedas, the terrible 'lord of cattle' who dwells in mountain and forest, combined with the ithyphallic Yogin of the Harappā seals to form the uncanny, paradoxical, and fascinating figure of the later Śiva.

Śiva and Vishnu are the great Gods of classical Hinduism. Śiva, as we have seen, is prefigured in the Vedic Rudra. How do matters stand with Vishnu? Six hymns only out of 1,017 are dedicated to him in the Rig-Veda, and three of these he shares with Indra, and from these we learn nothing except that he takes three miraculous steps with which he measures out the earth and supports the heavens. The first two steps can be seen and traversed by mortals, but only Vishnu knows the third and highest. Alternatively he paces out the world and allots what he has paced out as a habitation for the human race. It seems clear that in most contexts the three steps of Vishnu represent earth, sky, and what is beyond; and in this third step man is promised companionship with Vishnu.

All this amounts to very little. The three steps of Vishnu seem to indicate that the god thereby circumscribes the cosmos in space: he sets a limit to the finite world. So too in time he sets the 360 days and nights in motion 'like a self-revolving wheel'. This perhaps is a faint adumbration of the doctrine of *saṁsāra*, the endless flux of matter in ever-recurring cyclic time. This ever-moving universe is kept in being by Vishnu, though he mightily transcends it, for 'in body he grows outwards, beyond all measure, and none can attain to his greatness' (Rv, 7.99.1).

Hints of the shape of things to come there are in the Rig-Veda, but they are only hints and faint forebodings. Indra in some ways prefigures Vishnu's incarnation as Krishna, and Rudra already has many characteristics of the later Śiva while Varuna supplies yet more. The *ṛta*, too, looks forward to the later and more complex *dharma*, but that is all. There is no trace of a mother-goddess, later to become so prominent, nor do we hear anything of the key-concepts of *brahman*, *moksha*, *saṁsāra*, and *karma*. The Rig-Veda still looks back to its Indo-Iranian past: the key concepts of Hinduism have yet to make their appearance.

2
Brahman

THE WORLD OF the Rig-Veda was still the world of Indo-
European mythology, and the rise of Indra to his position as
'king of the gods' at the expense of Varuna is closely parallel
to the ousting of Kronos by Zeus in Greek mythology; and just
as Zeus was to maintain his predominant position in later
times, so was Indra to remain the undisputed prince of the
celestials throughout the classical period. His victory, however,
turned out to be nugatory, for with the close of the Rig-Vedic
period the gods, whose importance had always been bound up
with the sacrifice, were rapidly subordinated to it, and the
sacrifice itself, which was conceived of as being not only the
ritual representation of the ordering of the cosmos, but also
as the necessary concomitant of that ordering, without which
the cosmos itself would fall apart, lost its hold on men's
thoughts. The old myths and rituals associated with them began
to lose their savour: the gods had failed, and there were as yet
no new gods to set up in their place.

There is a tendency (which we were unable to avoid in our
last chapter) to isolate the Rig-Veda from the rest of the Vedic
scriptures and, therefore *a fortiori* from the scriptures (*smṛtis*)
of classical Hinduism; and to some extent this is unavoidable.
But for the Vedic Indians themselves the importance of the
Rig-Veda, like that of the other Vedas, lay not so much in itself
as in the use made of it in the sacrifice. Traditionally there are
four Vedas—Rig-Veda, Sāma-Veda, Yajur-Veda, and Atharva-
Veda. Of these the first three are directly connected with the
sacrifice, and are 'collections' (*saṁhitās*) or manuals used by the

different types of officiating priest, the *rig* being the 'words' uttered by the priest whose function was to recite, the *sama* being the 'chant' of the chanting priest, and the *yajus* being the sacrificial formulary employed by the Adhvaryu who presided over the actual sacrificial action. In addition the sacrifice took place under the general supervision of a Brāhman who usually stood by in silence.

The Sāma-Veda is composed almost entirely of strophes borrowed from the Rig-Veda, and has, therefore, no independent interest to the historian of religion. The Yajur-Veda, unlike the Rig- and Sāma-Vedas, which are entirely in verse, is partly in prose and partly in verse. Moreover, it exists in two recensions, commonly known as the 'White' Yajur-Veda (also known as the *Vājasaneyī Saṁhitā*) and the 'Black' Yajur-Veda which exists in three recensions the most important of which is the *Taittirīya Saṁhitā*. The former consists of prose and verse formulas only, whereas the latter includes much explanatory matter mixed in with the sacrificial formulas. This exegetic material was known by the name of *Brāhmana*. This word is derived from *brahman*, a word on which we had occasion to touch in our introduction and which we shall have to discuss more fully later. For the moment it will suffice to say that *brahman* in this context means simply 'sacred formula' or 'sacred action', and that a *Brāhmana* is a text which comments on these formulas and actions. The word *Brāhman(a)*, however, also means a person (more usually called 'Brahmin') who both supervises and embodies the sacred. In the Black Yajur-Veda, as we have seen, the Brāhmana texts are not separated out from the formulas themselves. In the case of the White Yajur-Veda, however, this is not so, and its Brāhmana (the enormous *Śatapatha* Brāhmana or 'Brāhmana of a Hundred Paths') forms a separate though dependent work. The same arrangement holds good for the Rig- and Sāma-Vedas, each of which has two Brāhmanas of importance attached to it.

Quite different from these 'Three Vedas' is the Atharva-Veda, which is certainly a later production since our earliest texts speak of only three Vedas. It is not directly concerned with the sacrificial ritual but with more personal matters— incantations and spells of every conceivable kind, spells to drive demons away, to cure diseases, or to procure the love of a woman. The authenticity of the Atharva-Veda was sometimes disputed in ancient times, and the frankly magical tone of the bulk of it has led some modern scholars to the conclusion that it is not of Aryan provenance. There is, moreover, a curious parallelism between the Vedas and the great classes or castes into which primitive Aryan society seems to have been divided. It is fairly certain that the Aryans themselves were originally divided into only three classes known as the 'twice-born' because they alone received the initiation which ranked as a second birth: these were the Brāhmans (priests), the Kshatriyas ('royal' warriors), and the Vaiśyas (the common people of the villages). The fourth class, the Śūdras ('servants' or 'slaves') was probably added later and recruited from the conquered indigenous peoples. So too it is possible that the Atharva-Veda emanated from the pre-Aryan stratum of the population, and therefore only gained its status as a Veda with difficulty.

The Brāhmanas, in addition to providing a running commentary on the sacrifice, also preserve much mythological matter concerning the origin of the universe and its development from an undifferentiated chaos into an orderly cosmos. In them creation itself is seen as a sacrificial act. At the end of the Brāhmanas, however, there appear portions of them called *Āranyakas* or 'forest treatises', which, though not yet entirely divorced from the sacrificial act, are esoteric in content and consciously concerned with the inmost nature of man and the universe of which he forms part. These again merge into the purely speculative Upanishads which constitute the *Vedānta* or 'end of the Veda' and which, despite their later date, are the real sacred book of classical Hinduism. They set the 'pantheistic' and 'monistic' tone that gives its distinctive flavour to Hinduism in all its phases, and their importance can scarcely be exaggerated.

It was once fashionable to contrast the inward-looking spirituality of the Upanishads with the crass sacrificial priestcraft of the Brāhmanas. This, however, is a gross oversimplification, for there is no hard-and-fast dividing-line between Samhitā and Brāhmana, and between Brāhmana and Upanishad: they merge imperceptibly into each other, and the earliest speculations about the origin and nature of man as microcosm, the universe as macrocosm, and the mysterious identity that was felt to exist between the two, are based on similar speculations concerning sacrifice and universe which are so prominent a feature of the Brāhmanas. In the two earliest Upanishads, the *Bṛhadāranyaka* and *Chāndogya*, this close connexion is particularly apparent, and it is very clear from these treatises that the final Upanishadic identification of the human soul (*ātman*) with the Absolute (*brahman*) develops out of the purely magical identifications of details of the sacrifice with various objects in the phenomenal world.

This kind of speculation is rare in the Rig-Veda itself, but not foreign to it. It becomes prominent in the tenth and last book which is usually considered to be of a later date, but it is present, though disguised, in the so-called 'riddle' hymns of the earlier books, the full meaning of which now eludes us. For the older stratum of the Rig-Veda creation is thought of as the forming and ordering of unformed matter, often called 'wood', a curiously exact parallel to the Greek use of *hylè* in the same sense. This creative activity is sometimes spoken of in terms appropriate to the building of a house and is attributed to a variety of gods including Varuna, Indra, and Vishnu. They 'measure out' and construct the universe much as an architect measures out and constructs a house.

Towards the end of the Rig-Vedic period, however, it becomes clear that a plurality of gods becoming ever less distinguishable from each other was beginning to be an embarrassment, for these later Vedic seers were becoming increasingly interested in what constituted the unitary and unifying principle of the universe, and in this quest the multitude of the gods was a scandal, creating many a problem and solving none. So according to the new way of thinking the personalities of the various gods shrank and became little more than mere names marking a single reality. This 'they call Indra, Mitra, Varuna, Agni, or again it is the celestial bird Garutmat. What is but one the wise call [by] manifold [names]. They call it Agni, Yama, Mātariśvan' (RV, 1.164.46). Here Vedic polytheism is already slipping into classical Hindu pantheism.

One of the results of the blurring of the distinctions between

the gods is that none of them succeeded in rising to the supreme
position of creator and sustainer of the universe: none became
identified with the One Being who was felt to emanate and
sustain the manifold. This function was indeed attributed to
many of them, but it was now felt that the function assigned to
the god was more important than the god himself and so it
was that functional gods came into existence whose names
described the creative functions they had to perform. And so
we meet with Viśvakarman, the 'maker of all things', Prajāpati,
the 'Lord of Creatures', and Bṛhaspati or Brahmanaspati, the
'Lord of Brahman or sacred power', and finally with Purusha,
the 'Male Person' whose sacrificial death gives rise to the
manifold cosmos. These late Rig-Vedic creation hymns mark a
new departure: they are no longer elaborating traditional
material, but are original and personal attempts to find a satis-
factory answer to the mystery of the origin of the universe. In
the two hymns to Viśvakarman (RV, 10.81, 82) the old idea
of the divine artificer fashioning the world out of a pre-existent
'wood' reappears, but this is combined with the ascription of
paternity to the god. A creation hymn to Brahmanaspati (ibid.,
72), however, goes beyond this: here Brahmanaspati welds the
worlds together like a smith, but the raw material on which
he works is 'being', and 'being' itself arises from 'not-being'.
What the poet understood by 'not-being' we do not know—
whether he meant literally nothing (which is foreign to the
later Hindu development) or whether he envisaged something so
nebulous and chaotic as not to be described as 'being' at all. In
any case the old dualism remains—the dualism between chaotic
and unformed matter and an intelligent agent who gives it
intelligible form.

There are three hymns in the tenth book of the Rig-Veda
which prefigure the pantheistic monism of the Upanishads.
These are RV, 10.90, 121, and 129. In 10.121 the poet gives
expression to what he feels to be the inadequacy of the mythological gods; he is groping after a real God to whom worship
can be offered not simply for reasons of tradition but because
he is the author of the universe and as such a fit object of
worship. 'Who is the god', he asks, 'whom I should worship
with the oblation?' 'In the beginning', he answers, 'was the

Golden Seed: once born he was the One Lord of [all] that is.'
The creator god himself, then, emerges from unformed, chaotic
matter—'the great waters came, conceived and gave birth to the
All as Seed and Fire. Thence did he, the One life-force of the
gods, arise.' This Golden Seed who, we are told in the last
stanza, is Prajāpati, the 'Lord of Creatures', is thus, once born,
identified with the All—he both *is* the universe and the life-
force that pervades it, he is both death and immortality; but he
is also creator and generator of heaven and earth, king and
lord of all that lives and breathes, and the ruler of all things
according to right and valid law (*satya dharma*). This myth
anticipates much of the cosmological speculation we meet with
in the earlier Upanishads, and the fusion of theism and monistic
pantheism which is so utterly characteristic of Hinduism here
appears for the first time. The light of consciousness symbolized
by the Golden Seed (the sun) and fire emerges from the 'waters'
of unconscious matter, becomes one with matter as its life-
force, puts order into chaos, and rules and controls it by firmly
established law—by *dharma* which is the *habitus* of the cosmos,
that by which it coheres and is what it is (*satya* 'true' from *sat*
'what is'). Prajāpati, then, the Lord of Creatures, is both a
transcendent God who rules according to law and an immanent
spirit who is the life of every living thing: he is both God the
Father and God the Holy Spirit, though as Lord of Creatures
he is predominantly the first.

No less famous and no less 'seminal' is the reverently
mysterious creation hymn RV, 10.129:

Then neither Being nor Not-Being existed, neither atmosphere, nor
the firmament, nor what is above it. What did it encompass? Where?
In whose protection? What was water, the deep, unfathomable?

Neither death nor immortality was there then, no sign of night or
day. The One breathed windless by its own power. Nought else but
this existed then.

In the beginning was darkness swathed in darkness: all this was
but unmanifested water. Whatever was, that One, coming into
being, hidden by the void, was generated by the power of heat.

In the beginning desire which was the first seed of mind over-
covered it. Wise seers, searching in their hearts, found the bond of
Being in Not-Being.

Their cord was extended athwart. Was there anything above or anything below? Givers of seed there were, and powers; beneath was energy (? *svadhā*) and above impulse.

Who knows truly? Who can here declare whence it was born, whence is this emanation. By the emanation of this the gods [came into existence] only later. Who knows whence it has arisen?

Whence this emanation (*visṛshthi*) has arisen, whether [God] created it or whether he did not, only he who is its overseer in highest heaven, knows. [He only knows] or perhaps he does not know.

In this hymn, inconclusive as it is—and its very inconclusiveness foreshadows the religious climate of the Upanishads—two ideas emerge which were later to be widely developed, first the generation of creation by heat, and secondly the primacy of desire in the creative process. The word for 'heat' (*tapas*) is also the word used in the later language to mean 'austerity' or 'ascetic practices', and throughout the whole long history of Hinduism ascetic practices, often carried to grotesque lengths, have been regarded with the greatest reverence and awe, for they are deemed to generate supernatural power that may be put to good or evil uses: they can create and they can destroy. In the creation myths of the Brāhmanas and early Upanishads we learn time and again that Prajāpati brings creation into existence by exercising the severest austerities, whereas in the later literature the gods themselves are distressed by the austerities of holy men, for such austerities make them more powerful than they are themselves. Desire (*kāma*) was later to be regarded as the basic drive that keeps the phenomenal world in being, it is the power behind *saṁsāra*. For classical Hinduism *saṁsāra*, *this* world, was if not evil in itself, then so little good as to make *moksha* or 'escape' from it the one true salvation of all existent things. Desire, then, though less roundly condemned than in Buddhism in that it is allotted its due place in the Hindu *dharma*, is generally deprecated *because* it is creative and therefore perpetuates the wheel of existence. Neither in the creation hymns of the Veda, however, nor in the Upanishads do we find this shrinking away from the forces of life: Hinduism was not at this state a world-denying religion. It stood on the threshold of world affirmation and world-denial, uncertain

which way to turn; and in the Atharva-Veda desire could still
be hailed as the first-born of creation (AV, 9.2).

There is one other creation hymn in the Rig-Veda which
was later to be vastly developed in the Brāhmanas because it
visualizes creation as a sacrificial act—the self-immolation of
the primal Being in order to produce the manifold world. This
Being is called simply *Purusha*, 'Man', and in the later literature
it was to be used both in the sense of the Supreme Being
seen as a 'person' and as the immortal substrate of the human
soul. The only hymn in which he is celebrated, the *Purusha-
sūkta*, goes beyond the creation hymns we have considered so
far in that there is no creator God to fashion an already existent
primal matter. 'God' and 'matter' are in this case one, and the
One is a primordial giant—Man—the victim and prototype of
all sacrifice.

Thousand-headed is Purusha, thousand-eyed, and thousand-
footed. Enveloping the earth on every side he exceeded it by ten
fingers breadth. Purusha is indeed this All, what has been and is yet
to come, and he is the Lord of immortality [and] of what grows by
[eating] food. Such is his greatness, and more than that is Purusha.
One-quarter of him is all contingent beings, three-quarters of him
is what is immortal in heaven. With three-quarters Purusha as-
cended, one-quarter of him came into existence again [down]
here. Thence did he stride forth on every side among all that eats
and does not eat.

So far the pattern is familiar: God both *is* the universe and
transcends it. In the case of Purusha the finite world only
accounts for one-quarter of his being, the remaining three-
quarters constitute immortality and are unaffected by the cosmic
sacrifice that is about to take place.

When the gods performed a sacrifice with Purusha as an oblation,
the spring was the melted butter, the summer its fuel, the autumn its
oblation. This sacrifice, Purusha born in the beginning, they
besprinkled on the strew; him did gods, Sādhyas, and seers sacrifice.

From this primeval sacrifice, the prototype of all sacrifice, all
things came into being, beasts of the field, beasts of the forest,
and birds of the air, *Ṛc*, *Sāman*, and *Yajus*, that is, the formulas
of the three Vedas, horses and cattle, sheep and goats. Further

the four great classes or castes (here mentioned for the first
time) arose from different parts of his body, the Brāhmans
from his mouth, the Kshatriyas or warriors from his arms, the
Vaiśyas or husbandmen from his thighs, and the Śūdras or
serfs from his feet. So too the moon was born from his mind,
the sun from his eye, Indra and Agni from his mouth, Vāyu,
the wind god, from his breath, the air from his navel, the sky
from his head, the earth from his feet, and the cardinal points
from his ear: 'thus did they fashion the worlds'.

The world, then, is nothing less than the dismembered body
of Primal Man: it is the completed sacrifice, and all sacrifice
is but a repetition and renewal of the creative act, and in the
material remains of the sacrifice, the Atharva-Veda (11.7)
tells us, the whole cosmos, both spiritual and material, is contained—heaven and earth, gods and Vedas, the whole sacrificial
system itself as well as *dharma* and truth, for 'the sacrificial
altar is the utmost ends of the earth and the oblation is the
navel of the earth' (RV 1.164.35).

The *Purusha-sūkta* combines two elements that are fundamental to the later speculation of the Brāhmanas and Upanishads, (i) creation is a sacrifice, and (ii) macrocosmic man is
the prototype of microcosmic man, and his various parts
correspond to the different organs of the human individual:
between man and the world there is analogy of being, and since
creation is a sacrifice on the macrocosmic scale, so is this
sacrifice renewed on the microcosmic scale a creative act which
ensures the continued orderly existence of the universe.

The *Purusha-sūkta* is probably a survival in myth of a
human sacrifice once practised. The Brāhmanas, however,
know only of animal sacrifices, and these were practised on a
huge scale. There was in addition the Soma sacrifice to which
reference has already been made, and offerings of milk and
vegetables were also common, and may even in that period have
been beginning to replace blood sacrifice. Originally the
sacrifice seems to have served three purposes; it was a gift to
the gods for which gifts were expected in return—long life, an
abundance of offspring, wealth, health, victory, and the
other good things of this world; it was intended to remove
'sin' incurred by contact with taboo objects or by incorrect

performance of the ritual; and it was a communal meal shared
with the gods in which their virtue passed into the faithful
through the consecrated flesh, Soma, or other sacrificial
species. In the period of the Brāhmanas the actual rite became
more important than the gods to whom it was offered, the
sacrifice ceased to be a propitiatory act but came to be regarded
as having cosmic importance in itself, and the gods, so far from
being the object to which the sacrifice was offered, became mere
celebrants along with men in this vital creative work. The
distinction between gods and men was already becoming blurred,
and already in the *Purusha-sūkta* we find gods and seers
(*Rshis*) appearing on equal terms. These *Rshis* it was who
originally 'heard' the Veda at the beginning of time and it is
they and the 'fathers' who originally instituted the sacrifice in
exact imitation of a pre-existent exemplar (RV, 10.130).

If sacrifice and the world process are in some sense identical,
then it becomes important that these correspondences or
identities should be correctly understood, and the compilers
of the Brāhmanas spend much of their time in establishing
identities between each and every sacrificial object and cosmic
phenomenon; sometimes it is the fire altar, sometimes the
sacrificial horse, sometimes the sounds uttered in the Sāman
ritual. Each portion of the sacred action is in some sense
identical with the whole universe. This 'magical' interpretation
of the universe starts in the *Purusha-sūkta* of the Rig-Veda:
in the Atharva-Veda it is already well-established. In a hymn
extolling the ox (9.7) we read:

Prajāpati and the highest Lord are his horns, Indra his head, Agni
his forehead, Yama his neck. King Soma is his brain, the sky his
upper jaw, the earth his lower jaw. Lightning is his tongue, the
Maruts are his teeth. . . . *Brahman* and *kshatra* ('royalty') are his
hips, strength his thighs . . . thought his heart, wisdom his liver,
ordinance (*vrata*) his pericardium, hunger his paunch, enjoyment his
rectum, the mountains his intestines, anger his kidneys, mettle his
testicles, offspring his penis.

And so on.

This one example will suffice to illustrate the passion for
identification of more or less everything in the whole wide

universe of spirit, mind, and matter with the individual parts
of a sacred animal or other sacred object that possessed the
authors of the Atharva-Veda and the Brāhmanas. Of more
interest, however, is the use here made of the term *brāhman*
so soon to become the key concept of Vedic religion. The
etymology of this word is still disputed, but the traditional
connexion with *bṛhat* 'great, large' can scarcely be maintained
since it does not at all fit in with the earliest meaning of the
word which is 'sacred word' or 'sacred formula', and thence by
extension the Veda in general. It is connected with Vāc, the
'Word' which makes a man a *Brahmán* (one possessed of *bráhman*) and which also proclaims itself as the first principle of the
universe (RV, 10.125).

In the cosmological hymns of the Rig-Veda we have cited
hitherto the first principle of the universe was a personalized
entity—Purusha, the Golden Seed, or Prajāpati. There is,
however, an opposite tendency which develops in the Brāhmanas and Upanishads, and that is to elevate some impersonal
force or entity to the position of supreme principle and ground
of the universe. In the Rig-Veda we found Vāc, the 'Word'
taking on this role; in the Atharva-Veda the same part is
played by breath, desire, time, and, of all things, the leavings of
the sacrifice. The same is true of *bráhman*, 'sacred utterance',
and it is largely a matter of chance that *bráhman* won the
day rather than 'breath' or 'food' both of which are repeatedly
extolled as the 'highest' in the earlier Upanishads. Or perhaps
it was not entirely a matter of chance, but a natural development
of the social stratification of Vedic society; for in the passage
from the Atharva-Veda we have quoted *bráhman* is contrasted
with *kshatra*, 'holy utterance' with secular power; and this of
course refers to the two upper classes or castes of Brāhmans
and Kshatriyas.

At this point it will be profitable to pause for a moment
to consider the various words connected with the root *bṛh*-
that we have encountered so far. First there are two words
identically spelt but differently accented, *bráhman* and *brahmán*
(nom. sing. *brahmā*). The first, neuter in gender, is the 'sacred
utterance' we have already discussed, while the second which is
masculine means primarily 'one imbued with the power of the

sacred utterance or word', and such a person may be either a
god or a man. In the former case the divine *brahmán* crystallized
into a single figure of that name whom orientalists have tended
to call Brahmā (using the nominative singular rather than the
root form in order to avoid confusion). This Brahmā, in the
later system, was to become the creator *par excellence. Brahmán*,
however, could also refer to a man—a Brahmin or Brāhman
—but in this sense the term was gradually replaced by the
kindred word *Brāhmana*, a member of the highest or priestly
class or Brāhman as we shall call him in this book. The word
Brāhmana is also the name of the sacrificial texts of the Vedic
corpus to which we have had occasion to refer.

This philological interlude is justified not only because it
will, it is hoped, clear the reader's mind of confusion, but also
because it illustrates the manner in which it was not only
possible but logical that the Brāhmans of a later period should
come to be regarded as gods among men. Originally they were
simply priests entrusted with the recital of the sacred word
(*bráhman*), the Veda, but once the *bráhman* had established
itself as the immutable and eternal ground of the universe the
significance of the Brāhman assumed literally infinite propor-
tions. Thus, though the warrior class or Kshatriyas were
continually struggling for supremacy, they had to rest content
with second place because the Brāhmans could claim to be the
possessors of an eternal and timeless dimension which was
denied to them. That this dimension has often been far from
apparent in them has been largely responsible for that tension
in Hinduism between what is and what ought to be, between the
'eternal *dharma*' that invisibly *is* and the *dharma* elaborated by
the Brāhmans here on earth.

From 'sacred utterance' *bráhman* took on the more general
meaning of 'sacred power' as such: 'who knows the *bráhman*
in man knows the highest Lord' (AV, 10.7.17). The *bráhman*
in man is, then, the same as the *bráhman* in God—the
bráhman in Brahmanaspati, the 'Lord of Brahman'. Of very great
significance in the development of the idea of *bráhman* is the
hymn of the Atharva-Veda, 10.2. This reads almost like an
appendix to the *Purusha-sūkta*, for it takes up the idea of
Purusha both as the Primal Person on the macrocosmic scale

and as individual man on the microcosmic. 'By what', the poet asks, 'does one attain to the highest Lord? . . . By what does one measure the year?' 'It is Brahman that attains the highest Lord. . . . It is Brahman that measures the year.' Again it is Brahman that pervades the gods and the gods' people, and it is Brahman that is true secular power (*kshatra*). 'The earth is sustained by Brahman, Brahman is the sky set above, it is the atmosphere, the broad expanse above, extending far.' Brahman is thus equated with the fine essence that pervades the entire universe and which enables man to 'grow into all the points of the compass'. Through Brahman he is omnipresent, for Brahman is 'enveloped by immortality' and man himself (*purusha*) is the 'city of Brahman'.

In this hymn it is implied that man, through his participation in Brahman, is co-extensive with the universe; in Brahman macrocosm and microcosm meet, but this union is only fully achieved in the Brāhman who is the depository of Brahman or in the Brahmacārin, 'the man who follows the path of Brahman', that is, the young Brāhman student. Already in the Atharva-Veda the apotheosis of man has begun.

In an extravagant hymn (AV, 11.5) the Brahmacārin is extolled, by virtue of the Brahman he carries within him, as Prajāpati, the creator of heaven and earth himself. 'He goes abroad setting the two worlds in motion; in him the gods become of like mind. He sustains heaven and earth and fills his teacher with the fervour of austerity (*tapas*). . . . He is the first-born of Brahman . . . and from him is born the highest Brāhmanical Brahman, all the gods, and immortality.' Here the identification of microcosm and macrocosm is complete; the Brahmacārin who on earth is known and seen as a young student of the Veda is roundly identified with the creator and sustainer of heaven and earth in all his aspects: as Prajāpati he reconciles the gods within himself, and as student he fills his teacher with ascetic fervour. His origin is Brahman but he also gives birth to Brahman in his turn: he embodies the whole of existence, both immortality and mortal life. The identification of microcosmic man not only with the universe but with the creator of the universe had already reached its extreme limit.

Brahman is one and yet many: this is already taught in the Brāhmanas. 'I praise what has been and is yet to come, the great Brahman, the imperishable One—the manifold Brahman, the imperishable One; for truly all gods, all beings pass into that imperishable: it is both the Brahman and the *kshatra* (the Brāhman and Kshatriya classes). The Brahman is Agni (the priest god) and the *kshatra* Indra (the warrior god); and the All-gods are Indra and Agni' (ŚB, 10.4.1.9). But the All-gods are also the peasantry: hence Brahman reflects and is reflected in the three great classes into which Aryan society was divided. Significantly there is no mention of the Śūdras. This passage is important for it shows the close interconnexion that, even at this early date, was felt to exist between the transcendental order of timeless and 'imperishable' Being in which all is one and the social structure of Brahmanical society: the latter receives its eternal sanction from the former.

It has often been said that the great achievement of the Upanishads is the so-called Brahman/Ātman synthesis, that is, the identification of the individual soul (*ātman*) with the ground of the universe (*bráhman*). This is an over-simplification since in many passages *ātman* means not the individual soul but the 'soul of the All' and is therefore merely another word for Brahman. To identify the two in this sense is pure tautology. So far as it is at all possible to summarize the teachings of the Upanishads we should say that they identify the deepest level of the subjective 'I' with the ground of the objective universe; either can be referred to as Brahman or Ātman or, for that matter, Purusha who is either man, the individual, or Cosmic Man. This idea is already adumbrated in the Atharva-Veda and the Brāhmanas, and the Upanishads merely take on a train of thought where they leave off. In one of the most obscure hymns of the Atharva-Veda (10.8) the identity between the objective Brahman and the subjective Ātman is already apparent. The hymn starts with an invocation of the highest Brahman 'who presides over what was and is yet to be', who keeps heaven and earth apart, and at the same time is 'this whole [world] that lives and breathes and is possessed of Ātman'. This is the macrocosm. The hymn, however, ends not with the macrocosm but with the microcosm, man:

In the lotus of nine doors (the human body) enveloped in the three strands there dwells a supernatural being (*yaksha*) possessed of Ātman; this do those who know Brahman know. Free from desire it is, wise, immortal, self-existent, delighting in [its own sweet] savour, no wise lacking. Knowing this Ātman, wise and ageless [yet ever] young, one has no fear of death.

Here in a nutshell we have the whole teaching of the Upanishads: it is the recognition within the human soul of an immortal something that participates in, is of the same nature as, or is actually identical with the immortal Brahman which sustains and ensouls the entire objective cosmos. Just how this relationship was to be understood and what room if any it left for God was to be the perpetual preoccupation of classical Hinduism.

Brahman—Ātman—Purusha: these three terms came to mean the same two things at the end of the period covered by the Brāhmanas and at the beginning of the Upanishadic era: all three can mean either the essence of the human soul which, because it has its being outside time, is immortal, or the changeless ground of the universe which is at the same time the source of all change. Thus in a justly famous passage from the *Śatapatha* Brāhmana (10.6.3) repeated almost verbatim in the *Chāndogya* Upanishad (3.14) we read:

One should venerate Brahman as the True.... One should venerate the Self (*ātman*) who consists of mind, whose body is breath, whose form is light, whose self is space, who changes his form at will, whose thought is swift, whose conception is true, whose resolve is true, in whom are all scents and tastes, who holds sway over all the points of the compass, who encompasses all this [world], who does not speak and has no care—like a grain of rice or a barley corn or a grain of millet or the kernel of a grain of millet is this Person (*purusha*) within the self, golden like a smokeless flame—greater than the sky, greater than space, greater than this earth, greater than all existing things. He is the self of breath (life), he is my own self. When I depart from hence I shall merge into that very self.

Or in the words of the *Chāndogya* Upanishad:

This my self within the heart is that Brahman. When I depart from hence I shall merge into it.

By the time of the Upanishads the word *bráhman*, though it retained its original meaning of 'sacred utterance' in the specialized senses of both the Veda and the Brāhman class which was the guardian of the Veda, ordinarily meant the Absolute, that is, what remains unchanged in a world of change. This, however, was not enough for the Upanishadic sages, and they tried to define more accurately what this something was. For the *Taittirīya* Upanishad the basic element was food, for the *Kaushītakī* breath. In more modern terminology it was matter for the former, spirit for the latter.

'Brahman is food.' This has a strange ring for modern ears, but the idea behind it is sound enough—and classically materialist; for 'contingent beings are born of food, once born they live on food, dying they enter food' (TU, 3.1[2]). Food, living matter, is the foundation of all life, and life itself manifesting itself in breath is dependent on it. Dependent on life again is the discursive intellect (*manas*); dependent on that again is spiritual awareness (*vijñāna*, the 'faculty of discrimination', or *buddhi* 'awareness'), and dependent on that again is joy (*ānanda*); and joy is supreme spiritual enlightenment and the experience of immortality. This purely spiritual ecstasy, however, is ultimately dependent on matter, or as the Upanishad puts it, on 'food'. Matter and spirit are inextricably intertwined and interdependent, and Brahman is both—both the formed and the unformed, the manifest and the unmanifest, the mortal and the immortal, the here-and-now and the beyond. The world-process itself is grounded in the deathless, and matter thereby has itself an infinite and immortal dimension. To see oneself as integrated in the world-process—not only as an 'eater of food' but as the 'food' of other living creatures—is to transcend individuality and to conquer death; for if it is true that the Being in the individual person and the Being in the sun are one (TU, 3.10[4]), then each individual man must partake in the immortality of the whole. This is a mysticism of union and communion with the totality of existence, not one of withdrawal and detachment as in the classical Yoga. In the *Taittirīya* Upanishad several 'selves' or Ātmans are spoken of—the selves of food, of breath (life), of mind, of spiritual awareness, and finally of joy. Matter, then, is prior to mind, and mind to spirit.

'Joy' is an extra-temporal spiritual ecstasy which is none the less only made possible by its being grounded in the lowest 'self', that of 'food' or matter. Without matter, the Upanishad implies, there can be no conscious spirit. Therefore 'one should not despise food' (3.7). Ecstasy is liberation both from the 'fetters' of space and time and from the knowledge of good and evil. 'Such a man does not fret [thinking]: "What good have I left undone? What evil have I done." ' (TU, 2.9). *Dharma* in any sense of that word has been transcended (KathU, 2.13–14), and the liberated mystic sees himself as beyond good and evil. So he is free to cry out:

O rapture, O rapture, O rapture!
I am food, I am food, I am food!
I am an eater of food, I am an eater of food, I am an eater of food!
I am a maker of verses, I am a maker of verses, I am a maker of
    verses!
I am the first-born of the universal order,
Earlier than the gods, in the navel of immortality!
Whoso gives me away, he, verily, has succoured me!
I who am food, eat the eater of food!
I have overcome the whole world! (TU, 3.10[6].)

We saw that even in the Rig-Veda personal and impersonal tended to be confused. This is even more true of the Upanishads. Brahman is neuter and is often simply called *tat*, 'That' or 'It', but Ātman and Purusha are both masculine as is Brahmā, the personified creator God. There are plenty of passages in the Upanishads which are purely pantheistic in the sense that everything is felt to participate in everything else and therefore to *be* everything else: Absolute, World-Soul, and the individual soul (*ahaṁkāra*) are all said to be omnipresent (ChU, 7.25) and therefore identical, but this is rather a harking back to the magico-mystical identifications of the Atharva-Veda and the Brāhmanas, for in the Upanishads even the most forthrightly monistic utterances are qualified. Let us take the most famous example of all, the celebrated *Tat tvam asi*, 'That art thou' of the *Chāndogya* Upanishad. This occurs in a long dialogue in which one Uddālaka is instructing his son in the nature of reality. Reality or the Truth (*satya*) is one, and all the rest is 'name and form'. 'Just as everything

made of clay can be known from one clod of clay—the modification is but a verbal distinction, a name—the reality is just
clayness, . . . so is the teaching' (ChU, 6.1.4), namely that the
'modifications' of the One True Brahman are, in the last
instance, verbal distinctions only—transient forms into which
the one reality transforms itself, though remaining ever essentially the same. The father then proceeds to treat the subject of
the differentiation of the many from the One in mythological
terms much as the Brāhmanas had done before. He starts by
denying categorically an earlier teaching that Being arose from
Not-Being and firmly asserts that, 'In the beginning this world
was just Being, One without a second'—and the One desired to
become many. He divided himself into three—heat, water, and
food—that is, the gaseous, the liquid, and the solid, for these
are the constituents of all material and spiritual things. The
human body which, though 'appropriated to death', is none the
less the support of the immortal, incorporeal Ātman, is itself
a sprout rooted in food; and food, through water and heat, is
rooted in Being. On death the soul rejoins the 'highest divinity'
which is Being. 'That which is the most minute, this whole
world has it as its self (ātman); that is the Self, that art thou.'

This is not the absolute monism that was later to be developed
philosophically as the examples that follow show. The World-
Soul (ātman) or Brahman cannot be described in spatial and
temporal terms; hence you can only say 'more minute than the
minute' or 'greater than the great', the 'infinite' or 'nothing
at all' in order to convey your meaning in ordinary language.
In order to illustrate what is meant by 'That art thou' a series
of parables follows.

Bees, for instance, are seen to collect the pollen of different
trees and the whole is reduced to honey, the different pollens
remaining unaware of what has happened to them. Individuality, then, is transcended in a higher reality to which it has none
the less made its individual contribution. Or it is like the sea
into which individual rivers flow, losing themselves and merging
in the greater whole. The two parables need to be taken in
conjunction, if we are to understand the teaching of the
Upanishads. In the parable of the bees, individual, differentiated
pollens of different savours and tastes are collected, and each

loses its individuality in the end-product, honey; but each pollen has none the less added its own distinctive flavour to the whole. In the second parable the opposite pole of the paradox is stressed: individual souls, compared to rivers, are identical in substance with the Absolute as the water in rivers is identical with the water in the sea. Interpreting the two parables together it would seem that though, on attaining to Brahman, the individual soul loses its individuality in the All with which it is substantially one, it brings to it its own individual perfume and flavour.

Again Brahman is likened to a great fig-tree. However much one may cut at it, the wound will heal and the tree live on; and even were the whole tree to wither up, the life will continue, for 'life does not die'. Brahman, then, is eternal life.

Again it is like the fruit of the fig-tree which you can cut up and separate seed from seed. These too you can further divide till there seems to be nothing left at all: that seeming 'nothing' is Brahman. Or again it is like salt dissolved in water until the whole watery mass is permeated with it and the taste of it in one place will be the same as the taste of it in another. It is present in everything that exists, yet so subtle is it that only the wise can discern it, for it is the Being that gives existence to all that appears to be other than itself. The search for it is likened to a blindfolded man from Gandhāra left alone in the desert. Once the bandage is removed from his eyes, he will, if he is a reasonably sensible man, ask the way to Gandhāra until he finds it. So too will the seeker after Brahman ask a qualified teacher to show him the way. The 'city of Brahman' is our home, and it is where we go to when we die. Passing into the 'highest divinity' we no longer know anything.

It would then seem that the highest bliss that consists in being merged in Brahman, is identical with complete nescience, a complete 'unknowing' akin to deep dreamless sleep—a simile that constantly occurs throughout the Upanishads. This is certainly true of most passages in the two earliest of them, the *Bṛhadāranyaka* and the *Chāndogya*, but the *Taittirīya* thinks differently. On attaining to the 'self that consists of joy' which follows on that of spiritual awareness the soul 'goes up and down these worlds, eating what it will, assuming whatever

form it will' (TU, 3.10[5]). There is a very similar passage in the
Chāndogya (8.12–13), but this is to anticipate the whole concept of *moksha* which will be occupying us in the next chapter.

In the Upanishads Brahman is both changeless Being beyond
space and time, the material cause of the universe, and its
efficient cause as well. The human soul is at one with It in so
far as, at its deepest level, it has its being outside time, but it is
distinct from It in that it does not share Its creative activity in
time. In Western terminology it partakes of Absolute Being,
but is not for that reason God. The dual nature of the Ātman-
Brahman appears most clearly in the rather late *Maitrī* Upanishad (6.15) which says: 'There are, assuredly, two forms of
Brahman, Time and the timeless. That which is prior to the
sun is the timeless; it is without parts. But that which begins
with the sun is Time, and this has parts.' Brahman is, then, both
primal matter and changeless spirit; and though it may be said
of the soul when it enters Brahman that it 'knows nothing', this
is certainly not true of Brahman itself, for It is the source of
mind and sense and must then understand what It has emanated. It pervades all things, yet is other than what It pervades,
controlling them from within: 'He is your Self, the Inner Controller, the Immortal' (BU, 3.7). 'He is the unseen seer, the
unheard hearer, the unthought thinker, the ununderstood
understander. Other than he there is no seer, other than he
there is no hearer, other than he there is no thinker, other than
he there is no understander. He is your Self, the Inner Controller, the Immortal' (ibid., 3.7.23).

The general teaching of the Upanishads is not that the
phenomenal world is unreal, as is sometimes supposed: it
emanates from the Absolute as sparks are emanated from fire
or as a spider's web is woven out of itself by the spider. The
'mortal' and the 'formed' are as much part of the 'partless'
Brahman as are the 'immortal' and 'unformed'. Complete
monism is found in the relatively late *Māndūkya* Upanishad,
but this is untypical both of the Upanishads themselves and of
most of the subsequent sacred literature. The conclusion that
nothing at all *is* except the One is arrived at by analogy with
sleep. In dreams the sleeper 'emanates' an 'objective' world out
of himself, and since the microcosm is an exact replica of the

macrocosm, it must be inferred that the world in which we live is Brahman's dream. In deep sleep (and in death), however, all becomes one; but this, according to the *Māndūkya* does not constitute unconsciousness but a 'mass of wisdom, composed of bliss'. This, on the macrocosmic scale, corresponds to the Brahman-Ātman in its capacity of creator of the world, the material cause from which the cosmic dream proceeds. 'This is the Lord of all, the knower of all, this is the Inner Controller, the womb of all, the origin and end of creatures.'

If, then, dreamless sleep in the microcosm corresponds to the Lord, the efficient and material cause of the universe, in the macrocosm, then there must be a fourth state in addition to the waking state, dream, and dreamless sleep which is absolutely identical with the Absolute One. There is: and this fourth state:

has cognizance neither of what is inside nor what is outside, nor of both together; it is not a mass of wisdom, it is not wise nor yet unwise. It is unseen; there can be no commerce with it; it is impalpable, has no characteristics, unthinkable; it cannot be designated. Its essence is its firm conviction of the oneness of itself; it causes the phenomenal world to cease; it is tranquil and mild, devoid of duality. Such do they consider this fourth to be. He is the Self; he it is who should be known.

This is the extreme form of the Brahman-Ātman identification. The ground of the objective universe and the essential human soul are absolutely and identically one. All terms referring to the Absolute in the earlier Upanishads that suggest action, will, or intellect—such terms as 'Inner Controller', Lord, King, or God, are no more than weak approximations to an ineffable reality, the only correct formulation of which is 'One without a second'. In this absolute non-duality culminates one great stream of Hindu thought.

3

Moksha

WHAT MOST SHARPLY distinguishes Hinduism, like its offshoot
Buddhism, from the religions of Semitic origin, is its un-
questioning acceptance of the doctrine of rebirth, reincarnation,
or the transmigration of souls. Of this there is no trace in the
Saṁhitās or the Brāhmanas, and it is only when we come to the
Upanishads that we first meet with this doctrine which was to
become central to all Hindu thought. In the Rig-Veda the soul
of the dead is carried aloft by the fire-god, Agni, who consumes
the material body at cremation, to the heavenly world where it
disports itself with the gods in perfect, carefree bliss. As in the
Iranian tradition the joys of the soul are conceived of in material
terms: the soul receives a new, more 'subtle' body, and its life
is a replica of human life on earth, though freed from all the
imperfections that are inseparable from it here. There will be
eating and drinking of heavenly food and drink, reunion with
father, mother, wife, and sons, the enjoyment of the delights
of love, eternal light and movement unrestrained, soft, cooling
breezes, and swift, refreshing waters, soft music and streams of
milk, Soma, honey, and wine (AV, 4.34.5–6). There will be
neither rich, nor poor, neither powerful nor oppressed, nor
will there be sickness, old age, or deformity of any kind.
The joys of the blest will be a hundred times greater than the
highest bliss on earth. So much is allotted to the righteous
dead.

Of the pains of hell the Rig-Veda says little. There is an
'abyss' below the three earths into which evil-doers will be
hurled. This, according to the Atharva-Veda, is the 'lowest

darkness', 'black darkness', or 'blind darkness'. In the Brāhmanas the idea of post-mortem judgement appears for the first
time: men's deeds are weighed in the balance, and they are
rewarded or punished in accordance with their good or evil
deeds. Righteous is separated from unrighteous in the presence
of Yama, the ancestor of the human race who was himself the
first to die and who was, in the later literature, to become the
king of the land of the dead and personified death. Far more
stress is laid on the lot of the blessed dead, however, than on
the pains visited on the unrighteous. The souls of the dead
are spoken of as the 'fathers'—ancestor spirits who claim
their share of the sacrifice as much as do the gods, though
the type of offering they receive is different. To die childless
is a terrible thing, for the 'world of the fathers' will not be
opened to the man who has no son to perform his funeral
rites.

In the Rig-Veda the 'fathers' feast with the gods (7.76.4)
and revel with Yama, their forbear (10.14.10). Their immortal
life is passed with the gods whom they resemble in all respects.
In the *Bṛhadāranyaka* Upanishad (6.2.15–16), however, a
distinction is made between the 'way of the gods' and the 'way
of the fathers'. The first is the way of those who have faith, the
second the way of those who have duly offered sacrifice, been
generous in their almsgiving, and performed austerities: the
first is the way of a spiritual *élite*, the second the way of those
righteous men who have done no more than follow the ordinances of traditional religion. The first, purified by the fire that
has consumed their gross bodies, pass on into the flame, the
day, the world of the gods, and thence into the lightning. 'A
spiritual (*mānasa*) person conducts them to the worlds of
Brahman. . . . Of these there is no return.' They have achieved
eternal bliss. The followers of the sacrificial cult, however, pass
on into smoke, the night, the world of the fathers, and finally
into the moon. There they become the food of the gods, 'but
when that passes away from them, they descend into space,
from space into the air, from the air into rain, and from rain
into the earth. When they reach the earth they become food.
Once again they are offered as an oblation in the fire of a man,
and thence they are born in the fire of a woman. Rising up into

the worlds, they circle round within them. But those who do not know these two ways, [become] worms, moths, and biting serpents.'

Here for the first time we meet with the doctrine of rebirth. Three classes of soul are distinguished—the soul that relies on faith (presumably in the eternity of the Ātman), the soul that performs its Vedic duties of sacrifice, almsgiving, and asceticism, and the soul that is ignorant of both these 'ways'. The first is liberated from the round of rebirth, the second returns to this world in human form, while the third is condemned to the life of an insect or reptile.

The technical term for a religious rite is *karma*; and, according to Vedic belief, every sacred act produces its appropriate result or 'fruit'; the rite, with the inevitability of the law of cause and effect, produces the result for which it was instituted, whether it be an abundance of sons, or of wealth, the destruction of an enemy, or the joys of paradise. Similarly a rite incorrectly performed will, by the same ineluctable law, bring about catastrophe: the rite has virtue in itself independently of men or gods. *Karma*, however, means not only a sacrificial 'act', it means also 'act' in general. The 'act' appropriate to a Brāhman is indeed sacrifice and the study of the Veda, but the act appropriate to a Kshatriya is the waging of war, that of a Vaiśya is to till the soil, to trade, and to make money, while that of a Śūdra is the service of the other castes. *Karma* thus comes to mean the acts appropriate to the four great classes, and then action in general, 'good' action and 'bad' action. So in another version of the passage we quoted above we are told that those whose conduct is 'delectable' (*ramaniya*) will enter the womb of a Brāhman, Kshatriya, or Vaiśya woman, but those whose conduct is 'evil-smelling' will enter the womb of a dog, a pig, or, what is quite as unclean and vile, an outcaste (ChU, 5.10.7). Actions, then, whether ritual or secular, invariably produce their own good and evil 'fruits'.

This doctrine which was soon to become the most distinctive feature of Hinduism was, at the time of the earliest Upanishads, still a closely guarded secret. In a well-known passage (BU, 3.2.13) in which Yājñavalkya, one of the foremost Upanishadic sages, is asked by a friend what survives when the body's

component parts are dissolved in their macrocosmic counterparts—when breath dissolves in the wind, eye in the sun, ear
in the moon, the 'self' (*ātman*) in space, and so on—he replies:
' "Artabhāga, my friend, take my hand. We two only will
know about this. We must not [speak of] this in public." So
they went away and discussed it. What they said was *karma*.
What they proclaimed was *karma*. A man becomes good (*punya*)
by good *karma*, evil by evil *karma*. Thereupon Artabhāga held
his peace.'

Since every action produces an effect or 'fruit' in the temporal
world, it follows that unless this chain of cause and effect can
be broken, there will be no end to the round of birth, death, and
rebirth. The Upanishads teach, however, that the human soul
in its deepest essence is in some sense identical with Brahman,
the unchanging something that is yet the source of all change.
This soul, then, must be distinct from the ordinary empirical
self which transmigrates from body to body carrying its load of
karma with it. How to realize this eternal soul and how to dis-
engage it from its real or imaginary connexion with the psycho-
somatic complex that thinks, wills, and acts, is from the time of
the Upanishads onwards the crucial problem facing the Hindu
religious consciousness.

The doctrine of *karma* which is so inextricably bound up
with that of transmigration because it is held to explain, as no
other doctrine can, inequalities of birth and endowment and the
visitation of suffering upon the innocent, does not fit naturally
into the Vedic conception of the afterlife according to which the
good are rewarded in heaven and the evil are punished in hell.
This doctrine was never abandoned but was combined with the
new doctrine in a not very harmonious synthesis. In the
Kaushītakī Upanishad (1.2–6) the souls of the dead ascend to
the moon which is the door of heaven; there they are questioned
as to their identity, and if they give the wrong answer, that is,
if they fail to realize their identity with Brahman, they are condemned to further empirical existence in human, animal, bird,
fish, or reptile form 'according to their *karma*, according to
their knowledge'. If, however, the soul gives the right answer,
saying, 'I am a season, . . . I am thou,' it enters into the way of
the gods. Thence it proceeds to the river 'Ageless' where it

shakes off its good and evil *karma* 'as a horse shakes off its hairs' (ChU, 8.13) and 'just as one driving in a chariot looks down upon the two chariot-wheels, so does he look down upon day and night, so [does he look down upon] what was well done and what was ill done and all the pairs of opposites. Such a one, divested of deeds well done and deeds ill done, knowing Brahman, draws near to (*adhiparaiti*) Brahman.' By knowing Brahman and by knowing that one *is* Brahman, all phenomenal existence is transcended, all the opposites are done away with, good and evil deeds no longer bind, and the 'self made [perfect] grows into (*abhisambhū-*) the unmade world of Brahman' (ChU, 8.13). From thence there is no return.

The great discovery of the Upanishadic sages was that the soul is immortal in that it has its true being outside space and time and that its connexion with the world of matter—the world of *saṁsāra* or perpetual flux—must therefore be transient and in some sense unreal. There have been mystics in all religions and even outside any religion who have vividly experienced timeless Being, but all religions do not believe in transmigration and do not therefore attach the overwhelming importance to this beatific experience that the Hindus undoubtedly do; for to those who have no belief in transmigration the experience would seem to be no more than a prefiguration of death which too must put a stop to any experience the soul can have in space and time. But, for the Hindu, life in space and time is without beginning and, unless the way of liberation is found, without end too; and eternal life in *this* sense becomes a crushing burden in its endless, pointless, senseless repetitiveness; and as the twin doctrines of *karma* and *saṁsāra* developed, the revulsion against never-ending life through never-ending death in a manifestly imperfect world became more and more extreme. For the Hindus the world was not created once for all nor was there any end to it: from all eternity it had been recreating itself and dissolving back into its unformed and 'unmanifest' condition, and these periods of evolution and devolution were called days and nights of Brahmā. Each day and each night of Brahmā lasts one thousand years of the gods, and each year of the gods corresponds to twelve thousand years of men. Thus every day of Brahmā which sees the emanation of

the universe from the divine substance and its dissolution back
into it lasts twelve million years, and for twelve million more—
the night of Brahmā—all remains absorbed in the One Brahman
in a state of pure potentiality waiting to be once more actualized. Each 'year of the gods' is in its turn divided into four
periods of *yugas* of varying length, the first or *Kṛta* age lasting
4,800 years, the second or *Tretā* lasting 3,600, the third or
Dvāpara lasting 2,400, and the last, the *Kali* age in which we
now live lasting only 1,800 years. The world on each renewal
emerges from the womb of Brahman perfect, and in it *dharma*
and Truth are 'four-footed' and entire, nor does any man gain
anything by transgressing *dharma*: the *dharma* as it exists in
eternity is faithfully reflected in time. This ideal and idyllic
state of affairs in which men's lives average 400 years, however,
never lasts. Theft, falsehood, and fraud creep in, and already
in the *Tretā* age man's life rarely exceeds 100 years. Such is the
Hindu concept of the cosmos—beginningless and endless in
time as well as in space—and the soul of man must ever anew
embark on this journey that has no end, passing from one life
and from one body into another like a caterpillar moving on
interminably from one blade of grass to the next (BU, 4.4.3).
Through each *kalpa* the soul pursues its wearisome course,
accumulating ever more *karma*, good and bad, and unloading
each in the appropriate heaven or hell, only to be born again to
shoulder the burden anew. When the universe is once again
absorbed into its source and the night of Brahmā sets in, the
soul is still not free, but merely unconscious, forgetful of its karmic
load; for once the twelve million years of the state of dissolution
have passed, it must once again take up its nightmare load. And
this will go on not for a few thousand years only but for
thousands and thousands of *kalpas* before the soul can hope
for its blessed release (MBh, 12.281.31). The heavens and hells
which classical Hinduism inherited from its Vedic past now
begin to proliferate, each heaven and each hell being appropriated to particular classes of holy men and malefactors. The
gods themselves are not exempt from the law of *karma*; they
too are subject to the laws of cause and effect, and a day will
come when the good *karma* to which they owe their exalted
estate will have worked itself out. Then they will be reborn as

men, for it is only through a human incarnation that *moksha* or final liberation can be achieved.

Saṁsāra is first described in detail in the *Maitrī* Upanishad (1.3–4), probably the latest of all the 'classical' Upanishads; and the description is not pleasant. The latest of the classical Upanishads were probably composed at about the same time that Hinduism's two great heterodox offshoots, Buddhism and Jainism, came into existence, and they are noticeably affected by the attitude of loathing and detestation that these two systems adopted towards the transient saṁsāric world. Man's body, once a microcosm of the divine, is fair in appearance only; in truth it is no more than a conglomerate of foul-smelling impurities, and what he calls his soul is fouler still. In it are 'desire, anger, covetousness, delusion, fear, depression, envy, separation from what is desirable and union with what is undesirable, hunger, thirst, old age, death, disease, and sorrow'. From the smallest insect to the mightiest god the whole world is in a perpetual state of suppuration and decay. Oceans dry up and mountains topple down: all things are vanity, and only man is fool enough to desire them. He thirsts for life and the fullness of it, not knowing that it is this very love of life that keeps him a bondslave to the twin evils of *karma* and *saṁsāra*— *saṁsāra* that is like a well without water and man the frog that helplessly struggles in it.

Saṁsāra is the endless prolongation of life and from the time of the *Maitrī* Upanishad life itself was deemed to be the evil from which liberation (*moksha*) was sought. 'There is nothing dearer than life,' the Mahābhārata repeatedly affirms. The strength of this instinct of self-preservation is recognized, but it is there to be overcome by the higher faculties of reason and self-control which distinguish man from the beasts. And reason itself must be disintegrated and transcended in the pure vision of the One which is the real 'self' and true Being. In the classic formulation of the Vedānta it is *sac-cid-ānanda*, 'Being, Consciousness, and Bliss,' a triad that transcends all triads, just as *moksha* transcends the three goals of life recognized by the Hindu tradition as being legitimate—*kāma*, *artha*, and *dharma*— 'desire or pleasure, the acquisition of wealth, and the pursuit of righteousness'. *This* world, the world of *saṁsāra*, is or should be

ruled by *dharma* which is binding so long as we are in the world
and of the world, but once *moksha* is achieved the fetters of both
dharma and *adharma*, 'righteousness' and 'unrighteousness',
right and wrong, fall away from us.

What is other than righteousness, other than unrighteousness, other
than the deed done and the deed left undone,
   What is the other than what has come to be, other than what is yet
to be—this that thou dost see, do thou proclaim (KathU, 2.14).

This is the cry of Naciketas, the seeker after knowledge, to
Yama, the god of death, who alone knows the secret of immortality. The incompatibility between *dharma* and *moksha*
and the tension between them is particularly conspicuous in the
Great Epic. The hero, Yudhishthira, the *dharma-rāja* or, 'King
of Righteousness', and thus the very embodiment of *dharma*,
represents the human conscience at its best: he hungers and
thirsts after righteousness, and his high sanctity is recognized
by all. At the same time he has complete faith and trust in
Krishna, the incarnate God; yet Krishna is always forcing him
and his to do actions that are contrary not only to *dharma*
as interpreted by the Brāhmans, but also to the *dharma* that the
King of Righteousness himself embodies and which the
common conscience of the human race acknowledges to be
true. For Krishna is God, the highest Brahman in personal
form, and therefore beyond all the pairs of opposites, beyond
good and evil. And so it is that after the most sanguinary battle
in all literature in which more than a billion men have been
slain in order that Yudhishthira may enter into his rightful
kingdom which he was, in any case, quite content to leave in
the usurper's hands, Yudhishthira asks Krishna to instruct him
in *dharma*, but Krishna declines to do so and delegates the task
to the dying Bhīshma who is the common 'grandsire' to the two
parties to the war. Further, when Bhīshma is questioned by
Yudhishthira on the subject of *moksha* his descriptions of this
state are so self-contradictory and vague that Yudhishthira, the
very embodiment of patience and self-control, shows signs of
weariness for his *karma* has not yet worked itself out and he is
therefore still interested in *dharma*, in right conduct, in doing
good, and in selfless service to his people: he is not yet ripe for

moksha which, he is told, he will not attain to until the next *kalpa* (MBh, 12.281.72–3) and which he in any case does not greatly desire, so void of content does it appear to be.

Bhishma can tell him all there is to be known about *moksha* and, following a tradition that is more common in opera than in epic, he does so at enormous length though he is in his death-throes, lying impaled on a bed of arrows. Krishna, however, who is a mere spectator at this scene, remains silent, though he holds the secret not only of *moksha* but also of the love of God for man that the liberated soul may enjoy if God so wills. Instead he imparts this saving knowledge to Yudhishthira's younger brother, Arjuna, whom he loves as dearly as himself, before the great battle begins, and his words on this occasion form the text of Hinduism's best-loved scripture, the Bhagavad-Gītā. But so little did these sublime words, which have moved the hearts of millions both inside and outside India, impress themselves on Arjuna that when the battle is over and won, he asks Krishna whether he would be good enough to repeat them since their purport has clean gone out of his head! Why, one wonders, did the Incarnate God elect to waste his words on Arjuna rather than on Yudhishthira who was athirst to hear them? The easy answer would be that Krishna and Arjuna were linked together by eternal bonds, for they were incarnations of the eternal sages Nara and Nārāyana who, either together or in the person of Nārāyana alone, were a manifestation of the Supreme Being. This, however, obscures the real issue. Yudhishthira's *karma* has not yet worked itself out: he must wait for it to 'ripen' and only then will he attain to *moksha*. To tell him the great secret prematurely would be to violate *dharma* itself, for the law of *karma* is inseparable from the eternal *dharma* and not even God can break it—let alone Yudhishthira who, embodiment of *dharma* though he is, might have been tempted to throw off the chains of *karma* and there-fore of *dharma* before his time, thereby entering into the pleasure of his Lord. For the last words of Krishna to Arjuna in the Bhagavad-Gītā were: 'Give up the things of *dharma*, turn to me only as thy refuge. I will deliver thee from all evil. Have no care' (BG, 18.66). To *this* temptation Yudhishthira might have succumbed, but his time had not yet come.

In a later phase of Hinduism which the Bhagavad-Gītā itself initiates, the grace of God could and did intervene to extricate man from the trammels of *karma*, but this was not to be the way of the 'King of Righteousness'. For him the wheel of existence was, or so he devoutly hoped, no senseless machine: each man had his own destiny to work out, his own *dharma* to fulfil, and only then could he lay aside the burden of duty, responsibility, and the patient endurance of wrong. This was not, indeed, the accepted *dharma* of his time, nor was it to be at all conspicuous in the history of Hinduism until India made contact with the immoral but moralistic West of the nineteenth century, for even the revitalizing of Hinduism by the *bhakti* cults of rapt devotion to God was concerned far more with escape from this life into God than in the pursuit of *dharma* in this world in accordance with the will of God.

For *dharma* is 'subtle' and 'hard to understand'. It is hard to understand because the world of *saṁsāra* is worse than 'a vale of tears', it is a terrible jungle full of wild beasts and venomous serpents which seek to devour you. In terror of these, hapless man vainly seeks a way of escape, but he loses his way and falls into a pit, the mouth of which is covered over with creepers. These fasten themselves round his limbs and he is left suspended head downward in the pit. But this is only the beginning of his troubles, for when his gaze is turned to the bottom of the pit, he sees a gigantic serpent patiently waiting for his fall, while at the mouth of the pit stands a huge elephant ready to trample him to death should he rise to the top again. But by good chance there grew on the edge of the pit a tree on which there was a honeycomb; and this honeycomb, though it too attracted stinging insects, dripped sweet honey which, if he were lucky, he could catch as it fell. This afforded him much comfort and diverted him from the terrors of the pit; but his comfort was short-lived, for he saw that the roots of the tree were being nibbled away by mice, white and black, the days and nights of all-consuming Time. And he saw that the tree must inevitably come crashing down and carry him off with it into the bottom of the pit where the mighty serpent lay eager to devour him (MBh, 11.5). Such is the parable of *saṁsāra* which the Hindus share with the Jains.

This extreme pessimism is more typical of the Jains than it is of the Hindus, for both the Jains and the Buddhists held this world to be a place of terror and pain. Pleasure was short-lived and illusory, masking for a moment the stern reality of pain which is the natural condition of mortal life. And so the main preoccupation of all three religions was to become the search for a sure way of escape from this saṁsāric world into something that is beyond the passage of time—the Nirvāna of the Buddhists, the Brahman-Ātman of the Hindus.

We have seen what a feeling of horror the world inspired in classical Hindu breasts (though the parable we have cited is extreme). How did they account for it intellectually? The major trend of the Upanishads is pantheistic, and this trend is perhaps best summarized in this verse from the Gītā (6.29):

Integrated in Yoga [the liberated man] sees the self as abiding in all things and all things in the self.

This means that the man who has achieved *moksha* can *see* the eternal in the temporal, and the temporal, therefore, as 'grounded' in the eternal and as participating in it. This indeed is explicit in the Upanishads for Brahman is 'formed' as well as 'formless', 'here' as well as 'beyond', 'Not-Being' as well as 'Being', 'mortal' as well as 'immortal'; and yet it is none of these, and however it is described, one can only reply, 'No, no' (*neti, neti*). Neither in the Upanishads nor in the Gītā is there a hard-and-fast line drawn between the eternal and the temporal.

In the classical period of Hinduism, however, the so-called Sāṁkhya analysis of reality came to be more and more accepted, and in the *Praśna* Upanishad (4.8) the essentials of the system are already present whereas the *Śvetāśvatara* and the *Maitrī*, generally regarded as the latest of the Upanishads, are thoroughly permeated by it. Its classical formulation, however, is in the *Sāṁkhya-Kārikā* ascribed to one Kapila who may or may not be identical with a sage of that name mentioned in the *Śvetāśvatara* Upanishad.

The Sāṁkhya (which means 'enumeration') divides existence into twenty-five categories. Twenty-four of these are evolutes of *prakṛti* or Nature and are subject to modification and change:

the twenty-fifth is *purusha*, the 'person' who is indestructible
and not subject to change; he is the soul. This term, as used in
the classical Sāṁkhya system, has nothing to do with the
Purusha or Primal Man we met with in the Rig-Veda and the
Upanishads, for in the Sāṁkhya there is not one 'great soul'
only but an infinity of individual souls each distinct from the
rest. The twenty-four categories of Nature are, besides Nature
herself, *mahat*, the 'great', also called *buddhi*, 'consciousness'
or 'intellect' (sometimes also called the 'great soul'); *akhaṁkāra*,
the 'ego-principle'; *manas*, 'mind', that is, the faculty that sets
in order the information transmitted through the senses, what
the Schoolmen called *sensus communis*; the five sensory organs
(sight, hearing, smell, taste, and touch), the five 'motor' organs
(speech, handling, walking, evacuation, and reproduction),
the five 'subtle' elements which correspond to the five sensory
organs (the objects of sight, hearing, etc.), and the five gross
elements which are said to proceed from the five subtle elements
(ether or space from sound, air from touch, fire from sight,
water from taste, earth from smell). *Mahat* or *buddhi* proceeds
directly from Nature, *ahaṁkāra*, the ego-principle from *mahat*,
while all the other categories derive directly or indirectly from
the ego-principle. The whole system can, then, be schematized
as follows:

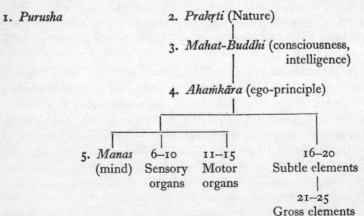

1. *Purusha*   2. *Prakṛti* (Nature)

3. *Mahat-Buddhi* (consciousness,
                                intelligence)

4. *Ahaṁkāra* (ego-principle)

5. *Manas*   6–10   11–15   16–20
   (mind)   Sensory   Motor   Subtle elements
            organs   organs

                                         21–25
                                     Gross elements

Here again no clear distinction is made between macrocosm
and microcosm. 'Consciousness' and 'ego-principle' are

common to the two and on the macrocosmic scale transcend the subject-object relationship. In this respect they would appear to be identical with Nature itself, also called the 'unmanifest'. This again would correspond to the macrocosmic Brahman of the Upanishads which is the 'unmanifest' source of all that is manifest, the formless behind the formed—in our terminology 'primal matter'. But Brahman is, as we have seen, eternal and unchanging spirit too. Here the Sāṁkhya entirely parts company with Upanishadic teaching; for, for the Sāṁkhya, *purusha*, the spiritual essence, and *prakṛti*, Nature or mind-bearing matter, are entirely distinct. Moreover, unlike the Purusha of the Rig-Veda and the earlier Upanishads, the Sāṁkhyan *purusha* is not one but many—it is each and every individual soul, and all of these are eternal in that they have their natural being outside and independent of *prakṛti*, outside the sāṁsāric world and outside space and time which condition that world. How these timeless monads ever got mixed up in matter is never explained, but it is the function of Nature who herself being feminine, is, as it were, in love with *purusha* 'man'— that is the soul—to extricate him from her embrace, against nature though this may seem to be.

More fundamental to the structure of *prakṛti* or Nature, however, than the twenty-four categories are the three 'strands' or *gunas* which permeate every corner of her being. These are called *sattva*, *rajas*, and *tamas* which can be literally translated as 'the quality of being, energy, and darkness'. Usually they are translated as 'goodness, energy, and dullness'. *Sattva* is the quality of purity and tranquillity, *rajas* is the active principle which initiates *karma*, and *tamas* is constrictive, obstructive, and conducive to lethargic apathy. It is *sattva* that most nearly approaches to the nature of *purusha* and is the agency through which Nature promotes *purusha's* liberation from herself while both *rajas* which promotes *karma* and thereby binds the *purusha* (soul) in yet tighter fetters, and *tamas* which blinds and stupifies it, impede his journey home.

The idea of *moksha* in the Sāṁkhya is, then, totally different from that of the Upanishads. It does *not* mean to see all things in the self and the self in all things; it means rather to *isolate* the self or soul—and the 'self' is not a universal, all-pervading Self

or World-Soul but one self among countless others—from all
other things, both the whole saṁsāric world and all other
'selves' which, like itself, are self-subsisting and autarchic
monads.

The importance of the Sāṁkhya system lies in this, that it
supplies a theory of the construction of the phenomenal
world out of twenty-four *tattvas* or elements and three *gunas*
or 'strands' which was to find almost universal acceptance in the
later literature, both philosophic and purely religious. More
important still, it was the theoretical basis on which Yoga
practice was built. It is utterly different from the dominant
pantheistic trend of the Upanishads in that it does not admit an
Absolute in which the temporal and the eternal are reconciled,
it does not admit the identity in any sense of the individual soul
with the Supreme Soul for the very good reason that it denies
the existence of the latter, it regards *moksha* not as a merging of
the soul into an impersonal Brahman but as its total isolation
within its own eternal and timeless essence. It is against this
background that we must consider Yoga, the technique devised,
possibly in pre-Aryan times, to bring about 'liberation' by
physiological and psychological means. Yoga was, moreover,
from the beginning taken up by the Buddhists and Jains
neither of whom conceded the existence of an impersonal
Absolute or a personal God, but only an extra-temporal something that inheres in all human souls—something left more or
less undefined by the Buddhists but classified as an atomic
monad by the Jains.

The word *Yoga* is used technically in two distinct senses. The
meaning most familiar to the West is the physical, mental, and
psychic technique practised in India by followers of the major
philosophical schools either for purely spiritual purposes or in
order to produce maximal physical, mental, and spiritual well-
being. The second sense in which the word is used is to denote
one of the six classical philosophical schools, the *Yoga-darśana*
or Yoga world-view. This Yoga philosophy is so closely akin to
the Sāṁkhya that the two together are usually called the
Sāṁkhya-Yoga—Sāṁkhya supplying the theoretical basis and
Yoga the technique for achieving the highest goal envisaged
by the Sāṁkhya, that is, the total *isolation* of the individual

monad which is the soul both from all other souls and from the whole domain of Nature.

In the Yoga system this ideal is reached in eight stages. The first two represent the ethical preparation, and the last six the contemplative *askesis*. The first stage inculcates the negative virtues of abstention from injury (*ahiṁsā*, Gandhi's 'non-violence'), truthfulness, abstention from theft, sexual purity, and the renunciation of property. In the second stage the more positive virtues are developed—purity, contentment, rigid austerity (*tapas*), the study of scripture, and 'devotion to God' (*iśvara-pranidhāna*).

The mention of God in this context calls for comment. The Sāṁkhya system proper admits of no God, and the declared aim of both Sāṁkhya and Yoga is not union with God (as many popular treatises on this subject would have us believe) but complete isolation of the soul in the soul. What then is meant by 'devotion to God' in this context? Let us see what the *Yoga-sūtras*, the classical textbook on this subject, have to say.

'The Lord (*iśvara*)', they say, 'is a special type of soul which is untouched by care, works (*karma*), the "ripening" of works, or hope. In him the seed of omniscience is perfect. He is the *Guru* even of the ancients since he is not limited by time' (YS, 1.24–26).

God, then, is no different from other souls in that he is eternal and unlimited by time, since that is the natural condition of all souls, but he *is* different from them in that he is never affected by matter or Nature. According to the commentaries he is also responsible for the maintenance of cosmic order, for the imprisonment of souls in matter and also for their eventual extrication therefrom. He is useful to the soul, however, rather as the ideal object of contemplation, for he is the divine exemplar of all human souls: by the contemplation of God one becomes *like* God: there is no question of the soul actually becoming God as is too often irresponsibly affirmed. *Moksha*, then, for the Sāṁkhya-Yogin means to become *like* God in his timeless unity, it does not mean to participate in him in any way. The goal is isolation, not union or fusion as in the Upanishadic concept of merging into Brahman.

It would, then, appear that the Yoga techniques were

originally designed simply to release and isolate the soul from the physico-psychic complex to which it is temporarily and unnaturally attached. From the point of view of technique *iśvara-praṇidhāna* or 'devotion to God' is simply one of the many means for preparing the mind for the more purely contemplative exercises that are to follow. Contemplation of God is useful, because God is the perfect Yogin in that he is never at any stage 'tainted' by matter. Purity, perfect contentment with whatever may be one's lot, ascetic training, and study of the scriptures under a competent Guru (spiritual preceptor) as well as contemplation of God as perfect exemplar, are one and all the mental dispositions required if further progress is to be made. Only if these are fully present from the beginning can the goal of isolation be achieved; for without them the purely physical aids to contemplation, the Yoga postures and techniques of breath-control, and the mental training that goes with them (steadying of the mind and deep meditation) may lead to quite unforeseen and disturbing results such as mental disequilibrium and nervous breakdown. If the course is pursued under the direction of a competent Guru, however, the Yogin will in the end achieve *samādhi* (lit. 'concentration' [of soul in soul]) which can be likened to 'sleepless sleep'. This is a state of pure isolation in which there is no sense of 'I' or 'mine', a consciousness of pure detachment both from the world and from other souls. This is the highest state the Yogin can reach: detached both from the world and from God he abides in his own essence alone.

For the *Yoga-sūtras* this state is higher than the state described in the Gītā as 'seeing the self as abiding in all things, and all things in the self'. This state the *Yoga-sūtras* take account of, calling it 'omniscience', the sense of both being the All and knowing the All; but this state, sublime though it may be, is no more than the dawn before the sunrise.

'Just as the effulgence of the sun is visible before the sun actually rises,' a commentator on the *Yoga-sūtras* says (3.33), 'so does the preliminary illuminative knowledge which has all things as its object arise before the [supreme] knowledge of the difference [between the eternal and the temporal] supervenes. This being so, he knows everything without recourse to any other form of Yogic concentration.'

The sense of being the All and knowing the All is only the prelude to the final stage of the isolation of spirit in spirit, the passage out of time into timelessness, from Time with parts to Time without parts, as the *Maitrī* Upanishad puts it.

Standing, philosophically, at the opposite pole from the dualist Sāṁkhya-Yoga is the *Advaita* Vedānta, the philosophy of non-duality derived from the *Vedānta* or 'end of the Veda', that is, the Upanishads. Advaita or pure monism is only one school of the Vedānta. From the philosophical point of view, however, it is still the most important in India, and it has been widely publicized by the Neo-Vedāntins of the Rāmakrishna Mission outside India. Outside the intellectual *élite*, however, it has exercised a far less profound influence than has the *viśishtādvaita* or 'differentiated non-duality', for it is this form of the Vedānta that supplied the intellectual framework of the *bhakti* cults with their often highly emotional worship of a personal God. The basic texts of the Advaita are the *Māndūkya* Upanishad, Gaudapāda's verse commentary thereon, and the *Brahma-* or *Vedānta-sūtras* which is a not very successful attempt to harmonize the teachings of the Vedānta. It was, however, Śankara, the founder of Advaita as a philosophical system, who first made it a watertight system of absolute idealism. Yet poles apart though the absolute monism of Śankara and the neat dualism of the Sāṁkhya and the *Yoga-sūtras* of Patañjali may be, they agree in this, that an absolute distinction must be made between the temporal and the eternal; but it is on the *nature* of both of these that the two systems so radically differ.

The Upanishads are a collection of speculative texts loosely strung together: they have no single authorship and they do not attempt to present a logically coherent view of reality. There are, however, two trends in them, one towards absolute monism which culminates in the *Māndūkya* Upanishad, the other towards a transcendent though still immanent theism which reaches its clearest expression in the *Śvetāśvatara* Upanishad. Originally the terms *brahman*, *ātman*, and *purusha* were used indifferently to denote the changeless ground of the universe abiding through all phenomenal change. In the later Upanishads with a theistic tendency, however, there is a movement towards assigning the highest place to Purusha, the 'Person', as being superior to the Brahman-Ātman in the macrocosm (KathU, 3.10–11; MundU, 2.1.2; 3.2.8; ŚU, 3.7–8) and more inwardly immanent than it in the microcosm (KathU, 4.12; MundU, 2.1.9; ŚU, 3.13); he is both the *antaryāmin*, the Inner Controller of the macrocosm and the 'innermost self or soul' (*antarātman*) of the self. These passages lend themselves to a theistic rather than to a monistic interpretation. Śankara, however, preferred to take his stand on what he considered to be the 'great utterances' of the Upanishads which express the absolute identity of the soul with the Absolute: 'That art thou' (ChU, 6.9ff.); 'This Ātman is Brahman' (MāndU, 2); 'I am Brahman' (BU, 1.4.10); and 'Consciousness is Brahman' (AitU, 5.3).

The starting-point both of Śankara and the Sāṁkhya-Yoga is the *experience* of the immortality of the soul; and immortality in this case does not mean the infinite prolongation of human life in time: that is *saṁsāra* which the Hindus regard rather as a living death; it is death-in-life, not life-in-death. It means rather an unconditioned and absolutely static condition which knows nothing of time and space and upon which death has no hold; and because it is not only pure Being, but also pure consciousness and pure bliss, it must be analogous to life. It is, then, life-in-death: it has the immobility of death but the consciousness of life. In man, the microcosm, the nearest approach to it is in dreamless sleep, but this, too, is not what *moksha* is.

In a celebrated dialogue between Prajāpati (now no more than a heavenly Guru) and Indra (the ancient war-god who now appears in the incongruous role of a seeker after Brahman) Prajāpati says:

'Now, when one is asleep, composed, serene, and knows no dream —that is the self, that is the immortal that fear cannot touch. That is Brahman.'

Indra is very far indeed from being satisfied with this, and says:

'Such a man has no present knowledge of himself (*ātman*) [so that he could say] "This I am", nor for that matter [has he knowledge of] things around him. He becomes as one annihilated. I see nothing enjoyable in that' (ChU, 8.11).

The monistic answer to this particular problem is supplied in the *Māndūkya* Upanishad in the words we quoted at the end of the previous chapter. This state is 'unthinkable' and 'cannot be designated. Its essence is the firm conviction of the oneness of itself; *it causes the phenomenal world to cease*; it is tranquil and mild, devoid of duality.' And this is the position to which Śankara adheres. Prajāpati's answer to Indra, however, is quite different. In *moksha* the soul severs its links with matter and therefore knows neither pleasure nor pain, it soars up to the highest light where, no longer merely serene, it becomes serenity (*samprasāda*) itself; but this is a personal serenity which preserves the soul's individual form (*svena svena rūpena*). 'He is the highest person (*uttama purusha*). There he goes around laughing, playing, enjoying himself with women or chariots or friends, remembering nothing of this body which was appended to him' (ChU, 8.12).

This may sound crude, but it is at least one of the Upanishadic views of the nature of *moksha*: and it is totally at variance with the monism of Śankara. It asserts not only personal survival in an extra-temporal state but also the survival of personal relationships. This, however, was a view of *moksha* that had little future; and the purely monistic view of *moksha* as the complete isolation of the eternal from the temporal was long to hold the day. But in the case of the Advaita the 'eternal' was not simply the eternal essence of one single soul as it was in the Sāmkhya-Yoga, but Absolute Being or, in Western terminology, the impassible Godhead behind the Creator God. For in Śankara's opinion there was only one reality, Brahman, and this was identical with every human soul, first because Scripture said so ('I am Brahman', etc.) and secondly because, whatever else one may doubt, one can scarcely doubt one's own existence. The Creator God who is so frequently mentioned in the Upanishads as being both the efficient and the material cause of the universe, cannot be wholly identical with Brahman because he is the source and cause of multiplicity. Hence Śankara introduces the concept of *māyā* which he arbitrarily interprets as 'illusion' or 'appearance' to explain the 'apparent' though not real relationship between the One and the many, although the word *māyā* is never used in this sense either in the Vedic corpus or in the *Brahma-sūtras*.

The simile he never tires of using to illustrate this concept is that of a rope which one may take for a snake in the dark. The 'snake' is imposed on the rope through the creative 'ignorance' of the person who sees the rope. For him, and for him alone, the snake is real right up to the moment he discovers his mistake; but once verification exposes the snake as an optical illusion, it is realized that the snake does not exist at all. So too in a dream, the dreamer, again through creative 'ignorance', experiences the dream as real, but when he wakes up he realizes that it was not so and thinks no more about it. The only difference between dream and the phenomenal world is that a dream is the individual illusion of one man, whereas the phenomenal world is a collective illusion shared by all souls which have not yet attained to liberation; and this illusion is the product of *māyā* and of God who is the author of *māyā*.

In actual fact the *māyā* of the Advaita corresponds exactly to the *prakṛti* or Nature of the Sāṁkhya—and this identification is roundly made in the Upanishads (ŚU, 4.10) where *māyā* and *prakṛti* are simply alternative expressions for the phenomenal world; but whereas in the Sāṁkhya *prakṛti* is a separate *principle* independent of soul, *māyā* in the Advaita is a collective hallucination superimposed on the One reality considered as object by the same reality considered as subject and diversified by the same *māyā* into an apparent multiplicity of individual souls. But for the deceitful operation of *māyā*—and in non-technical texts the ordinary meaning of *māyā* is 'deceit'—all souls would realize that they are not many but one, and not one only, but *the* One without a second—Brahman-Ātman. *Moksha*, then, for the Advaitin, does not mean that the soul merges into Brahman as a river merges into the sea, but that it realizes itself as it eternally is, that is, as the One Brahman-Ātman, which is Absolute Being, Consciousness, and Bliss. With the realization of this, *māyā* disappears and is shown to be totally unreal. Real and verifiable from the point of view of the soul still in bondage to matter, it is unreal to the soul which has realized the true oneness of itself. All this amounts to little more than saying that the phenomenal world, both as macrocosm and as microcosmic man with his body, mind, and emotions, is not Being in an absolute sense nor not-being in the sense of the 'horns of a hare' (i.e. something that has never been observed), but something indefinable between the two, what we in the West usually call 'contingent being'. It is not this that separates Śankara from the theists (for the *māyā/prakṛti* argument amounts to little more than a verbal quibble) but the fact that he admits of no distinction at all between the liberated soul and the Absolute or the liberated soul and God *quâ* Absolute. He does not deny the existence of the Creator God on the empirical level nor does he identify the soul with this God on any level. Creation, omnipotence, and omniscience are the attributes of God as seen by man while still in the bondage of *māyā*: let us call these attributes *māyā* (*a*). Dependence, limited knowledge, and limited power are among the attributes of the man not yet liberated: let us call them *māyā* (*b*). God, then, will be Brahman + *māyā* (*a*), man Brahman + *māyā* (*b*). But from the absolute point of view *māyā* does not exist; so man and God must be identically Brahman. On the relative level, however, they are distinct since their *māyās* are different. The identity, however, is the reality, and this is what *moksha* reveals.

Śankara's formulation of the state of *moksha*, however, is far more extreme than the general trend of the Upanishads would seem to warrant, nor does the long section of the twelfth book of the Mahābhārata devoted to the subject of *moksha* bear him out. In this book and in the *Anugītā* in Book XIV where Krishna instructs Arjuna once again since he had already forgotten what he had told him in the Bhagavad-Gītā, there are endless descriptions of *moksha*. The soul becomes or 'is conformed to' (*kalpate*) Brahman, infinity, deathlessness, or the one Self of all things; it is free from all thought of 'I' and 'mine'; it casts off its lower self in order to enter into possession of the higher; it transcends all the opposites, fear and time, sorrow and joy; 'it goes to [a state] where it does not grieve or die, where it is neither born nor reborn, where it does not change, where is that highest Brahman, unmanifest, unmoving, steadfast, unformed and effortless, immortal and unfractionable (*aviyogin*), where men are not negated by pairs of opposites or by mental work (*karma*), where [all] are always like-minded (*samāḥ*) and friendly, and where they rejoice in the well-being of all creatures' (MBh, 12.241.11–14). To achieve this the lower self must be left behind.

You must rigorously control the rebellious senses with your intellect (*buddhi*) as a father controls his children so prone to fall. To draw the mind and the senses together into a single point [of concentration] is the highest form of asceticism (*tapas*). That is better than any other way of perfection (*dharma*), it is said to be the highest such way. Concentrating the senses and mind in the contemplative intellect (*medhā*), rejoicing in yourself, sit down, not thinking overmuch. Once the senses have been brought back from their pastures and have been shut up in the stable, then will you of your own self see the highest eternal Self, the Self of All, the Great Self, like a smokeless flame. . . . Just as a mighty tree complete with flower and fruit and many a branch, knows not of itself where its flowers and fruits may be, so does the [little] self not know whither it goes or whence it has come. But other is the self's inmost Self (*antarātman*) which surveys all things. Light the lamp of wisdom and behold the [Great] Self by thine own self. Having seen the [Great] Self, knowing all things, become selfless and, like a snake that has sloughed off (*vimukta*) its skin, slough off all evil things (MBh, 12.250).

The discourses on *moksha* in the Great Epic progress from a modified Sāṁkhya-Yoga position in which one great Purusha tends to take the place of the numberless individual *purushas* of the classical system to a more frankly theistic position. In this God (Vishnu) tends to be exalted above Brahman and the Great Ātman; so while it is possible to *become* Brahman one can do more than enter into God. But whether souls become Brahman or enter into God, it is not clear whether, once their empirical personality, their 'I' or lower self, has been destroyed, anything at all corresponding to personality remains; and it is this that Yudhishthira who is 'King of *dharma*', not of *moksha*, would dearly like to know. The answers he receives are vague, for this is a state, the text tells us, which is neither oneness nor multiplicity, but certain similes are repeatedly used to describe what can only be called unity-in-diversity. The liberated soul is like a fish in the sea, permeated within and without with water, or it is like a maggot in a fig, enveloped by the fig,

living on it, and almost of the same texture as it (ibid., 12.310);
purified from all taint of *karma* and 'isolated' (*kevala*) it unites
with the permanently pure and isolated (ibid.). In theistic
terms the soul enters into the Lord, or it is united with him as
two suns might unite in the sky. Or again it is like molten iron
which takes its form from the mould or is transmuted into fire
when heated in the fire (ibid., 14.18). The soul, then, in the
Great Epic as in perhaps a majority of passages in the Upanishads, is not identical with the One, but is 'oned' with it
when liberated, divested of its purely human personality
which militates against the divine, but 'conformed' to the
divine in that it partakes of its timelessness and, in the theistic
versions on this theme, of its love and wisdom.

4
God

MOKSHA MEANS 'liberation, freedom, release'. As a snake
is 'released' (*vimukta*) from its old skin, so is the arrow of the
Ātman released from the bow of the mystic syllable *Oṁ*
into the target of Brahman (MundU, 2.2.4): it is freedom to
range at will as a bird flies freely through the unobstructed air
or as a fish swims through the boundless ocean (MBh, 12.328.
30–31); it is freedom from the body and the trammels of space
and time which fetter the body, freedom to laugh and play in
the infinite, as the *Chāndogya* Upanishad puts it. Only in the
Advaita Vedānta and the Sāṁkhya-Yoga does *moksha* imply
the total isolation of the soul within itself, whether this isolation
is interpreted as that of the Absolute or simply of one individual soul.

In the Upanishads there are two trends of which the drift
towards monism is one. The other is a trend towards a more or
less clear-cut form of theism. We have no space to trace this
tendency in detail here, but must be content to say that the
Brahman-Ātman is spoken of not only as the imperishable, the
All, and so on, but also as the Lord and king of all, the 'Inner
Controller' who indwells the cosmos yet is other than it. The
shift towards theism becomes more marked when we find the
authors of the Upanishads using once again the term *deva*
'god', but not now in the sense of *a* god as in the Rig-Veda,
but of 'God', the omnipotent, omniscient ruler of the universe.
This tendency culminates in the *Śvetāśvatara* Upanishad
where we once again meet with the Vedic god Rudra-Śiva,
but this time not as the terrible archer of the forests who seeks

whom he may devour, but as the Supreme Lord who is master over the perishable and imperishable alike (1.10)—a personal God, then, who transcends both the finite and infinite which together constitute the 'city of Brahman'. Of this city he, the Other, is absolute Lord (5.1): he is 'the One—they admit of no second—who rules all the worlds with his ruling powers. Over against his creatures he stands. He, the Protector, creates (*saṁsṛj*-) all things and welds them together at the end of time' (3.2). He is:

The beginning, the efficient cause of the conjoining [of soul and matter],
Seen as beyond the three times (past, present, and future), without parts too.
Worship him who takes on all forms, becomes becoming,
The adorable God who dwells in your own thoughts, primeval.
Higher and other than the [world-] tree, time, and form.
Is he from whom this compounded world proceeds.
Righteousness (*dharma*) he brings, rejecting evil, he, the Lord of good fortune.
Know him as the Self-subsistent, the immortal base of all.
Him, the Supreme, the great Lord of lords,
Supreme divinity over [all] divinities,
Supreme Master of masters, beyond the beyond,
Him let us know as God, Lord of the universe, adorable.
The effects [he causes] and the tools [he works with] cannot be known.
No equal to him is seen, no superior.
His high power (*śakti*) is famed as various indeed,
And from his own essence are his works of wisdom and strength. . . .
As a spider envelops itself with the threads [of its web],
So does he, the One God, envelop himself with [threads]
Sprung from primal matter (*pradhāna*) out of his own essence.
May he grant us entry into Brahman.
The One God, hidden in all creatures,
Pervading all, the Inner Self of all contingent beings,
The overseer of *karma* abiding in all creatures,
Witness, aware (*cetā*), solitary (*kevala*), free from all qualities,
The One in whose power are the many—[the many] which are themselves incapable of action—
[The One] who makes the one seed manifold—

Him do wise men behold as self-subsistent (*or* standing in themselves);

[And so beholding him] they, no others, have eternal happiness
(*sukha*).

Eternal among eternals, conscious among conscious beings,

One among the many, disposer of desires—

He who knows him as the God who is the cause of all, to be
approached by Sāṁkhya and Yoga,

He is released from all fetters (6.5–13).

The achievement of the *Śvetāśvatara* Upanishad is that it
welds together the teachings of the earlier Upanishads,
Sāṁkhya theory and Yoga practice, as well as the insights of the
creation hymns of the Rig-Veda, into a theistic framework. Its
God, Rudra-Śiva is no longer one god among many, but the
First Cause who emanates, sustains, and reabsorbs the universe
into his own substance. Though himself inactive and impassible, he is ceaselessly active through his 'power', his
śakti, through which the world comes into being and is again
destroyed. He, the Great Lord (*maheśvara*), does not disdain
to dwell in the human heart, and 'whoso knows him with heart
and mind as dwelling in the heart, becomes immortal' (4.20).
Moreover, the Great God, Rudra-Śiva, bridges the dualism of
the Sāṁkhya system, for he is the supreme Purusha among
many *purushas*, 'eternal among eternals', and at the same time
Lord of both these manifold eternal *purushas* or souls and of
Nature or *prakṛti*.

In the Great Epic Śiva is both the great ascetic and the
ithyphallic God who delights in the worship of his *lingam*
or phallus. As ascetic he is eternally at rest, 'isolated', and rapt
in the contemplation of his own unfathomable Being, while in
his phallic capacity he is eternally productive of forms. In him
the finite and infinite meet, and in him all the opposites are
reconciled.

With the one unborn Female, red, white, and black (symbolizing
the three *gunas*) who produces many creatures like herself,

Lies the One unborn Male, taking his delight: another unborn
Male leaves her when she has had her pleasure of him (4.5).

Both the one and the other male are Śiva, for he is forever
involved in *saṁsāra* and forever unaffected by it: he is the

exemplar of the human soul both when it is 'fettered' and when it is 'liberated'. In him there is no distinction of persons, male and female coalesce into wholeness. 'Thou art woman. Thou art man. Thou art the youth and the maiden too,' the Upanishad says (4.3) quoting the Atharva-Veda (10.8.27). As woman he is *śakti*, *māyā*, and *prakṛti*, the creative power inherent in Nature, and as man he is Purusha,—unchangeable, eternal Spirit. In the Upanishad *māyā* is neither illusion nor appearance, but the power by which God creates a real universe which is the manifestation and materialization of his power. Man is made in the image of God: he is both 'fettered' in the temporal world and 'free' in the eternal, and it is by 'knowing God' that he is freed from his fetters. *Moksha*, then, consists in *knowing* God, that is, in experiencing him as 'abiding in your heart'. This can be expressed as having access to Brahman (6.10), as being merged in Brahman (1.7), both of which mean no more than participating in eternal being, or as 'isolation' as in the Sāṁkhya-Yoga (1.11). The relationship between Ātman, Brahman, and God in the experience of liberation is, however, best formulated in 2.14–15:

Even as a mirror smeared over with dirt shines brightly once it has been cleaned,
So does the soul (*dehin*) once it has beheld the quiddity of its own Ātman become one, its goal achieved and free from sorrow.
When the integrated man (*yukta = Yogin*) beholds the quiddity of Brahman by means of the quiddity of his Ātman, as with a lamp,
Then does he know the unborn, abiding, pure God who is devoid of all quiddity, [and knowing him] he is released from all fetters.

Just as the Great God transcends both the finite and infinite, *prakṛti* and *purusha*, *māyā* and Brahman, so is he more intimate to the soul of man than the soul itself: transcending the infinite he yet indwells the soul. All this was later to be formalized in the theology of the *Śaiva Siddhānta* in the Tamil-speaking lands in the extreme south of India in the thirteenth century A.D.

In the *Śvetāśvatara* Upanishad the Absolute is for the first time identified with a personal God, in this case, Rudra-Śiva. Though Śiva indwells the soul, he is not identical with it, he is the 'Person of the measure of a thumb, the innermost soul (*antarātman*) ever seated in the heart of creatures' (3.13); but since he is God worship is due to him as it is not due to an impersonal being (2.17), and it is therefore legitimate to invoke his protection and his grace (*prasāda*). The highroad to the knowledge of God which brings about *moksha*, however, is considered to be Yoga. The Yoga described in the *Śvetāśvatara* Upanishad is basically the same technique as that of the *Yoga-sūtras* and the Bhagavad-Gītā; it aims at mastering the senses and the mind, so that the mirror of the soul, unsullied by all temporal concerns, may perfectly reflect the God who is 'hidden in the heart'. The immanent God is thus to be known (*jñāna*) by Yoga, the transcendent God to be worshipped with loving devotion (*bhakti*).

Once, however, the Absolute—the supreme Brahman, Ātman, and Purusha—was identified with a particular god, it inevitably came to be associated with all the mythological accretions that in the course of time had converged to form the personality of that God. Śiva is no exception; and in him are combined the terrible Rudra of the Rig-Veda and the ithyphallic Yogin of the Harappā seals, and however much his worship may be spiritualized, these basic characteristics never leave him.

In the Great Epic it is not at all clear whether Śiva or Vishnu is to be regarded as the supreme Deity. Śiva's appearances are rare, but when he does appear, Krishna, the incarnation of Vishnu, invariably seems to take second place. Throughout there is tension and rivalry between the two gods, and this is never wholly dissipated even when they are fused into the single figure *Hari-hara*, *Hari* being one of the names of Vishnu and *Hara* of Śiva.

There are three passages in the Mahābhārata which describe the Great God Śiva in detail: these are 7.202–3, 12.285–6, and 13.14–18. The word *Śiva* means 'mild' or 'auspicious', but this is not the quality that first strikes us in this uncanny god. Unlike Vishnu whose benevolence is rarely in doubt Śiva is wrathful, incalculable, jealous in the Old Testament sense of that term, and devoid of comeliness. He loves to haunt the cremation-ground, clad in elephant-hide or tiger-skin, his neck encircled with a necklace of skulls, with serpents in his hair.

He wears the matted locks of an ascetic and the austerities he performs are terrific. Once the god of love had the impudence to disturb his Yogic contemplation with the vulgar lures of sex. With a glance of his third eye—the eye of contemplative wisdom situated above the bridge of the nose—he reduced the impudent godlet to ashes, and would only consent to take his consort Parvatī, the 'lady of the mountains', to be his wedded wife after she too had performed the fiercest austerities.

But this fierce asceticism is only one side of his character; he is also *natarāja*, the 'Lord of the dance'. His dance is two-fold: either he dances in the sheer joy of overflowing power—he dances creation into existence; or else, in the Tāndava dance, he careers down the mountain-side frenzied, like a madman or a drunkard, surrounded by a rout of half-human, half-animal creatures who urge him on in his mad career. This dance represents the destruction of the world. Sometimes he dances alone, sometimes he is partnered by his consort variously called Parvatī, Umā, Kālī, or Durgā.

Śiva is the reconciliation of all opposites: therefore he is both creator and destroyer, terrible and mild, evil and good, male and female, eternal rest and ceaseless activity. His consort is really only part of himself—his *śakti*, the 'power' by which he creates, sustains, and destroys. In the so-called *Śākta* cults which worship the female Śakti rather than the male Śiva who, being ever immersed in a Yogic trance, is deaf to the prayers of men, Śiva's consort is worshipped to the exclusion of Śiva himself. Usually she is represented not as the mild Umā or Parvatī but as the dreadful Durgā or Kālī who, with lolling tongue, drinks blood out of a human skull and who, to this day rejoices in the bloody sacrifices of goats at her great temple in Calcutta.

In the full figure of Śiva, however, the male and female principles are united, and he himself is said to be half man and half woman. The emblem under which he particularly delights to be worshipped is the *lingam* or phallus which is always erect. *Lingam* and *yoni* (the female organ) represent the totality of his nature and the totality of all created existence. Unlike the discus of Vishnu or the thunderbolt of Indra they are the *natural* symbols of supreme Deity for they are to be found throughout the whole created order. Hence even the gods bow down in worship to the all-creating and all-sustaining phallus of Śiva.

Śiva is also *paśupati*, the 'Lord of animals', and there is scarcely an animal whose form he will not assume. Usually, however, it is as a bull that he is worshipped, and when in human form the white bull Nandin is his mount. Although the title *paśupati* is found in the Atharva-Veda, Śiva claims to have founded the religion of the *Pāśupatyas* which took no cognizance of the Vedic division of society into the four great classes or the four stages of life laid down by the Brāhmans (MBh, 12.286.123ff.). This and other evidence suggests that there is much in the figure of Śiva that derives from non-Aryan sources. Brāhmanism, however, can absorb almost anything into itself, and so the rivalry between Śiva and Vishnu was resolved by the creation of a largely artificial *Trimūrti* or 'One God in three forms', Brahmā—Vishnu—Śiva, a trinity in which Brahmā is the creator, Vishnu the preserver, and Śiva the destroyer. This compromise was, however, without effect on popular religion, and Hindus are to this day predominantly worshippers of either Vishnu or Śiva or Śiva's *śakti*, each of which their devotees regard as the supreme Being.

There are too many threads that go to make up the disconcerting figure of Śiva for us to attempt to summarize his significance. Despite the fact that he was later to inspire the tenderest love among his devotees, he remains a *mysterium tremendum et fascinosum*: he terrifies and he fascinates. Unlike Vishnu and his incarnations there is little that is human about him; he transcends humanity, and the violence of the contradictions that he subsumes into himself gives him a sublimity and a mystery that no purely anthropomorphic figure could evoke. Permanently ithyphallic, yet perpetually chaste: how is one to explain such a phenomenon? The Śāktas[1] of a later time sought to realize in themselves the perfect union of the male and female principles in the One by combining the strictest control of the senses with the sexual act itself. A man and a woman, representing Śiva and his Śakti, would lie in close embrace but with the senses under such perfect control that no seminal discharge took place. Thus, it was claimed, the complete

[1] Worshippers of Śakti.

fusion of the male and female principles, of Purusha and *prakṛti*, was realized in the One and indivisible Śiva who, though ever chaste, is yet ever ithyphallic. In this close embrace which imitates the inseparable unity of Śiva and Śakti, there is no distinction between liberation and creativity, between *moksha* and *saṁsāra*, because the opposites are felt to have been transcended. The close union of the sexes is thus the most perfect representation in the saṁsāric world of the divine transcendence of all opposites.

From the sixth century onward the cult of Śiva was making increasing progress in the Tamil-speaking lands of south India where Jainism and to a lesser extent Buddhism were by now firmly entrenched. This movement, which was deeply devotional in character, reached its climax with Sambandhar who converted the local king from Jainism in the seventh century and in Māṇikka Vāśagar (Skt. Māṇikya Vācaka) who in the ninth century composed some of the loveliest hymns in praise of the love of God that have been written in any language. These and the other Tamil Śaivite[1] saints together with their Vaishnavite[2] counterparts started the great *bhakti* movement which was later to sweep across all India and which will engage us in a later chapter. The theology of the Tamil Śaivites, known as the *Śaiva Siddhānta*, was systematized by Maykandar Karulturai in the thirteenth century in his *Śiva-jñāna-bodham* which claims to be the quintessence of the *Āgamas*, as the sacred books of the Śaivites are called, and by Arulananti (Arunandi) Śivācārya, his pupil, in his *Śiva-jñāna-siddhiyār*.

Rather earlier than these two great teachers but later than the original upsurge of Śiva-worship in the south a similar movement took place in Kashmir in the extreme north. This is associated with the names of Vasugupta and Somānanda who probably lived in the ninth century A.D. Unlike the parallel movement in the south the system of the Kashmir Śaivites resembled that of Śankara, though it differed from it in three important respects—first the Absolute is now Śiva, not Brahman, secondly the divine personality is far more subtly and

---

[1] 'Śaiva' or 'Śaivite' = worshipper of Śiva.
[2] Worshipper of Vishnu.

elaborately conceived, and thirdly *māyā* is not in any sense unreal since logically the super-eminently real, Śiva, cannot co-exist with what is illusory or in some sense unreal. There is no space in this little book to enter into the elaborate theology of this interesting sect which, in its intricacy, resembles some of the Gnostic speculations of the West. Suffice it to say that the liberated soul becomes one with Śiva and his five *śaktis* or 'powers' which are eternal relationships existing within the Deity itself and through which multiplicity is eternally present in the divine unity. Thus though Śiva and Śakti are indissolubly one, they have these five powers—the power of conceiving of themselves as separate, absolute satisfaction in their profound unity, and the eternal prototypes of will, knowledge, and action, all of which are actualized in *māyā* or the phenomenal world.

The *Śaiva Siddhānta* of the South is far more deeply permeated with the devotional spirit from which it sprang. Its whole conception of God and his relationship to the world stands nearer to Christianity than does any other system, for in it God *is* love (S, 3.1.47) and his every action springs from his loving care for his creatures. We saw that as early as the Atharva-Veda Śiva was called *paśupati* the 'Lord of cattle' and we saw how he had taken over the *pāśas* or 'fetters' of the Vedic Varuna. In the *Śaiva Siddhānta* all existence is divided into *pati*, *paśu* and *pāśa*, the Lord, his cattle or chattels, and the fetters with which the latter are bound. Śiva, the Lord, is wholly transcendent and other than both the souls who are his cattle and the fetters which bind them. These fetters are three in number—*māyā* which, as in the northern school, is real and without beginning in time, *karma*, the acts of individual souls and their good and evil 'fruits' to which, again, no beginning can be assigned, and *ānava*, literally 'the quality of being minute' which, being the principle of individuation, keeps the soul shut up within itself. This principle is utterly at war with the soul since it separates it from God: it is far more destructive of the soul than *māyā*, for *māyā* can be used by God to liberate the soul. The soul, on its side, can do nothing without the prompting of divine grace, and the love of God is thus the supreme virtue and the highest *dharma* is obedience to his command. God himself, though in theory impassible, has but

one desire, and that is 'to do you good' (S, 3.2.27). This being
so, and since God's law is love, 'the virtues of loveless men are
sinful' (ibid., 29).

God alone is transcendent and wholly independent. The
world (*māyā*), human souls, and what they do are therefore
dependent on him: though not created in time they are logically
posterior to him, and but for him would be pure non-existence.
It can never be said that the soul *is* God or God the soul as the
followers of the Advaita would have us believe. Though the
Śaiva Siddhānta, like other systems, speaks of God's action
in the world as a 'game' or 'sport'—and the dance of Śiva
symbolizes this 'game'—the 'game' has a purpose, and that is the
divinization of man, the transforming union of his soul into
God, in which the soul is not annihilated or even negated, but
fused into the likeness of God. God, on his side, is no absolute
blank, but supremely self-aware and effortlessly active though
ever at peace. His activity is his Śakti, his eternal consort,
through whom he creates and loves what he has created. 'Śiva
begets Śakti and Śakti begets Śiva. Both in their happy union
produce the worlds and souls. Still Śiva is [ever] chaste and the
sweet-speeched Śakti remains [ever] a virgin. Only sages can
comprehend this secret' (S, 3.2.77). And the secret is this,
that just as Śiva and his Śakti are eternally one and united in
substantial love, yet eternally distinct in that without distinction love is impossible, so is the liberated soul oned with and
fused in Śiva-Śakti, but still distinct in that it knows and loves
what it can never altogether become.

Throughout endless ages God is in loving pursuit of the soul,
and the soul must respond to the call of grace by entrusting
itself wholly into the hands of God. In its lowest state it is
apparently wholly identical with *āṇava*: this is the state of
kaivalyam or 'isolation' which, as we have seen, the Sāṁkhya-
Yoga regarded as the *highest* state the perfected Yogin could
reach. In this state 'the soul is non-intelligent, it is *formless*,
imperishable; . . . it is *actionless*, *markless*, it is not a self-agent;
it cannot enjoy fruits; it is united to *āṇava*; and it is *vibhu*,
omnipresent' (S, 3.4.38). Here we find all the attributes of the
highest Brahman of the Vedānta attributed to the soul at its
least developed stage; and this is deliberate. The state of purely

negative isolation and undifferentiated oneness at which both
the Sāṁkhya-Yoga and the Advaita Vedānta aim is, according
to the *Śaiva Siddhānta*, simply the state of the human embryo
or that of pure potentiality as in the 'night of Brahmā' that
separates the world ages. It is the lowest of all states, and
precedes the *sakala* state which the soul enjoys when united to a
body. Only in the 'pure' state that follows and in which it is
freed from the triple 'taint' of *ānava*, *māyā*, and *karma*, is it
ripe for *moksha* which is the transforming union into God.

Just as the king's son taken and brought up among savages did not
know himself to be different from the others till his true father came,
and separating him from his wild associates, acknowledged him as
his own, and had him respected even as himself. So also does our
Lord appearing as the gracious Guru separate the sorrowing soul,
which is caught among the savages of the five senses and is unable
to know its own greatness or that of this Friend from its sensory
environments, and purifying it of its dross and transforming it even
into his own glory, places it under his Flowery Feet (S, 3.8.1).

God is the father of the soul, and the soul once it is transformed
into one substance with him, can thus say *Soham* 'I am He', but
this can *never* mean identity, since even in *moksha* the soul is
still a servant, united with God but under his feet. This state of
union with God can be called *sāyujya* ('conjunction'), *sārūpya*
('conformity'), *sāmīpya* ('proximity'), or *sālokya* ('sharing the
same "world" or nature'). 'They will so unite with God that
they will never leave God, and God will never leave them; and
dwelling in him, they will perceive only God in everything'
(S, 3.8.29). Entering into the fullness of God the soul 'becomes
one with that fullness and all in all' through God's absolute
Being, awareness, and bliss. The soul melts in God (ibid., 30)
as iron is melted by and transformed into fire: it is not destroyed
for it continues to experience its ineffable union with God (S,
3.11.9); nor is the simile of water being poured into water
adequate, for the soul is only partially of the divine substance,
being but a half-way-house between God and matter (*māyā*).
Rather it is transmuted into the divine as copper is transmuted
into gold by the philosopher's stone, or it is drawn to God as a
piece of iron is drawn to a magnet through the power (*śakti*) of
magnetism which both have in common (ibid., 10, 12). United

with God it is united with all other liberated souls in something not unlike what Christians call the Communion of Saints, and all its actions will henceforth be divine. For, 'in order that men may know him the Lord gives his devotees his form, and they know him and are in him. So he is visible in his devotees who know him, as ghee is visible in curds' (B, 12.3).

The *Śaiva Siddhānta* presents perhaps the highest form of theism that India was ever to develop, for Śiva, even as a mythological figure, gives an overwhelming impression of 'otherness' and transcendence which the much milder and more superficially attractive figure of Vishnu rarely does. Vishnu is very much nearer to man and becomes incarnate as man.

The figure of Vishnu is even more complex than that of Śiva as he seems to have subsumed several other deities into his person. In the Great Epic we meet him in his incarnation as Krishna, the chieftain of the clan of the Yādavas, who allies himself with the Pāndavas in their fratricidal struggle with their cousins, the Kauravas. Already in the Epic Krishna, son of Vasudeva, and therefore called 'Vāsudeva', has become identified with the Ṛshi Nārāyana who is said to have 'heard' the *Purusha-sūkta*, thereby becoming one with the All (ŚB, 12.3.4; 13.6.1.1). This combined figure is epigraphically attested as early as the second century B.C.

Vishnu is the god who from time to time becomes incarnate in order to rehabilitate the world. 'For the protection of the good and the destruction of evil-doers, and for the [re-]establishment of *dharma* I come into being in successive ages' (BG, 4.8). The number of these incarnations or 'descents' (*avatār(a)s*) is not fixed, but those most commonly mentioned are his *avatārs* as a fish, a boar, a man-lion and a dwarf, as Paraśu-Rāma, who exterminated the Kshatriya class twenty-one times, as Rāma, the hero of the Rāmāyana, the shorter of the two Sanskrit epics, and as Krishna, one of the heroes of the Mahābhārata, the Greater Epic, and finally, and most surprisingly, as Buddha. At the end of this era he will reappear as Kalkin who will inaugurate a new and better age. None of these incarnations need detain us except those of Rāma and Krishna.

In the original Rāmāyana of Valmīki which was probably written in the fourth century B.C. it is only in the first and last

books which are generally agreed to be later additions that
Rāma appears as an incarnation of Vishnu—and there only as a
partial one. Rāma is the ideal of Indian chivalry—loyal,
patient in affliction, obedient to higher authority, the ideal
husband, son, and brother, and the chastiser of evil powers. It
was only gradually that he came to be accepted as a full incarnation of Vishnu, but in the later reworkings of the original poem,
notably the Sanskrit *Adhyātma-Rāmāyana* of the fourteenth
century and the immensely popular seventeenth-century Hindi
version of Tulsī Dās, Rāma is fully deified and his name is used
to mean simply 'God'.

Yet important as Rāma is in the development of the devotional
religion associated with Vishnu, Vishnu's incarnation as
Krishna is, at least in the earlier period, more important still,
for it is Krishna who speaks the most 'seminal' of all Hindu
scriptures, the Bhagavad-Gītā. If the *Śvetāśvatara* Upanishad
is the rock on which the fabric of Śaivite theism rests, this is
doubly true of the Bhagavad-Gītā not only in its relation to the
cult of Vishnu but also in its relation to the whole subsequent
development of Hinduism. Though it does not rank as *śruti*
as the *Śvetāśvatara* does, its influence has been far in excess
not only of the *Śvetāśvatara* but probably of all the Upanishads
put together; for though there are adumbrations of divine
grace and divine love in the Upanishads, they are the faintest of
adumbrations only: in the Gītā they became much more
explicit. There are plenty of didactic passages in the Mahābhārata, but only on this one occasion does Krishna deign to
reveal the full truth about himself, and this in great secrecy to
Arjuna, his closest friend, at the most solemn hour of his life.
True, he had been acclaimed as the Supreme Being by friend
and foe alike time and again before, but nowhere else does he
reveal himself as such or give instruction in the manner in which
men should live their lives.

The Gītā can conveniently be divided into three parts: the
first (Chapters I–VI) deals with the different ways in which the
soul may win through to liberation, the second deals with the
nature of God and ends up with the grand theophany in
Chapter XI, while the last part, after going over much of the
previous ground, ends up with what is a new gospel, not hitherto

proclaimed in India, the gospel of the love of God for man. In the *Śvetāśvatara* Upanishad the transcendence of the personal God over and above the impersonal Brahman was affirmed, but God was seen rather as the exemplar of the soul than as the supreme object of loving devotion. Only with the advent of the *Śaiva Siddhānta* was the transcendent and rather aloof God of the *Śvetāśvatara* united to the highly personal God Śiva who claimed man's total devotion, service, and love. The Gītā was probably composed in the third or fourth century B.C., and it is thus our first literary source for *bhakti*, as devotional religion is called in India. The word *bhakti* derives from a root *bhaj-* the first meaning of which is 'to share or participate in' and this meaning is still present in the Gītā where Krishna is said to 'participate in' his devotees as much as they participate in him (4.11). The word is also very frequently used for sexual love and sexual union, and this aspect of it tends to be emphasized in the later *bhakti* sects: in the Gītā, however, there is no faintest suggestion of this.

The Gītā is not an easy text to interpret as it is not consistent with itself. The climax of the book is, however, the theophany in the eleventh chapter, in which Krishna, the incarnate God and inseparable friend of Arjuna, reveals himself to the latter in his 'supreme form as the Lord', and this revelation inspires the terrified Arjuna to confess Krishna as being 'more to be prized even than Brahman' (11.37). The theology of the Gītā, then, continues that of the *Śvetāśvatara* Upanishad. Brahman is both the timeless state of being which characterizes *moksha* and the source and origin of all that has its being in space and time. It is, then, both time and eternity. God, however, in the Gītā transcends both, and because he is personal you can never say that the liberated soul actually *becomes* God as you can say that it becomes Brahman; for the word *brahman* when used in this context means no more than 'eternal' as it normally does in the early Buddhist texts from which the term *brahmabhūta* 'become Brahman' seems to have been borrowed. *Moksha* means no more than to have been liberated from the bonds of *saṃsāra* into the freedom of immortal life; and because God is by definition beyond space and time, it also means that the soul participates in God's mode of existence without for that reason being identical with him, for though God, like Brahman, pervades all things both temporal and eternal, he transcends both as their overseer (9.10; 13.22). Though he is what is most inward in them and more characteristic of them than they are of themselves, he stands apart from them, contemplates them, and approves of them. He is the foundation of both eternal and temporal being. He is 'the foundation of Brahman, of the immortal and the imperishable, of the eternal *dharma*, and of absolute bliss' (14.27).

To understand the message of the Gītā properly one must see it in its setting. The great war between the Kauravas and the Pāndavas which King Yudhishthira, the eldest of the Pāndava brothers, had done everything in his power to prevent, is about to begin, and the two armies face each other for the fray. This time it is Arjuna, Yudhishthira's younger brother and Krishna's bosom friend, not Yudhishthira, whose heart sinks at the thought of the slaughter of many of those who are nearest and dearest to him and are yet ranged on the other side. Krishna's prime purpose in the Gītā is, then, to persuade Arjuna to go into battle with a clear conscience. He argues first that though you may kill the body you cannot kill the soul because it is eternal, and that since, according to orthodox teaching, the soul of a warrior slain in battle goes straight to heaven, he is really doing a service to his kinsmen in ridding them of their bodies. Secondly in refusing to fight he would be violating the *dharma* of his caste, the Kshatriyas or warriors, and thirdly that he would be accused by his enemies of having opted out of the war because he was afraid. If he goes through with the battle he cannot lose: either he will be killed, in which case he will go straight to heaven, or he will conquer, in which case he will inherit the earth. Arjuna, however, had already seen the heaven of Indra, who was his father among the gods, and had been but little impressed by what he had seen there, nor was he much more interested in inheriting the earth than was his other-worldly brother, Yudhishthira, who was not interested at all. Higher inducements had, then, to be offered. So Krishna proceeds to instruct him first on how final liberation can be won even by a warrior engaged in battle and secondly on how liberation need not necessarily conflict with and negate the deep attachment that bound Arjuna to himself. The first, he teaches, can be achieved by a total dissociation of one's 'self', which is eternal and not therefore responsible for acts committed in time, from acts performed by a temporal body at the behest of a temporal will, both of which are mere evolutes of matter (*prakṛti* or *māyā*). In so doing he attains to the same separation of spirit from matter that is the reward of the most accomplished Yogin. In the heat of battle, then, he will be no different from the Yogin whose mind is stilled and to whom 'supreme bliss draws nigh, his passions stilled, for he has become Brahman and is free from strain. . . . Seeing himself in all things and all things in himself, he sees the same thing everywhere' (6.27, 29). He will have passed beyond pleasure and pain, the sense of 'I' and 'mine' and all the opposites, for he will understand that since he has his true being outside time and space, he cannot die.

It is at this point that Krishna makes the transition from the teaching concerning the immortal soul and Brahman to the teaching concerning himself, that is, God. 'For him who sees all things in me and me in all things, I am not lost nor is he lost to me. The Yogin who participates in (*bhajati*—loves, is devoted to) me who am present in all contingent beings, who, grounded in unity, is yet engaged in all manner of occupations, abides in me.' The nature of God he can infer from the experience of liberation in which time and space are abolished, and he can thus feel himself present everywhere. His mind and thoughts intent on God he attains to the 'peace that culminates in Nirvāna and subsists in God' (6.14–15), for only when it is itself released from the bonds of *saṁsāra* can the soul draw nigh to God (9.28). Both the way of 'knowledge' (*jñāna*), that is, intensive Yogic concentration aimed at dissociating the eternal from the temporal in man himself, and the way of devotion (*bhakti*) are said to lead to the 'Nirvāna of Brahman' and so to God (6.14–15, 27–32), but *bhakti* is the easier way (12.5–7) and, unlike the ways of salvation prescribed by the Vedas and Upanishads which remained in the exclusive possession of the three 'twice-born' classes, it is open to all men including Śūdras and women.

Not only is the personal Lord higher than Brahman, he,

like Varuna in the Rig-Veda, has also the power to bind and to loose—he can save his devotees from the effects of their own *karma*, or, in Christian terminology, he has the power to forgive sins and to remit the punishment due to sin. 'If even a man whose conduct is most evil devotes himself to me and none other, he should be considered good, for his intention is right. Very soon will he become righteous in soul (*dharmātmā*) and gain [thereby] eternal peace (9.30–31).' This does not mean that virtue goes unrewarded: on the contrary, it is its own reward, for 'all those whose evil deeds have come to an end and whose actions are good are released from the delusion of the opposites and participate in me, firm in their resolve' (7.28). The eternal *dharma*, then, is the one sure way to *moksha* within a world still bound. It is through God's grace alone, however, that the *karma* attaching to a soul can be cancelled out and that it can 'become Brahman' and through becoming Brahman be in a fit state to draw near to God.

Nor is God's grace limited to his devotees, for faith in *any* deity is God's own gift and will not fail of its reward (7.21), since all worship is really directed to the true God. This emphasis on grace is something new, for though divine grace is mentioned in the later Upanishads and becomes explicit in the *Śvetāśvatara*, it is made the main theme of the Gītā. Man 'who fears *saṁsāra* and desires *moksha*' (MBh, 14.35.12) need no longer grope alone in the darkness of matter towards the light of liberation, for he can now rely on the helping hand of a saviour God to lead him into the freedom of the elect. It would, however, be wrong to suppose that the Krishna of the Bhagavad-Gītā is primarily a God of love: his preference is not for the passionately devoted worshipper but for the wholly detached sage who yet acknowledges his overlordship.

'The man', he says, 'who has no hatred for any creature, is friendly and compassionate, unconscious of what he has or is, indifferent to pleasure or pain, patient, contented, ever disciplined (*yogin*), self-controlled, of firm resolve, his mind and intellect fixed on me, devoted to me—such a man is dear to me. The man from whom other people do not shrink and who does not shrink from other people, who is free from joy, impatience, fear, and excitement, liberated—such a man is dear to me. The man who is unconcerned, pure, capable, indifferent, unperturbable, and who gives up all active enterprises in his devotion to me—such a man is dear to me. The man who neither rejoices nor hates, who knows neither pain nor desire, and who abandons both what is pleasant and what is unpleasant, though full of devotion—such a man is dear to me. The man who makes no difference between friend and foe, who does not care whether he is commended or despised, whether it is hot or cold, or whether he experiences pleasure or pain, who is a stranger to attachment, indifferent to praise and blame, holding his peace, content with whatever comes his way, who has no home and whose mind is steadfast though full of devotion—such a man is dear to me. But those who reverence this immortal *dharma* as I have now declared it, who have faith in me, and for whom I am the highest end, such devoted men are exceeding dear to me' (12.13–20).

Here there is only the slightest shift from the ideal of 'holy indifference' typical of the Upanishads to a somewhat warmer relationship between God and man. The doctrine of love which is called the 'most secret of all' is held in reserve for the last lines of the last chapter of the Gītā, yet even there there is the utmost restraint. The perfect man is the one who has dutifully performed the duties of his caste (in Arjuna's case the ruthless prosecution of a just but senseless war) yet knowing all the time that these actions are in no sense 'his'. Such a man's 'consciousness is wholly unattached, he has conquered self, desire has left him, and by renunciation he attains to that absolute perfection which consists in the disappearance of action (*karma*). And as he wins this perfection so does he win Brahman . . . which is the final goal of knowledge. Integrated, his intellect made clean, resolute in his self-control, putting behind him the senses and their objects, love (*rāga*) and hate, cultivating solitude, eating lightly, with body, speech, and mind controlled, constantly engaged in meditation, wholly dispassionate, abandoning all thought of self (*ahaṁkāra*), force, pride, desire, anger, and acquisitiveness, thinking nothing his own, at peace, [the perfected man] is conformed to becoming Brahman. Having become Brahman, his soul assuaged, he knows neither grief nor desire' (18.49–54).

To become Brahman or rather to realize that one always was and is Brahman had been the main purport of the teaching of the Upanishads, and no state higher than this could be conceived

(6.22). But at the very end of the Gītā Krishna discloses the
true nature of *bhakti*; for whereas in the early stages of the
spiritual Odyssey *bhakti* may prove a short cut to *moksha*, it is
only once that *moksha* has been achieved that the real life of
bhakti which means participation in God's life can begin.

Indifferent to all creatures he receives supreme devotion to me.
Through devotion to me he comes to know me, who and how great I
am in my very essence. Then knowing me in my essence he forthwith enters me. Though he be ever engaged in works (*karma*),
relying on me, he reaches the eternal, undying state by my grace.

Even so, though to enter God may be a yet higher destiny
than to 'become Brahman' there is as yet no suggestion that it
means to love him and be loved by him. This is reserved for the
very end, and it is Krishna's 'most secret doctrine of all' and his
ultimate word.

Hear again the most secret [doctrine] of all, my ultimate word.
Because I greatly desire thee, therefore shall I tell thee thy salvation.
Think on me, worship me, sacrifice to me, pay me homage, so shalt
thou come to me. I promise thee truly, for I love thee well. Give up
all the things of *dharma*, turn to me only as thy refuge. I will deliver
thee from all evil. Have no care.

It is these last words that represent a decisive turning-point
in the history of Hinduism, for the whole point of the teaching of
the Gītā right up to the last had been that man's ideal course was
to perform the duties imposed on him by the *dharma* of his caste
while remaining all the time perfectly detached, with mind and
soul fixed upon the eternal Brahman and on God. Now,
however, at the very end, we are told that detachment and
exalted indifference are only the first steps on the path that
leads to union and loving communion with God: and it is this
that is totally new.

The full significance of this aspect of the Gītā was first
brought into relief by Rāmānuja, the great theistic philosopher
of the eleventh century who did so much to make *bhakti*
philosophically respectable. For Rāmānuja, as for the *Śaiva
Siddhānta*, the phenomenal world is real and *māyā* is God's
mode of operation in it. The soul, as in all Hindu thinking, is
eternal and timeless, spiritual, unfractionable, pure conscious-

ness (*cit*), and of the same substance as God. There are as many souls as there are bodies to house them, and souls, though like God and like each other in that they are eternal, are none the less distinct from each other and from God who is their origin. Only on achieving *moksha*, however, do souls enter into possession of their true, timeless nature. God is the Supreme Soul and all creation forms his 'body'—both the souls in eternity and the world in time. At the same time he is in a different category and wholly other than all that is not himself. In Scripture God as well as Brahman is repeatedly spoken of as being *nirguna* 'without qualities or attributes', but according to Rāmānuja he is wholly good, and *nirguna* can therefore mean no more than that he is devoid of bad attributes. Moreover, God is a person, and as a person he is possessed of all good qualities to a superlative degree.

[God's] divine form is the depository of all radiance, loveliness, fragrance, delicacy, beauty, and youth—desirable, congruous, one in form, unthinkable, divine, marvellous, eternal, indefectible, perfect. His essence and nature are not to be limited by word or thought. He is an ocean of boundless compassion, moral excellence, tenderness, generosity, and sovereignty, the refuge of the whole world without distinction of persons. He, the one ocean of tenderness to all who resort to him, takes away the sorrows of his devotees. [By his incarnation] he can be seen by the eyes of all men, for without putting aside his [divine] nature, he came down to dwell in the house of Vasudeva, to give light to the whole world with his indefectible and perfect glory, and to fill out all things with his own loveliness. (R, on BG, 6.47.)

As in the *Śaiva Siddhānta* so in the Gītā and Rāmānuja God imprisons souls in matter only to release them and unite them with himself. This constitutes his adorable 'game' (*krīdā, līlā*). Moreover, just as the devotee longs for God and loves him, so does God long for the soul. 'Whoever loves me beyond measure', God is represented as saying, 'him will I love beyond measure [in return]. Unable to bear separation from him, I cause him to possess me. This is my true promise: you will come to me' (18.65). God needs the soul as much as the soul needs God, and this means that the soul is neither annihilated nor absorbed in the liberated state, but experiences unending and ever-increasing love. The devotee, 'though he has come to possess me, is not himself destroyed, and though I give myself to one who worships me in this wise, it seems to me that I have done nothing for him' (9.2). In Rāmānuja God's love is unconditional.

Rāmānuja, like Śankara, called himself a Vedāntin; but his differences from Śankara are radical, and he knew it. Śankara saw in *bhakti* no more than a step on the ladder that leads to the realization that the One alone exists and that all human souls are this One, neither more nor less. Once this ineffable unity is realized, the soul is utterly at peace, beyond all the opposites and all experience: and since it is the One Reality itself, plainly, once this is realized, no further spiritual progress is possible. Worship of God or the gods is thus seen to be illusory, for it means no more than that you are worshipping yourself. Hence *bhakti* is a very inferior, because unreal, substitute for 'knowledge' (*jñāna*), that is, the realization of absolute unity. Rāmānuja will have none of this. For him liberation means no more than the transcendence of time and space—a transcendence that is the birthright of every human soul: it is no more than the 'isolation' spoken of in the Sāṃkhya-Yoga in which the soul becomes *like* God, but has no personal relationship with God. The love of God is a different and entirely new experience, and it takes place in eternity not in time. Liberation may be an excellent thing, but compared to the love of God it is as a mustard seed beside Mount Meru, and the selfish cultivation of one's own immortal soul is contemptuously dismissed as fit only for those who do not know how to love (R, on BG, 12.11–12).

Rāmānuja called his system *viśishtādvaita* 'non-duality in difference', and he is only the first of Vaishnavite philosophers, of whom Madhva, Vallabha, Nimbārka, and the followers of Caitanya are the most important, who rejected Śankara's pure monism as being destructive of religion. Madhva, who lived in the thirteenth century, went much further than Rāmānuja and was not afraid to describe himself as a 'dualist' (*dvaita*). He makes a threefold distinction between God who alone is absolute and independent, human souls which are eternal, though subject to him, and matter. He differs from all other

Indian thinkers in that he distinguishes three classes of soul—
first those few elect spirits who are destined for liberation and
for loving communion with Vishnu, his consort Lakshmī,
and Vāyu (the Vedic wind-god, now transformed into the Holy
Spirit), secondly the majority of souls which are of indifferent
quality and can only look forward to an endless series of re-
births, and lastly souls of such hopeless depravity that they can
only expect eternal punishment in hell. This extreme reaction
against both Śankara and Rāmānuja with its emphasis on the
activity of Vāyu as Holy Spirit and on the *eternal* pains of hell
is generally thought to be due to Christian influence. It is
certainly wholly untypical of Indian thought and never succeeded in capturing more than a fraction of the devotees of
Vishnu. Rāmānuja's influence, however, bore fruit a thousand-
fold in the medieval flowering of the *bhakti* cults.

5
Dharma

BETTER TO DO ONE'S own duty (*dharma*) though void of merit than to do another's duty, however well performed. Doing the works (*karma*) that inhere in one's own condition (*svabhāva-niyata*) one remains unsullied. One should not lay aside the works that are inborn in each of us, even though they involve demerit (*sadosha*), for all enterprises are associated with demerit as is fire with smoke (BG, 18.47–48).

Karma, though it must be transcended by a total detachment from its 'fruits', is, nevertheless, inherent in the very nature of things: *sannyāsa* ('renunciation' or 'abandonment') does not necessarily mean opting out of the world in fervid, selfless, and yet selfish asceticism, but rather living in this world in the sublime consciousness of not being *of* this world. Though the soul be not yet free (*mukta*, 'liberated'), it should behave in the body *as if* it were free and cultivate the virtues of dispassion that are natural to the liberated man. In this a man would simply be doing what God does, for Krishna says in the Gītā:

I need do nothing at all in the three worlds, nor is there any goal that I have not attained, and yet I am engaged in the doing of works (*karma*). For were I not to engage in works tirelessly, all men would follow my example, and these worlds would fall into ruin were I not to perform works. Then would I be a worker of confusion and a destroyer of these [my] creatures (BG, 3.22–24). The system of the four great classes was generated by me together with the virtues (*guna*) and works attached to each. Worker of all this though I be, know that in eternity I do no work at all. Works do not defile me nor have I any desire for their fruits. He who knows that such is my nature, is not bound by [any] work [he may perform]. You must know that works were performed even by the ancients engaged though they were in the quest for liberation. So do you too perform works even as did the ancients in time long past. . . . You must see inaction in [the context of] work and (action and) work in [the context of] inaction. The man who does this is wise, integrated, the worker of all works (BG, 4.13–18).

God originates and sustains the world and reabsorbs it into himself: this is his *karma* (work) and his *dharma*. And man who, according to the Gītā, is a particle of God, must imitate him in his activity as well as in his eternal rest. To opt out of the active life and to sink oneself into the timeless peace of Brahman is to 'become Brahman' and thus to become like God who is the origin of Brahman, but it is to become like God in only half his being: it is a refusal to become a perfect image of God in his totality. Nor should it be supposed that God has no purpose in what he does: he has, and his ultimate purpose is the final liberation of all souls from the trammels of matter which is itself his own 'lower nature' (BG, 7.4–5). He binds that he may loose and that he may lead all souls back to himself whether they like it or not. This is the eternal 'game' that he plays with his creation; but like any game it has its own rules, and the rules of the game are called *dharma*. God alone knows the rules, but he can and does on occasion reveal them to man as Krishna did to Arjuna, and man, in his turn, obeys the rules willy-nilly, for he is conditioned by his own *karma*—the works that follow him from lives lived long ago into his present life with the same blind instinct that enables the calf to find the mother-cow wherever she may be in the herd—and by God's own purpose which manifests itself as Fate and Time (*kāla*) and against which it is useless to struggle. Arjuna may not understand with his finite intellect why a fratricidal war involving the slaughter of millions is both necessary and right and therefore part and parcel of 'eternal *dharma*' itself, but loath though he may be to take his cousins' lives he is not in fact a free agent, and must. However wrong the *dharma* imposed on you by your caste and by circumstances may appear to you, you are none the less in duty bound to do it, and if you refuse, then Fate, that is, God's will, will take you by the forelock and make you.

'If you persist in hugging your ego', Krishna says to Arjuna, 'and
[obstinately] refuse to fight, vain is your resolve, for Nature will
compel you. Bound by your own *karma*, you will be forced to do
what, in your deluded state, you do not want to do. The Lord of all
creatures stands in the heart of all, making them move hither and
thither like cogs in a machine by means of his uncanny power
(*māyā*)' (BG, 18.59–61).

To emanate, to sustain, and to reabsorb into himself—this
is the *dharma* of God which he repeats ever again for all the
cycles of eternity. In the 'night of Brahmā' God lies in dreamless sleep, there is no activity, and all is fathomless rest and
boundless peace. The 'day of Brahmā' dawns and God awakes.
In the mythology of the Vaishnavas during the night of Brahmā
Vishnu lies, unconscious and recumbent, on the cosmic serpent
Śesha, and as dawn approaches a lotus blooms miraculously
from his navel, and from this lotus springs the creator-god
Brahmā, while Śiva, the Destroyer or rather the agent of re-
absorption (*saṁhāra*), springs from his head. From these
beginnings the universe evolves through the four *yugas* (p. 62)
until it is once again ripe for dissolution. No man has seen the
dissolution of the world save only the great seer Mārkāndeya
who, being born again in another age, lived to tell the marvellous
tale.

At the end of this age, in the *Kali yuga*, the last, shortest, and
nastiest age in each world-cycle, evil proliferated and *dharma*
was wellnigh extinct in a world given over to luxury and vice.
Women forgot all modesty and even Brāhman ladies took to
themselves men of low caste and even outcastes; caste duties
were not observed, and Śūdras who, according to the sacred
dharma, had no other duty than to serve the other castes,
lorded it over Brāhmans, and the lives of men became ever
more brutish and short. When this extreme of degeneration
had been reached a fearful drought afflicted the earth, and men
died in their thousands. Then seven scorching suns appeared in
the sky and drank up all the waters of the earth, the rivers and
the seas. Wood, grass, plants, and trees were all reduced to
ashes, and the earth was stricken, parched, and desolate. Then
did a mighty conflagration appear which ate its way into the
regions of hell below the earth and consumed the denizens of

hell; and from thence it flared up into the heavenly regions
themselves destroying the gods with all their pomp and splend-
our. And now that the whole universe had crumbled asunder
beneath the flame, huge clouds appeared in the sky, garlanded
with lightning and bellowing with thunder: and the rains came.
For twelve long years did it rain until the great fire of dissolution was altogether put out. The oceans overflowed their
bounds, the mountains tottered and fell in fragments, and the
earth sank down under the boundless deep, and all was water,
endless water, everywhere.

And in that dread One Ocean in which all moving and unmoving
things had been destroyed, in which gods and Asuras, Yakshas and
Rākshasas had met their end, in such a world bereft of men, bereft
of beasts and trees, bereft of atmosphere, did I, [Mārkāndeya,]
wander stricken. . . . Long did I flounder in the waters of the One
Ocean—tirelessly though tired, finding no refuge anywhere. And
then somewhere in the massy expanse of water did I descry a mighty
fig-tree, broad and huge; and on its bough I beheld a cradle laid,
bespread with coverlets celestial, and lying therein I saw a little
child whose face was like a drop of water on the petal of a lotus and
whose eyes were wide-expanded as the full-blown lotus-flower.
And I was mightily amazed, marvelling at the child and how he lay
there though all the universe was no more. Meditate though I might
in all austerity, knowing though I did all that was and is and is yet
to be, I could not divine the mystery of the child. . . . Then did that
radiant child whose eyes were like unto two lotuses speak these
words to me, delightful to the ear. 'I know thee, Mārkāndeya, and
thy weariness and how thou fain wouldst rest. Pray sit thee down
here for as long as thou wilt. Enter into my body and sit thee there,
for there there is a dwelling prepared for thee; this favour have I
granted thee.' And when the child spake these words to me, I became
wearied of long life and of my human condition. Then on a sudden
did the child open his mouth, and I, helpless beneath the power of
Fate, was made to enter in' (MBh, 3.188).

And as Markandeya entered into the Lord's belly he beheld
there the whole wide world with all the kingdoms and cities
thereof—its rivers and seas and the weird monsters that dwell
in them, the heavens with the sun and moon that adorn them,
the earth with its trees and flowers, the mountains, and all the
beasts that roam the earth. There too did he see Brāhmans

performing lawful sacrifice, warrior kings attending to the
needs of all the castes, merchants, and peasants pursuing their
lawful avocations, and Śūdras bent on humble service. And he
saw that all evil was turned to good (ibid., 3.189.38).

And a new age dawned. But this in its turn must decline in
ruin. Brāhmans will neglect their sacrifices, sons will slay
fathers and fathers sons, private property will be confiscated
and wars unleashed by self-conceited, deluded men, the earth
will be ruled by men who are strangers to the eternal *dharma*,
property and wives will be held in common, and all men without distinction will be ranked together in a single caste. Brāhmans will be ill-treated, and Śūdras, not content to serve, will
themselves preach an abominable *dharma*. These are the signs
of another end, but this time all will be made well again, for
Vishnu, whose will it is that *dharma* shall never perish from the
earth, will clothe himself in human flesh again, and in this his
last incarnation, as Kalkin, sprung of Brāhmans in a Brāhman
family, he will restore their rightful dignity to the Brāhmans,
bring peace and prosperity to the stricken world, and utterly
destroy the tyranny of outcastes who had dared to set themselves up in the place of the Brāhmans. So does God ever
engage in works, bringing into being and reabsorbing into
himself the countless worlds that go to make up the universe.

God's *karma* fulfils itself in time, and time in the Great
Epic is identical with fate. God controls fate and man is power-
less before it: 'it is not man who is the doer of good and evil
works, for man is not independent. He is made to act like a
wooden puppet. Some are motivated by God, others by chance,
and yet others by the works they have performed in former
[lives]' (MBh, 5.158.14–16). What, then, is the relationship
between fate and the load of *karma* that man drags along with
him in the saṁsāric world? Though the Mahābhārata stresses
time and again the primacy of fate over human effort, it none
the less compares the two to the rain which prepares the ground
and the seed that man puts into it (5.78.2–5): the two are interdependent and work in harmony together. Human *karma* is but
a fraction of the *karma* of the whole universe, and this totality of
karma adds up to fate, and fate itself is under the control of God.
Fate is the cosmic *dharma* from which man cannot escape; and

in the long run it is man's co-operation with fate which is but another word for God's will that justifies him and earns him a place in heaven or that causes him to enter into God. This is made plain throughout the Epic. It is Krishna's will that the entire Kshatriya class should perish in atonement for their over-weening pride and to relieve Mother Earth of the excessive burden of an overpopulated world. In order that this may come about enmity must be sown between the Kauravas and the Pāndavas—the hundred sons of Dhṛtarāshtra on the one hand and the five sons of Pāndu on the other, the most illustrious of whom are Yudhishthira, the king of *dharma*, and Arjuna, Krishna's dearly beloved friend and comrade. The principal characters act out their lives like marionettes in a puppet-play —their own characters are their undoing, and their characters are in turn but the fruit of the *karma* of their past lives: they are what they are because they have done what they have done. Yudhishthira himself is driven on by fate and by his own *dharma*, which makes it impossible for him to break a vow under any circumstances whatever, to accept an invitation to a game of dice in which he loses all his kingdom. For twelve years he and his brothers are sentenced to exile in the forest, and for one more year they have to live in concealment. All this they do in fulfilment of their *dharma*, and in return they were to have received their share of the kingdom back. But the eldest son of Dhṛtarāshtra, Duryodhana by name, who has ruled the king-dom alone for thirteen years, will have none of it, for the taste of power is sweet. Yudhishthira who loathes nothing so much as the senseless slaughter of war, declares that he will be content with a mere five villages, one for himself and the rest for his brothers, and sends the Lord Krishna himself on an embassy to the Kaurava court, but Duryodhana's heart is hardened. Though he knows that Krishna is Almighty God, he hates him as much as he hates the King of Righteousness in whose anxiety for peace he sees only cowardice. He at least will not shirk his *kshatriya-dharma* which bids him go to war, to kill or to be killed. So too the blind king Dhṛtarāshtra, though he knows full well that war will spell the utter ruin of him and his, gives way to his dear son's insensate pride and lets things take their course. Thus, in their different ways, Yudhishthira's

refusal to go back on a foolish vow, Duryodhana's overweening
pride, and Dhṛtarāshtra's excessive affection for his son—all
resulting from their *karma* in former births—conspire to fulfil
the will of God, that the Kshatriya class should be utterly
wiped out in accordance with the *dharma* of that very class.
But it is not Duryodhana or Dhṛtarāshtra nor yet Yudhishthira's
brothers who raise their voice against this logical dénouement
to the warriors' *dharma*, but Yudhishthira himself who is the
god Dharma incarnate.

The Mahābhārata is a strange book, for it contains both
passages that are rigorously orthodox in their defence of the
system of the four classes and passages which expose its injustice and absurdity, and it is almost always with the latter that
Yudhishthira shows sympathy. The basis of the Hindu way of
life used to be considered the so-called *varnāśrama-dharma*,
'the *dharma* of class and the stages of life'. The first mention of
the *varnas*, as the four great classes are called, is in the *Purusha-
sūkta* of the Rig-Veda (p. 43) where it is said that the Brāhmans
issued from the mouth of Purusha, the primal giant, the Kshatriyas or warriors from his arms, the Vaiśyas or peasants from
his thighs, and the Śūdras or serfs from his feet. The word used
for the four great classes is *varna* which means 'colour', and
according to the Epic and the law-books all the hundreds of
castes and sub-castes that later developed were due to inter-
marriage between the four great classes, though this is now
considered to be extremely unlikely. The fact that the name for
the four great classes is *varna* 'colour' probably means that a
distinction was drawn between the light-skinned Aryan
invaders and the darker-skinned aboriginals. These were
probably enslaved and formed into the Śūdra or 'serf' class.
How the four great *varnas* proliferated into the hundreds of
castes (*jātis*) that exist today is not wholly clear. In some
cases whole tribes would form a new caste on being received
into the Hindu system, or again new castes might be grouped
around a certain trade. In any case efforts were made to group
new castes and sub-castes into the general framework of the
four *varnas* which, in the law-books, are considered to constitute the social framework of Hindu society. The proliferation
of castes led to the social segregation that has been characteristic

of Hindu society in historical times and to all the familiar social taboos which made it impossible for people of different castes to eat together, let alone to intermarry. Out of the same system grew the curse of untouchability which degraded a large section of the population to a state of permanent ritual impurity that put them on a par with dogs and other unclean animals.

Ideally, however, Hindu society was divided into the four great classes only, and membership of them was hereditary. According to the ancient Hindu *dharma* men are not born equal; they are born into that station of life for which their past *karma* has fitted them. The inequalities that the system imposed and made permanent were not, then, generally felt to be unjust since they were quite simply the result of good or bad deeds performed in former lives, and it was only with the advent of the *bhakti* cults and their devotion to a personal God who could save anyone by an act of pure grace from the bondage of *saṁsāra* that any social mixing of castes took place. In the great texts of classical Hinduism the mixture of castes was considered the most appalling sin and, as we have seen, one of the signs that the end of the world is nigh.

In the earliest period there seems to have been some rivalry between the two highest classes, the Brāhmans and the Kshatriyas, but very soon the Brāhmans emerged triumphant, and they arrogated to themselves powers and privileges that it would be difficult to parallel in any other civilization. This they were able to do because they claimed to be the depositories of Brahman itself—of the sacred power that keeps the world in being. They were gods among men and are even spoken of as gods of gods: indeed it is said in the *Laws of Manu*, the most authoritative of the Hindu law-books, that they have the power to make and unmake gods at their pleasure, for they are the lords of creation and 'forms' of *dharma*.

Of [all] creatures the animate are said to be the best, of animate beings those who live on their wits, of those who live on their wits men, and among men Brāhmans are the best. . . . The very birth of a Brāhman is an eternal form of *dharma*; born for the sake of *dharma* he is conformed to becoming Brahman. When a Brāhman is born he is born superior to the whole earth, he is the lord of all creatures, and he has to guard the treasury of *dharma*. Everything that exists

throughout the world is the private property of the Brāhman. By
the high excellence of his birth he is entitled to everything. What
he enjoys, what he wears, and what he gives away are his own
private property, and it is through the mercy of the Brāhman that
others enjoy [anything at all] (*Manu*, 1.96–101).

Seldom indeed in the history of the world can a single class of
men have arrogated to themselves such more than divine
honour. Moreover, by the mere fact that he is a Brāhman and
engaged in sacred rites which are themselves Brahman, the
Brāhman can be considered to be already in a state of liberation
from the bonds of *saṃsāra*.

The Brāhman's duties are purely religious: he must study
and teach the Veda and the *smṛtis* and he must sacrifice both for
himself and for others. For this he must be recompensed, and
one of the most highly meritorious deeds a Kshatriya or a
Vaiśya can perform is to lavish gifts on the Brāhmans, for in so
doing they sanctify themselves. The gift of a Śūdra, however,
would defile the holy man.

The Brāhmans were and are the custodians of the Veda,
and they should instruct the other two 'twice-born' classes in
Vedic lore, but on no account should instruction be given to a
Śūdra, let alone an outcaste: that would be an appalling sin and
is punished by the pains of hell. The Śūdras, indeed, were
regarded as being so impure that they were denied all access to
the Veda, they might not sacrifice or have sacrifice offered on
their behalf, nor might they associate with the twice-born.
The Śūdra was created a slave, and even if manumitted by his
master, a slave he remains, for no merely human agency can
alter the eternal *dharma* as interpreted by the Brāhmans. Of the
four great classes the Śūdras alone were not 'twice-born',
that is to say, they were not admitted to the initiatory rites
through which the other classes received the sacred thread and
were born again.

The Kshatriyas were the warrior class, and at the head of
them stands the king. They were the secular power responsible
for the enforcement of the *dharma* laid down by the Brāhmans.
The king's first duty is to protect his subjects, but he has also
the duty to expand his kingdom by fair means or foul, if
necessary by war. The duty of the ordinary Kshatriya is to take

part in war, to kill or be killed while facing the enemy, and it
was this sanguinary duty so utterly at variance with the precept
of *ahiṁsā* which forbade the taking of the life of any living
thing that roused Yudhishthira to violent protest against the
whole *kshatriya-dharma*. The remaining class, the Vaiśyas,
probably formed the majority of the community, their lawful
occupations being agriculture and trade. The hierarchy of caste
was said to reflect the three strands or *gunas* which pervade the
whole of *prakṛti* or Nature. The Brāhmans, of course, reflect
the strand of *sattva* or 'goodness', the Kshatriyas *rajas* or
'energy', and the Śūdras *tamas* or 'dullness', while the Vaiśyas
were a mixture of 'energy' and 'dullness'.

Just as there are four classes, so are there four stages in the
ideal life of the twice-born. On attaining the age of reason and
being invested with the sacred thread the youth should leave
home and study the Scriptures with a Guru until he is proficient
in them. During this period the student or Brahmacārin as he
is called leads a life of absolute celibacy, he 'fares (*carati*)
according to Brahman', he must treat his Guru as his father and
as a god, giving him absolute and willing obedience. At the end
of this period he should return to his father's house, take a wife
and found a family, raising up sons so that his line may continue
and so that there will be someone to perform his funeral rites
when he is dead. In the married state the wife is wholly subject
to her husband whom she should revere as a god: she should rise
before him in the morning and retire to rest after him; and she
should not presume to eat until he has finished. A man was
entitled to at least one wife, though rarely to more than four,
but no woman was entitled to more than one husband. The
only exception to this rule is said to have been Draupadī
who was solemnly wedded to all the five Pāndava brothers, a
special dispensation having been granted from heaven for this
very exceptional family. The wedding-bond was absolutely
binding particularly on the woman, who might not re-marry
after her husband's death. In later days child-marriage became
a regular practice, and if the husband died when still a child,
the young widow's lot was rarely enviable, for she was expected
to spend the rest of her life mourning her departed lord and
interceding for his soul. If, however, she preferred to join her

husband immediately to share with him celestial joys, she was free to mount his funeral pyre and win eternal merit thereby. As late as the seventeenth century the Jesuit missionary, de Nobili, witnessed such scenes and was touched by the ecstatic devotion with which many of these young widows went to their deaths. The spirit in which they did so he found admirable though he felt it could have been expended in a better cause. The lady who so sacrificed herself was known as a *satī*, a 'real or true woman', one who sacrificed bodily life to a higher reality. The term *satī* appears in Anglo-Indian as *suttee*, and the widow's self-sacrifice has thus, incorrectly, come to be known as 'committing suttee'. It is true that a widow's lot was frequently so miserable that even death may have seemed preferable to a life in which she was all too often held up to contempt and that she might be forced by public opinion to take the extreme step, but this must be regarded as a perversion of a *dharma* which regarded voluntary self-sacrifice as the highest virtue.

A woman, according to the Hindu *dharma*, is never *svatantra*, she never 'has a thread of her own': she is not her own mistress. In childhood she is subject to her father, in marriage to her husband, and after his death to her eldest son. The highest standards of modesty and decorum were expected from her, and the *Laws of Manu* (8.371) lay down that if she committed adultery, she should be thrown to the dogs 'in a place frequented by many'. The perfect relationship of husband and wife is illustrated by the relationship of Rāma and Sītā in the Rāmāyana. The husband is all tenderness and kindly consideration, the wife all humble duty, submissiveness, and self-effacing, self-sacrificing love. The woman, though she may never claim to be her own mistress, has a dignity of her own, particularly when she becomes a mother, and it is even said (MBh, 13.105. 15) that a mother is worth ten fathers. The husband, on the other hand, is not forbidden to take another wife should his own die; indeed if an earlier wife has failed to produce male offspring, he is in duty bound to take another wife that he may raise up a son to continue his line, for the son is the father's second self.

Despite the immense emphasis that Hinduism puts on the

efficacy of ascetic practices, on self-restraint, and the control
of the senses, it does not advocate celibacy, for a man's first
duty is to raise up sons for himself, and the state of the householder is therefore considered to be the 'root' of all the other
three *āśramas* or states of life. But 'when a householder sees
that wrinkles are beginning to appear and that his hair is
growing grey and when his sons are themselves fathers of sons,
then should he betake himself to the forest'. He may either
leave his wife with his sons or take her with him. In the forest
he should live on fruit and roots only, he should perform
sacrifice with them and wear only a skin or tattered garment.
The austerities prescribed by the *Laws of Manu* seem extreme
even by Hindu standards, for during the grilling heat of an
Indian summer the forest-dweller is recommended to expose
himself to the heat of five fires; during the monsoon he should
live unsheltered under the open sky, and in winter he should
wear wet clothes, and he 'should gradually increase the rigours
of his austerities' (*Manu*, 6.23). These austerities combined with
a diligent reading of the Upanishads were designed to detach
the ascetic's soul from the burden of the flesh and to magnify it
in the world of Brahman where there is neither grief nor fear
(ibid., 32). This is the beginning of the end, for when the
forest-dweller has reached this stage, he becomes a full *sannyāsin*. He has now discharged his three 'debts'; he has absorbed
the teaching of the Veda, has reared up sons to continue his
line, and has offered sacrifice according to his ability. Still in the
world though not of it he is now ready to fade out into a timeless
bliss.

He will desire neither death nor life, but will await his appointed
time as a servant awaits his wage. . . . He will patiently bear with hard
words, despising none, nor out of attachment to the body will he
bear enmity to anyone. To one who is angry with him he will not
show anger in return, and him that curses him will he bless, nor will
he utter any untrue word. [Calmly] seated, rejoicing in the things
of the soul (*ātman*), caring for nothing, eating no meat, with the soul
his one companion, intent on happiness [eternal], so will he live. . . .
By curbing the senses, by destroying affection (*rāga*) and hatred, by
doing no harm to any living thing (*ahiṁsā*), he will conform himself
to deathlessness. . . . He will understand that the soul's involvement

in sorrow while it is still in the body arises out of what is other than *dharma* (*adharma*) and that its bond with happiness is eternal because *dharma* is its goal. By Yoga he will perceive the subtle nature of the Supreme Soul and how it permeates all bodies, the lowest as well as the highest. . . . He will abandon this originated abode whose central pillar is bone, which is held together by tendons, whose mortar is flesh and blood, whose thatch is skin, which is evil-smelling and full of urine and faeces, infected with old age and grief, the home of disease, sick, unquiet, and perishable. . . . Thus by gradually giving up all attachments, liberated from all the pairs of opposites, he will abide in Brahman (*Manu*, 6.45–81).

Such is the ideal life prescribed for the three 'twice-born' classes, though it is doubtful whether even Brāhmans fulfilled these exacting duties at all often.

We have already had occasion to notice that there is a certain fondness for the number three in Hindu classifications: 'all things proceed in a threefold way', as the Mahābhārata (14.39. 21) says. There are three twice-born classes, three stages in their lives culminating in that of the *sannyāsin* which completes and negates them all, three strands in Nature, and three aspects of Brahman—Being, Awareness, and Bliss. So too in human life there are three legitimate pursuits—the pursuit of pleasure, the pursuit of wealth, and the pursuit of righteousness or *dharma*, and the three of them culminate in and are negated by the goal of all life, *moksha*.

Once upon a time when the great war between the Kauravas and the Pāndavas had ended in the total destruction of the Kauravas and when Drona's son, Aśvatthāman, goaded on by the Great God Śiva, and to avenge his father's blood, had butchered the victorious Pāndava hosts as they lay besottedly asleep, the five Pāndava brothers sat down with the wise Vidura and discussed which of the three legitimate pursuits of man was the highest. Was it *dharma*, *artha*, or *kārma*—righteousness, wealth, or pleasure? (MBh, 12.167) Vidura opened the discussion and said that *dharma* was manifestly man's highest goal on earth: it was by *dharma* that the sages of old entered into Brahman, and it is on *dharma* that the three worlds are based; by *dharma* did the gods become gods, and by *dharma* is wealth itself acquired. And by *dharma* we must understand mastery of the Veda, asceticism (*tapas*), renunciation, faith, sacrifice, patience, purity of temperament, compassion, truthfulness, self-control, and self-improvement. From this wholly orthodox point of view Arjuna ventured to diverge, putting in a strong claim for the supremacy of wealth of which, he said, righteousness and pleasure were but the two wings. The two youngest brothers who were twins preferred to compromise. *Dharma*, they said, should be pursued in the first instance, then wealth should be acquired in accordance with *dharma*, and last of all should men's thoughts turn to pleasure. Bhīma, however, who was second to Yudhishthira in age though far below him in virtue—for he was violent, gluttonous, and cruel—thought differently. Satisfaction of desire (*kāma*), he boldly declared, was the first duty of man. Speaking in the spirit of the Vedic hymn that saw in desire the source and origin of all things (pp. 41–42), he said that without the desire to achieve all achievement is impossible. How had the great sages of old won through to liberation? They had desired it, and through the fervour of their desire they had won the prize. Desire is the secret of all success, whether material or spiritual, and only a hypocrite would deny it. Yet there must be equilibrium between the three. 'Dharma, wealth, and desire (or pleasure) must be pursued equally; the man who is devoted to one of them only is inferior. The man who is skilled in only two is said [by scripture] to be mediocre, but the superior man is he who rejoices in the whole triad (*trivarga*).'

The King of *dharma*, Yudhishthira, however, could agree with none of them, for the slaughter of millions of men in accordance with what men called *dharma* had made him despair of *dharma* itself. He said:

There is no doubt about it, you have all formed your opinions from the books on *dharma* and you know your authorities well. I, however, desire to know [the truth]. You have had your say and I have listened to your considered opinions. Listen to me without allowing yourselves to be distracted though I speak only under duress. Only he who takes no pleasure in evil or in good, in wealth, *dharma*, or pleasure, only he who is free from [all] taints (*dosha*), to whom a clod of earth and a piece of gold are all one, only he is freed alike from pleasure and from pain, from riches and success. Birth and death are the very soul of all created things; all are subject to decay and change. Or again they may be made alert by many [a wise teacher] and prate of liberation, yet we know not what it is. Did not the Self-subsistent Lord himself say that there can be no liberation for the man who knows the bond of love (*snehena yukta*)? Wise men make Nirvāna their goal, doing neither what is pleasing nor what is displeasing [to themselves]. That is the fundamental rule, not doing what you would. Even as it has been ordained for me, so do I act. Fate controls all creatures: and Fate is the stronger. Be very sure of that. Not by any action [of his own] can a man attain a goal that is beyond his reach. Know that what is to be will be in very truth.

These are the words of bitter disillusion, and it is strange that the King of *dharma* itself should reject *dharma* in favour of meek submission to an incomprehensible fate and the quest for Nirvāna which puts a stop to all *dharma* as to all contingent things. But Yudhishthira's dilemma is real: he is *dharma* incarnate and everyone admits this and reverences him as such. But he is not at ease in a world where the traditional *dharma* so obviously conflicts with the dictates of conscience and compassion. He has no quarrel with the ten commandments which sum up what is obligatory on all men irrespective of class and caste for these are in accordance with his own nature— 'fortitude, patience, self-control, not to steal, purity, control of the senses, insight (*dhī*), wisdom, truth, and the avoidance of anger' (*Manu*, 6.92). What he protests against time and time again is the *dharma* peculiar to the warrior class particularly as it applies to kings. He was driven into a most bloody war not only by his wife and brothers who wanted vengeance but also by the incarnate God, Krishna, who was determined to wipe out the whole warrior class. The war is won, but the whole earth has been made desolate, and so sick at heart is Yudhish- thira that he would fain renounce his kingdom and retire to the forest in search of spiritual freedom. Immense pressure, however, is brought to bear on him, and he is finally per- suaded to accept the throne, but he does so with a sad heart and an uneasy conscience, for he has been told at very great length by Bhīshma, his dying grandsire, that the *dharma* of kingship involves not only wars of aggrandisement but also lying, cheating, and spying on the grandest possible scale; and it was Yudhishthira's proud boast that he had never told a lie.

Only once had he done so, and it had caused him bitter remorse. Nor would he even then have dreamt of doing something so utterly at variance with his character, had he not been ordered to do so by the Lord Krishna: and Krishna was God. It was during the heat of the battle and things were going ill for the Pāndavas because Drona who had been the well-loved preceptor of both them and the Kauravas and had sided with the latter in the great war, was making havoc of their forces and could not, even with Krishna's help, be certainly defeated. So Krishna bade the unscrupulous Bhīma slay an elephant whose name was Aśvatthāman, for Aśvatthāman was the name of Drona's son. This Bhīma did and told Drona that his son was dead so that all his zest for battle might desert him. But Drona would not believe him because all men told lies except only Yudhishthira who was the embodiment of *dharma* and truth. And Yudhishthira, egged on by Krishna, told Drona that Aśvatthāman was dead but mumbled indistinctly that he spoke of the elephant, not of Drona's son. And that it might be plain to all that there is such a thing as eternal *dharma* that is higher than men and higher than the incarnate God himself, a marvellous thing occurred, for whereas the King's chariot had previously never touched the ground but remained poised four inches up in the air on account of his righteousness and wholehearted love of truth, no sooner did he utter a half-true word than his chariot came to rest on the solid earth: and Yudhishthira became as other men.

Yudhishthira told a lie in obedience to God, and Krishna was swift to justify himself. *Dharma* is subtle and hard to understand, and there are exceptions to all the obvious rules, and so in the matter of truthfulness it is right and proper to tell lies where women are concerned, in marriage, in defence of cows or Brāhmans, or to save life; and was not Drona wantonly destroying the Pāndava hosts? But the King of Righteousness was not convinced, for, whatever God might say, something higher than God told him that he had sinned. And this nagging doubt was to pursue him for the rest of his life, for it became ever more plain that the *dharma* taught by the Brāhmans and

practised by God incarnate was not the same as the *dharma*
he bore in his own soul. What was the use of his being told that
the highest *dharma* was to abstain from injuring living creatures
if in the next breath he were bidden to slaughter animals in
sacrifice or to preside over the supreme blood-sacrifice of war?
For war, like the self-immolation of widows, is a sacrifice and
pleasing to the gods. No, he says, and he repeats it time and
again throughout this mighty Epic, 'There is nothing more
evil than the Kshatriya's *dharma*,' and many a Hindu has
thought like him since. Or how can *dharma* be equated with
Truth as it so often is, if God himself can urge him to tell a lie?
And it is this that hurts most, for Yudhishthira has deep and
abiding faith in the divinity of Krishna, but there is so much in
what he says and does that by the highest standards (which are
his own) is purely and simply wrong. Yudhishthira is full of
doubts about what the eternal *dharma* can really be, but it is
left to his wife Draupadī openly to challenge the wisdom and
goodness of God. Yudhishthira had gambled away not only his
kingdom, but his brothers, his wife, and himself. Reduced to
the status of a slave Draupadī was dragged half-naked into the
Kauravas' assembly-hall and cruelly misused by the Kaurava
brothers. Slaves, however, have no rights, and so did Yudhishthira, bound by the fetters of *dharma*, utter not a word. But
later when the Pāndavas were exiled in the forest Draupadī
gave vent to her feelings and hurled defiance at the All-Highest.

As a man splits log with log, stone with stone, iron with iron—
things that [of themselves] can neither move nor think—so does the
Lord God, the Self-subsistent, the primal Grandsire, hurt one
creature by means of another, establishing for himself an alibi.
Joining things together only to disjoin them again the Lord acts at his
own good pleasure, playing with his creatures as children play with
dolls. He does not treat his creatures as a father or a mother would,
but acts in raging anger; and since he acts so, others follow his
example. . . . Beholding the disaster that has overtaken you and the
prosperity of Duryodhana, I accuse the Creator who looks on at such
injustice. And what benefit has the Creator from granting prosperity
to the cruel and greedy son of Dhṛtarāshtra who has violated the
Aryan code and degraded *dharma*? If it is true that deeds (*karma*)
once performed follow the doer and none other, then by those evil
deeds is the Lord himself defiled (MBh, 3.31.34–41).

Yudhishthira is horrified at this blasphemous outburst, but he has no counsel to offer except to show patience in adversity; for Yudhishthira's virtues are the virtues that a Brāhman should display, not a Kshatriya, and with this he is continually upbraided by his wife, his brothers, and by Krishna himself. He is 'steadfast, self-restrained, chaste, patient, ever devoted to *dharma*, high-spirited, he honours and gives hospitality to guests, relatives, servants, and all who resort to him: he is truthful, generous, ascetic, and brave, at peace with himself, wise, and imperturbable; the soul of *dharma*, he never commits an injustice out of desire or under the influence of impetuosity, out of fear or to promote his own interests' (MBh, 12.55.5–9). Such a person could scarcely be an ideal Kshatriya, and Yudhishthira knows it. All his instincts draw him towards detachment and non-violence (*ahiṁsā*); he loathes war and violence of any kind and he does not relish the bloody sacrifices kings are expected to offer. But he is the first to pay due reverence to Brāhmans, for though it is of course true that there can be very bad Brāhmans as there are bad priests in other religions, reverence is nevertheless due to them in their sacramental capacity as being the human repositories of Brahman, the eternal principle and source of *dharma*. But he is also told (and he believes it) that the Brāhman who fails to practise the virtues of self-control and who has not conquered desire, anger, lust, and the other passions is no better than a Śūdra, while the Śūdra who leads a holy life must be deemed to be a Brāhman.

Before the war when Yudhishthira was exiled in the forest he had asked his heavenly father, the god Dharma, for one boon only: 'that I may ever vanquish greed, delusion, and anger, and that my mind may ever dwell on giving, austerity, and truth'. All this came naturally to him, however, but these were not the qualities most desirable in a king. Thus when victory once again restored his kingdom to him, his massive sense of guilt and unworthiness impelled him to renounce the kingdom and to spend the rest of his days as a forest-hermit. Not all his brothers' pleas nor those of the dying Bhīshma nor yet Krishna himself could persuade him to go back on his resolve, until Krishna told him brutally that he must renounce renunciation itself if he is to be worthy of liberation: he must win the final battle against himself.

Just as you had to fight against Drona and Bhīshma, so now the time has come to fight against your own mind. You must enter into battle so that by dint of [self-] discipline and your own deeds [you may reach] the farther shore of what has the form of the unmanifest. There neither arrows nor servants nor kinsmen can help. You must fight against yourself alone; the battle is on. If you lose this battle, what will your condition be? Recognize [how wretched it will be, and once you have done so] you will have done your duty. Make your decision [bearing in mind] the coming and going of [all] contingent beings, and rule your kingdom as your fathers and fore-fathers did before you. There is no salvation (*siddhi*) in giving up external goods; in giving up the possession of your body there may or may not be salvation. Whatever *dharma*, whatever pleasure the man may enjoy who has divested himself of external goods though he still clings to the body, may that be the lot of those who hate you. Death is spelt out in two syllables, the eternal Brahman in three. Death is *mama* ('this is mine'), the eternal is *na mama* ('nothing is mine'). So death and Brahman reside within the self; unseen they control [all] creatures, have no doubt of that. If it is true that the soul cannot be destroyed, then to slay the body of others must be the same as refusing to do injury (*ahiṁsā*). Though you have conquered the whole earth with all that it contains of moving and unmoving things and yet have no thought that it is yours, what will you do with it? Or if a man choose to live in the forest subsisting on forest herbs, yet considers things as his own, then is he ripe to enter into the mouth of death. Consider the nature of your internal and external enemies; in so doing you will be freed from the great fear [of death] (MBh, 14.12–13).

In the Bhagavad-Gītā Krishna had bidden Arjuna go into battle with a mind wholly detached so that he could slay his enemies with equanimity. Arjuna needed the lesson, for he was not by nature detached and 'uncommitted' as was his brother. He had no instinctive yearning for liberation, so he had to be told of liberation and, that it might appear less frigidly exalted, of Krishna's abiding love for him and for all creatures. With Yudhishthira things were different; for here was a man both detached and compassionate by nature, devoted to *dharma* as traditionally expounded but more devoted still to the eternal *dharma* that was mirrored in his conscience—a man who, against his will and conscience, had been driven into a war of total extermination and whose remorse and bitter grief at the slaughter of both his own side and that of the enemy was well-nigh inconsolable. His Kshatriya's *dharma* which he hated and repeatedly cursed had led to the loss of millions of lives, and Krishna's assurance that all was well since the slain warriors were already experiencing unspeakable joys in Indra's heaven afforded him no comfort, for he was at last beginning to understand that of all the *dharmas* preached by traditional religion there was one which, though more typical of the heretical Buddhists and Jains, superseded them all, and that was *ahiṁsā*, the command that thou shalt do no injury to any living thing in thought, word, or deed. Yet long before the war broke out the holy sage, Mārkāndeya, had told him of a saintly fowler who, though a Śūdra, had given instruction to a proud and stiff-necked Brāhman; and he had told him that so long as one lives in this world, this absolute ideal can never be realized for even a pastime so apparently innocuous as agriculture involved the destruction of countless living things. Thus he saw that if he were to accept kingship once again, he would not be able to practise perfect *ahiṁsā*: therefore he would abdicate and lead a hermit's life in the forest. Krishna realizes that no appeal to his Kshatriya *dharma* can now have any effect, so he strikes him in his Achilles' heel, his thirst for renunciation, and he tells him that until renunciation is itself renounced, he is still the slave of desire; and, to drive the point further home, he tells him that even the liberated man is not free from desire, for desire 'dances and laughs [even] for the man who delights in liberation' (MBh, 14.13.19). This lesson Yudhishthira did not forget when his time came to enter into his rest.

Yet whatever Krishna might say, right up to the end Yudhishthira could not reconcile himself to his Kshatriya *dharma*. In the event the god Dharma himself confirms his intuition that the days of this violent *dharma* are numbered; for after he had allowed Arjuna to celebrate the great horse-sacrifice which is incumbent on victorious kings, and while he was receiving the congratulations of Brāhmans and others for the lavish gifts he had distributed in accordance with the custom of kings, a blue-eyed

mongoose one half of whose body was of pure gold mysteriously appeared before him and said: 'Your [whole] sacrifice
is not worth as much as an ounce of barley' (MBh, 14.90.7).
And the mongoose told him the story of a family of poor
Brāhmans who gave all their tiny stock of food to entertain a
stranger, leaving nothing for themselves; and he explained:
'Dharma takes no pleasure in gifts given in the expectation of
great rewards in heaven, he delights in little gifts honestly
come by and purified by faith.' Then the mongoose revealed
himself as the god Dharma himself, Yudhishthira's heavenly
father; and Yudhishthira knew that the blood of beasts slain in
sacrifice was no longer acceptable in heaven.

And more than this he learnt; for he had been told how the
great sage Viśvāmitra, during a great famine, had tried to force
an outcaste to give him the flesh of a dog to allay his hunger, but
the outcaste had protested that it ill beseemed a Brāhman to
accept forbidden food from an unclean man. So Viśvāmitra
took it away saying that even evil deeds could not harm a
Brāhman. And Yudhishthira understood that there can be
more righteousness in an outcaste than in even so great and
holy a Brāhman as was Viśvāmitra, and he said: 'If a frightful
act that is contrary to faith and truth is prescribed, [am I to do
it]? Am I to disregard the standards of [this righteous] slave?
If *dharma* has indeed become as flabby as this, then am I
utterly at sea and sunk in depression' (MBh, 12.142.1–2).
For Hudhishthira hungered and thirsted after righteousness
and for a teaching that was not of the scribes.

For fifteen years Yudhishthira ruled, but the light had gone
out of his life; and when he learnt that the incarnate God,
Krishna, had departed this world, he abdicated from his
kingdom which had brought him no happiness. Then once
again he cursed the Kshatriya *dharma* and force and violence
and kingship 'and ourselves who while yet alive are dead'
(MBh. 15.38.8); and so saying he laid aside his kingly robes
and departed into the forest with his four brothers and Draupadī, his wife. One by one they fall by the wayside, Draupadī
first, then the twins, then Arjuna, and lastly Bhīma, the eldest
next to Yudhishthira himself. So Yudhishthira is left alone—
yet not quite alone, for just as the brothers set out from their

capital city, a little dog attached himself to them and would not leave the side of King Yudhishthira.

And as Yudhishthira pursued his weary course alone, the great god Indra appeared in a fiery chariot and bade Yudhishthira enter into the heavenly gates, but Yudhishthira would not, for he had no desire to enter paradise now that his wife and brothers had fallen by the way. But Indra reassured him, they had already entered in and awaited Yudhishthira there. But Yudhishthira was not satisfied.

Yudhishthira: 'This dog is ever loyal (*bhakta*) to me. Let him come with me, for I have compassion on him.'

Indra: 'Thou hast cast off mortality and art now my equal. All glory and great fulfilment has thou now won. Today wilt thou taste of the joys of paradise. Renounce the dog, there is nothing cruel in that.'

Y.: 'Difficult indeed is it for a man of chivalry to do an unchivalrous deed. Such glory do I nowise covet for which I must renounce a creature loyal to me.'

I.: 'In paradise there is no place for men with dogs. . . . Renounce the dog, there is nothing cruel in that.'

Y.: 'It has been said that to renounce one who is loyal to you is an infinite evil, as evil as the slaying of a Brāhman. Hence will I by no means whatever, seeking my own pleasure, renounce this [dog] today. I cannot give up one who is in danger or loyal to me or friendless and afflicted or unskilled in his own defence or in danger of his life though it should cost me mine. This is my unbreakable vow.'

I.: 'Dogs are ever swayed by anger. No sooner do they see a gift [offered to the gods], or the sacrificial meat, or the oblation, if these are uncovered, than they carry it off. Do thou, then, renounce this dog, for thereby wilt thou attain the world of the gods. Thou hast renounced thy dearly beloved brothers and Draupadī too. By thine own works hast thou conquered the world. Yet wilt thou not renounce this dog, bent on total renunciation though thou art. Indeed thou art distraught today.'

Y.: 'Among dead men there is neither peace nor war, or so we believe on earth. Never can I bring them to life again. While yet they lived I did not renounce them. To abandon a loyal [friend], methinks, is as bad as to frighten off one who seeks sanctuary with you, as the murder of a woman, as the theft of a Brāhman's goods, or to violate a compact.'

This too Yudhishthira had learnt in a life devoted to the *dharma* that was engraved in his heart, that no chivalrous man, no Aryan, may desert a loyal and devoted creature even though he be a dog. This dog, however, was no ordinary dog, but the god Dharma himself who revealed himself to Yudhishthira and led him into paradise; and there he was sat in a place of great honour, for he had been faithful and true and had shown compassion to all creatures save, perhaps, to himself.

But when he entered he was struck dumb with astonishment, for he saw Duryodhana feasting in great pomp—Duryodhana, whose wicked obstinacy and pride had made the war inevitable. And the same old answer came: he was there because he had faithfully fulfilled his Kshatriya *dharma*; he had ever fought fairly and never flinched in the face of the foe. Then Yudhishthira was taken to hell, and there he saw his brothers and Draupadī tormented in a stinking pit. This was more than he could bear, and he did what he had never done before except at the height of the battle—he lost his temper and cursed the gods and their *dharma* too. But in so doing he was disloyal to the eternal *dharma* of which he was himself the embodiment, for in that *dharma* anger, even though it may call itself righteous indignation, has no place. So Yudhishthira was bathed in the peace-bringing waters of the heavenly Ganges, purged of anger though not yet of affection, that last taint of earthly life. For this he would have to be born on earth again so that at last he could win through to *moksha* and the complete passionlessness that is both freedom and peace.

6

Bhakti

'SUCH GLORY DO I nowise covet for which I must renounce a creature loyal to me,' Yudhishthira had told the great god Indra as he reached the doors of paradise, and Indra had reproved him for still being subject to human love, for in *moksha* there is no love.

Yudhishthira's dog was *bhakta*, 'loyal and devoted', and *bhakti* is the term used for a type of religion that seems to have originated in the Dravidian south; later it was to sweep the whole of India and utterly transform the face of Hinduism. In the Bhagavad-Gītā three paths to the Absolute are offered to the man who seeks liberation—the path of 'knowledge' (*jñāna*), the path of action (*karma*), and the path of *bhakti*. By 'knowledge' is understood not simply book-learning which, according to the Upanishads, leads you nowhere, but the intuitive apprehension of Brahman—a term which is variously interpreted by the philosophers but which in the Gītā means the direct apprehension of timeless Reality and the inter-connexion of all things as cohering in the 'Great Self' and therefore also in the individual 'self' once it is liberated from its mortal bonds. To speak of a 'path of action' as far as the Gītā is concerned is misleading, for this does not mean that the active life, as against the contemplative, has value of its own, but that it is possible and desirable to pursue the life of con-templation while still engaged in an active life, be it the sacred ministration of the Brāhman, the warfare of the Kshatriya, the business actiyity of the Vaiśya, or the menial service of the Śūdra. All these activities are good and each of the four great classes should carry out the duties of their station, for this is the *dharma* prescribed by the law-books and the will of God, but the zealous performance of caste duty can never lead to liberation, for action breeds its own reward or punishment, and the 'fruits' of *karma* bind whether they be good or bad; they 'attach to good or evil and therefore militate against detachment which is the *sine qua non* of liberation. Hence we are repeatedly told in the Great Epic that to achieve liberation one must transcend all the opposites, including good and evil. The goal of the 'path of knowledge' and the 'path of action', then, is the same— the realization of an eternal dimension in yourself. The way of 'loyal devotion', 'loving devotion', or *bhakti*, however, introduces a new element into Hinduism. At its lowest, as in the *Yoga-sūtras* (which however, avoid the technical term *bhakti*) it means no more than concentrating on the idea of God as being the eternal exemplar of the liberated soul, but in the commentaries on these *sūtras* God actively helps the soul to liberation by the exercise of his grace. In the Gītā this divine activity is far more pronounced: God leads the souls not only to liberation, the 'state of Brahman', but also to participation in himself—he 'causes them to enter' him. He in return loves the soul and asks to be loved by it.

The Gītā forms part of the Great Epic which claims to be the 'fifth Veda'. At about the same time that the Epic was assuming its final form perhaps in the fourth century A.D., a whole mass of new sacred literature was taking shape. This literature is known as the *Purānas*. The *Purānas*, of which eighteen are recognized, are huge mythological epics which extol the greatness of Vishnu or Śiva, their emanations, incarnations, and manifestations. Together with the two epics properly so called they constitute the bulk of the non-Vedic scripture known as *smṛti*. From the purely religious point of view by far the most important of them is the *Bhāgavata Purāna* compiled probably in the ninth century.

Already in the Mahābhārata Krishna appears as Vishnu incarnate but he is not the central figure of the Epic, and we hear very little of his early life. This deficiency was made good in the *Harivaṁśa* which purports to be a supplement to the Epic. In the *Bhāgavata Purāna* the legend is carried a stage further, particular emphasis being laid on the childhood and youth of the God-Man. Marvellous stories are told of how he was preserved from the machinations of the wicked king Kaṁsa, how he was brought up among cowherds, and how, when he grew to manhood, he sported with the cowherds' daughters (*gopīs*) who were distraught with the love of him. The *gopīs*' love for the youthful Krishna became the symbol of the love of the soul for God, and this self-abandonment to the divine became central to the cult of Krishna. Every stage in the divine hero's life, however, was utilized to excite the loving devotion of his worshippers. As the divine child he appealed to the maternal instinct, as a youth he became the lover of the soul, as a young warrior the trusted companion who is ever at your side, and in his maturity he became the universal father of all. It was, however, his love of the *gopīs* and their love for him that gave the cult of Krishna its special flavour: God is in love with the soul, and the soul with God. In this divine love-affair God is necessarily the male, the soul the female: God takes the initiative and the soul must passively wait for the divine embrace. The Krishna of the *Bhāgavata Purāna* is a very different person from the rather austere Krishna of the Gītā; he is not a teacher, but a lover, the handsome and wayward shepherd-boy who beguiles the soul with the sweet strains of his flute.

It was in the Tamil lands of south India that the cult of Krishna first came into prominence. Certainly during the eighth century and probably much earlier a great spiritual revival was initiated by persons describing themselves as 'Ālvārs', 'men who have intuitive knowledge of God'. These men seem to have sprung from a section of the Dravidian population which had remained unaffected by the pantheism of the Upanishads, so intensely personal is their attitude to God and so deeply emotional is their worship of him. Certain it is that for them caste did not count, for of the ten recognized 'saints', some were Śūdras, some outcastes, and one a woman. Moreover, the language they used was not Sanskrit but Tamil. This distinguished them from other non-Vedic sects like the Smārtas whose sacred books were the Sanskrit *smṛtis*. The movement probably started outside the Brāhmanical fold, but

like all the subsequent movements that sought to do away with
caste it was very soon reabsorbed into the caste system.

Among the Ālvārs only the most famous of them, Nāmm'-
ālvār, who flourished in the first half of the ninth century,
has left anything like a systematic account of their beliefs.
For the first time since the early Vedic age Nāmm'ālvār
denied that man's highest goal is liberation, for to him the loveless technique of Yoga had no meaning, or if it had, then it
meant no more than that the soul experienced its own essence in
isolation as one among many servants of God. The soul
is, indeed, a very wonderful thing because it reflects God, or is a
'mode' of him. 'It is not possible to give a description of that
wonderful entity, the soul—the soul which is eternal, and is
essentially characterized by intelligence (*jñāna*)—the soul
which the Lord has condescended to exhibit to me as a mode of
himself—for I am related to him as is the predicate to the
subject, or attribute to substance.' The soul, then, for Nāmm'-
ālvār, as for the whole stream of Hindu orthodoxy, is something that is indestructible because it does not exist in time:
it is utterly dependent on God, and to God it should aspire with
every atom of its being. In contradistinction to the Yogin and
Vedāntin who concentrate all their energies on uncovering the
timeless soul within, Nāmm'ālvār starts where they leave off,
for the state of quiet (*śānti*) which the Yogin enjoys is the
original virginal state of the soul which belongs to it from all
eternity, but which in *moksha* is recovered and disclosed. 'He
goes on to explain', Surendranath Dasgupta tells us, 'how,
through cessation of all inclination to other things and the
increase of longing for God *in a timeless and spaceless manner*,
and through the pangs of separation in not realizing him
constantly, he considers himself as a woman, and through the
pangs of love loses his consciousness.' This is a very far cry
indeed from the *tyāga* 'renunciation' and *vairāgya* 'passionlessness' of the Gītā. To the Ālvārs this passionlessness can
only be compared to that of the immature virgin who has yet
to be awoken by the touch of the bridegroom. Until the soul
had made itself 'female', it cannot receive the love of God.
Being but a 'mode' of God it has nothing of itself to give, and it
must therefore remain completely passive in order to receive

God's inflowing grace. Krishna's dalliance with the *gopis* may not seem to us the most sublime image of the love of God for man, but it unleashed such a flood of passionate spirituality in the Indian soul that it would be idle for anyone who sees value in this mysticism of love to deny its tremendous power. This mysticism, in its frank sexuality, is really comparable to that of the great Christian mystics like St. Teresa and St. John of the Cross in a way that the introspective mysticism of the *Yoga-sūtras* and the Vedānta is not.

To win through to liberation is only the first step on the mystic's path as Rāmānuja, who was very strongly influenced by the Ālvārs, was later to emphasize: it is only the *via purgativa* which precedes the *via contemplativa* in which all action is left to God, his grace, and his love; the soul can do no more than yearn that God will have mercy on it, and long and bitter though the intervening states of aridity may be, the soul knows that God cannot in the end but be merciful, however sinful it may be. Through his mercy God is not absolutely free, for, as the Advaitins well knew, love means total commitment and is the biggest fetter of all. 'O mercy,' cries Nāmm'ālvār, 'thou hast deprived God of the freedom of his just will. Safe under the winds of mercy, no more can God himself even of his will tear himself away from me; for, if he can do so, I shall still exclaim, I am victor, for he must purchase the freedom of his will by denying to himself mercy.'

The total attachment that the Ālvārs demand, however, does not exclude compassion for men still bound in the saṁsāric world, for the Lord Krishna is full of compassion for all his creatures. The soul, being a 'mode' of him, must reflect his whole nature, but it can only do this when it has been touched by the Lord's grace. Without God man is nothing, nor can he of himself benefit the Lord's creatures. Yet even without enlightenment man is not alone in the world, for the world itself is the body of God and its beauty is therefore a reflection of the beauty of God.

The poems of the Ālvārs with which they are said to have sung the 'atheistic' Buddhists and Jains out of southern India are as full of mythological detail as they are of devotion. Vishnu is still the bearer of the discus, sounder of the conch, consort of

the goddess Lakshmī and so on, but the mythological trappings
are used as an aid to devotion and fill out the personality
of the deity for the popular mind.

The worshippers of Vishnu-Krishna, however, did not have
it all their own way in south India, for a parallel movement
developed among the worshippers of Śiva. Śiva was in origin
at least partly un-Aryan, and it is not surprising therefore that
the earliest worshippers of Rudra-Śiva we know of, the
Vrātyas, did not observe caste rules and customs. No more did
the Kāpālikas who in addition drank wine and ate meat in their
rituals and made use of the sexual act to symbolize the eternal
union of Śiva with his *śakti* or creative power. These practices
were later inherited by the so-called left-hand Śāktas who made
sacramental use of all that was taboo to the Brāhmans—meat,
fish, wine, and sexual intercourse. These cults, however,
represent a deviation from the Śaivite norm, for in general the
worshippers of Śiva attached greater importance to chastity
than did the worshippers of Vishnu. By the end of the eighth
century the cult of Śiva had spread throughout the length and
breadth of India. His worshippers had their own corpus of
scripture known as the *Āgamas*, much of which has been lost,
and though they were to be found in all parts of India their
greatest strength was in the south, in Benares, and Kashmīr.

It was, however, again in the Tamil lands that Śaivism
developed its characteristic devotional form. This was the work
of a series of saints who spread the gospel that salvation could
only be won by a total self-surrender to Śiva. By the end of the
eleventh century the hymns of these saints had been collected
together and given the title of *Devārām*, and this together with
the *Tiruvācakam* or 'Sacred Utterance' of Mānikka Vāśagar
and ancillary writings came to be known as the 'Tamil Veda'.
These Śaivite hymns are distinguished from their Vaishnavite
counterparts by the extreme sense of unworthiness that the
devotee feels in the face of the all-holiness of God. The philosophy of the *Śaiva-Siddhānta*, which we have had occasion
to refer to, is based as much on the *Śvetāśvatara* Upanishad as
it is on the writings of the Tamil saints, but it was the influence
of the latter that made the writers of the *Śaiva-Siddhānta*
attach such enormous importance to the doctrine of grace freely

given and the impossibility of spiritual progress without love. The whole movement is an impassioned cry against the ossified ceremonial religion of the Brāhmans and the ideal of 'passion-lessness' that they shared with the Buddhists and Jains. It was against these last that they launched their passionate crusade in the name of the One True God, Śiva. In the following stanzas Appar, perhaps the most moving singer of them all, denounces the hollowness of purely mechanical religion in terms that bring to mind the much later reformer, Kabir.

> Why bathe in Ganges' stream, or Kāviri?
> Why go to Comorin in Kongu's land?
> Why seek the waters of the sounding sea?
>   Release is theirs, and theirs alone, who call
>   In every place upon the Lord of all.

> Why chant the Vedas, hear the Śāstras'[1] lore?
> Why daily teach the books of righteousness?[2]
> Why the Vedāngas[3] six say o'er and o'er?
>   Release is theirs and theirs alone, whose heart
>   From thinking of its Lord shall ne'er depart.

> Why roam the jungle, wander cities through?
> Why plague life with unstinting penance hard?
> Why eat no flesh, and gaze into the blue?
>   Release is theirs, and theirs alone, who cry
>   Unceasing to the Lord of Wisdom high.

> Why fast and starve, why suffer pains austere?
> Why climb the mountains doing penance harsh?
> Why go to bathe in waters far and near?
>   Release is theirs, and theirs alone, who call
>   At every time upon the Lord of all.

The Bhagavad-Gītā had taught that the love of God is open to all, irrespective of caste and sex, but it had also taught that each man should perform the duties dictated to him by his station in life. For Appar, however, who was himself of low caste, all distinctions between man and man were done away with in the worship of Śiva, and once one had confessed oneself Śiva's slave, all sins, even the slaying of a Brāhman or a cow, would be wiped out.

[1] Sacred texts.   [2] Law-books.
[3] Subsidiary disciplines connected with the study of the Vedas.

Though they give me the jewels from Indra's abode,
 Though they grant me dominion o'er earth, yea, o'er heaven,
If they be not the friends of our Lord Mahādev,[1]
 What care I for wealth by such ruined hands given?
But if they love Śiva, who hides in his hair
 The river of Ganges, then whoe'er they be,
Foul lepers, or outcastes, yea, slayers of kine,
 To them is my homage, gods are they to me.

What, however, distinguishes the Tamil Śaivite saints from almost all the other *bhakti* cults is their intense sense of personal guilt; man, as he exists apart from God, is evil and horribly corrupt, he is the slave of his *ānava*, his egoism.

Evil, all evil, my race, evil my qualities all,
Great am I only in sin, evil is even my good.
Evil my innermost self, foolish, avoiding the pure,
Beast am I not, yet the ways of the beast I can never forsake.
I can exhort with strong words, telling men what they should hate,
Yet I can never give gifts, only to beg them I know.
Ah! wretched man that I am, whereunto came I to birth?

The realization of one's abjectness makes the freely given grace of God seem all the more wonderful, for what has the wholly self-sufficient to gain from association with one so foul? This wondrous self-giving of God is the theme of this stanza of Mānikka Vāśagar:

  Thou gav'st thyself, thou gained'st me;
   Which did the better bargain drive?
  Bliss found I in infinity;
   But what didst thou from me derive?
  O Śiva, Perundurai's God,
   My mind thou tookest for thy shrine:
  My very body's thine abode;
   What can I give thee, Lord, of mine?

The Tamil Śaivite saints even more than the Ālvārs see in Nature the reflected glory of God, and the mating of animals brings to their minds the inseparable unity of all apparent opposites in the transcendental union of Śiva and Śakti. This does not mean that the sexual principle was arbitrarily introduced into the divine but that sex itself is seen as holy because it

[1] The 'Great God': Śiva.

reflects an essential polarity in God which is the source of his
creativity and joy.

I'll follow those who going to the shrine their praises sound,
With blooms and water for the God who wears the moon so mild
All lovely in his locks, a garland wreathed his neck around,
   And with him sing they Parvatī, the mountain god's fair child.
Once as I went to Aiyāru, with light and reverent tread,
I saw come two young elephants, male by loved female led,
And in that sight I saw God's foot, saw secret things unsaid.

Śiva has his terrible and his gentle aspect: he dances in sheer
joy and creation comes to be, and he dances in maniacal frenzy
and all the worlds crumble into ruin. Even though he appear as a
raving madman, his devotee sees in him nothing but love and
grace.

> O madman with the moon-crowned hair
>   Thou lord of men, thou fount of grace,
> How to forget thee could I bear?
>   My soul hath aye for thee a place.
> Venney-nallūr, in 'Grace's shrine'
>   South of the stream of Pennai, there,
> My father, I became all thine;
>   How could I now myself forswear?

The soul loses its reason in the divine madness and surrenders
itself totally to the 'foolishness of God' as St. Paul puts it.
God becomes all in all and man sees himself as nothing. All
thoughts of liberation are put aside in a passion of adoration for
the dancing God. In the words of Mānikka Vāśagar:

> I ask not kin, nor name, nor place,
>   Nor learned men's society.
> Men's lore for me no value has;
>   Kuttālam's lord, I come to thee.
> Wilt thou one boon on me bestow,
>   A heart to melt in longing sweet,
> As yearns o'er new-born calf the cow,
>   In yearning for thy sacred feet?

I had no virtue, penance, knowledge, self-control. A doll to turn
At another's will I danced, whirled, fell. But me he filled in every
  limb

With love's mad longing, and that I might climb there whence
   is no return,
He showed his beauty, made me his. Ah me, when shall I go
   to him?

> Fool's friend was I, none such may know
>   The way of freedom; yet to me
> He shew'd the path of love, that so
>   Fruit of past deeds might ended be.
> Cleansing my mind so foul, he made me like a god.
> Ah who could win that which the Father hath bestowed?
>
> Thinking it right, sin's path I trod;
>   But, so that I such paths might leave,
> And find his grace, the dancing God,
>   Who far beyond our thought doth live,
> O wonder passing great!—to me his dancing shewed.
> Ah who could win that which the Father hath bestowed?

It was the Bhagavad-Gītā that set in motion the transformation
of Hinduism from a mystical technique based on the ascetic
virtues of renunciation and self-forgetfulness into the impassioned religion of self-abandonment to God, but the strictly
religious impulse which gave momentum to the whole *bhakti*
movement stemmed from the Tamil lands of south India. From
the tenth century on all that is most vital in Hinduism manifests
itself in the form of *bhakti*. The cult of Śiva gained new impetus
in the twelfth century when a Brāhman called Bāsava became
Prime Minister of the principality of Kalyān not far from the
modern Bombay. Bāsava founded the sect of the Lingāyats
or Vīra-Śaivas who, though at first not opposed to caste,
later denounced both caste and image-worship. As time went on
they developed extreme puritanical and anti-Brāhmanic
tendencies. Outwardly they were and are distinguished by the
wearing of Śiva's symbol, the *lingam*, round the neck, while in
the matter of doctrine they rejected all that was most characteristic of Brāhmanical orthodoxy. They rejected the authority
of the Vedas and, for the first time since early Vedic times, the
doctrine of transmigration; they objected to child marriages
and did not prevent the remarriage of widows. In this way they
anticipated much that was to be characteristic of the reform
movements of the nineteenth century.

The renewal of Hinduism in the south came just in time to prepare the ancient Hindu *dharma* for the greatest trial of strength it has ever been called on to face—the coming of Islam. In the past Hinduism had had its ups and downs. Religions had grown up in its midst which rejected the social system of which the Brāhmans were the custodians; the principal of these were of course the Buddhists and the Jains, and with the conversion of the Emperor Aśoka in the third century B.C. Buddhism for a long time became the religion of the ruling house.

Both Buddhism and Jainism were proselytizing religions, but since both believed fervently in the principle of *ahiṁsā*, that is, that it is clean contrary to *dharma* to injure any living creature, their propaganda on behalf of their faiths was on the whole pacific. It is true that fanatics arose from time to time and that occasionally there was violence, but the responsibility for this was more often on the side of the Hindu counter-reformers than of their rivals. Moreover the social fabric of Brāhmanism was never seriously threatened by the Buddhists and Jains because their organization was essentially monastic and they made little appeal to the broad masses. When the Tamil counter-reformation came, then, it was only a matter of time for their always precarious hold on the local populace to relax and finally to disappear. Again, on the philosophical front, the advent of a galaxy of brilliant philosophers, of whom Śankara and Rāmānuja are only the brightest stars, provided Hinduism with a variety of philosophical systems that were fully capable of holding their own against the Buddhists. Philosophy, moreover, had never been divorced from religion in India, and so it was that Śankara founded monasteries throughout India in which the teaching of the theory of Advaita was regarded as no more than a *propaideutikon* to its practical realization. Other philosophers followed suit and monasteries began to spring up throughout the land in which the contemplative life could be actively pursued.

The advent of Islam, however, brought with it quite different problems and quite new dangers. There had, of course, been many earlier invasions of India, but the invaders were in each case easily assimilated and fitted somehow or other into the caste system, but the Muhammadan invasions were different, first because Islam is, of all the world religions, the least adaptable, and secondly because the Muslim invaders were of Turkic stock and of all the converts to the new faith the Turks were the most fanatical. The original wave of Arab conquest in the seventh and eighth centuries had affected India only to the extent that it detached the extreme north-western province of Sind from the rest of the sub-continent. It was, however, at the beginning of the tenth century that the Muslim incursions into India started in all seriousness. Mahmūd of Ghazni (997–1030) made some seventeen raids into India, looting, burning, and pillaging wherever he went. War against the Hindus was regarded as a sacred duty, for Islam, though tolerant of the 'people of the Book', that is, the Jews, Christians, and Zoroastrians who were considered to be the recipients of true revelation, abominated idol-worship which was scathingly denounced in their sacred book, the Koran. Moreover, war against the unbelievers, if they refused conversion, was a sacred duty, and Mahmūd, though certainly not indifferent to plunder, was no doubt sincere in his belief that in destroying the great temples of northern India he was rendering a service to God. His raids succeeded in wresting the Punjāb from the Hindu fold but, apart from their very considerable nuisance value, left the rest of India relatively undisturbed.

With the advent of the Ghūrids towards the end of the twelfth century Muslim pressure on India became continuous, and by the middle of the fourteenth century the Muslim sultanate of Delhi had extended deep into the Deccan and even included a section of the Malabar coast. After 1340, however, the frontiers of the Delhi sultanate contracted, and the growth of a new Hindu kingdom in Vijayanagar in the Deccan checked for the time being the advance of the Muslim power. The respite, however, was shortlived, for a second great wave of Muslim aggression was soon to start when Bābar, the Moghul ruler of Kābul, invaded India in 1525. Success followed success and the Moghul power became firmly established in Delhi, and by 1691 the officers of the Emperor Aurangzeb were in a position to levy tribute from Tanjore and Trichinopoly in the far south. It was only in the second half of the seventeenth century that the Hindus succeeded in mounting a counter-offensive. The hero of the movement was a Marāthā, Śivajī by name, who, himself a religious man, enlisted the moral power of a renascent Hinduism in his struggle against an essentially alien régime, and the songs of the Marāthā 'saints' played a not wholly negligible part in the establishment of the Marāthā polity. This second wave of the *bhakti* movement, then, was a natural response to the aggressive impact of a religion that challenged everything that Hinduism had stood for throughout the centuries.

The advent of Islam in India, however, did not have only a negative side, for the more astute of the Muslim leaders realized that Hinduism could not be simply extinguished. The most enlightened, if the most quixotic, of them all, Akbar (1556–1605) sought to reconcile the two religions and went so far as to open a 'House of Worship' in which representatives of all the religions of India were invited to take part in debate. This eirenic venture, however, was not a success and the debates petered out in 1582. Of more lasting effect were the efforts of Kabīr, a born Muslim, and Nānak, the founder of the Sikhs, to bridge the gulf between the two religions. The Muslims, on their side, were able to make many converts from among the Hindus. Frequently, in their zeal for saving souls, they resorted to force, but many conversions were voluntary particularly among the outcastes or untouchables who saw in conversion a way of escape from an intolerable social degradation. Further, Islam is a supremely simple religion and its uncompromising monotheism offered an attractive alternative to the complexities and imprecisions of the prevailing *dharma*. Hinduism's reaction to the Muslim aggression was to withdraw into itself: the caste system, which alone gave Hinduism its identity, became more not less rigid, and in addition the Hindus took over from Islam one of its least attractive customs, the veiling of women.

The *bhakti* cults originated in South India where their popular appeal was emphasized by the use of the vernacular in place of the time-hallowed Sanskrit. This trend was to maintain itself as the movement made its way to the north and from the fourteenth century we find an independent religious literature springing up in Hindī, Marāthī, and Bengālī to mention only

the most prominent languages. In some ways the *bhakti*
movement is comparable to the Protestant Reformation in
Europe; the centre of interest passes from the hierarchical act
of sacrifice and the hierarchy which mediates it to the laity to a
direct and personal relationship between the worshipper and his
God. As a natural corollary to this the language of the liturgy
which only the priests could understand was replaced by the
vernacular, and the singing of vernacular hymns gradually
supplanted and replaced the priestly liturgies. Here, however,
the analogy ends, for though there was often hostility to the old
order as represented by the Brāhmans, no clear break was ever
made with it. The Vedic rites which accompanied at least the
'twice-born' castes from their conception to their cremation
continued to be performed by Brāhmans, but personal religion
tended to evade their control and passed into the hands of the
'sect' which was headed by a 'Guru' who might be of any caste.
The ritual of the various sects naturally varied, but the *kīrtan*
or rhythmical singing of hymns usually to the accompaniment
of dance was characteristic of most of them. The object of the
kīrtan was to induce a state of ecstasy in the devotee in which he
believed he had established direct contact with the divine. The
quality and content of this ecstasy would be argued about *ad
nauseam* by the philosophers, but it was the emotional experience that mattered to the devotee. All this is reminiscent
of the 'enthusiasm' of the less orthodox Protestant sects that
were peripheral to the main stream of the Reformation, but
what the *bhakti* sects conspicuously lacked was the deep moral
earnestness and the grave preoccupation with sin that marked
the main stream of the European Reformation. The Tamil
Śaivites were the exception, for in general it can be said that
the Christian concept of 'sin' as an offence against God did not
enter into the Hindu way of thinking until contact with the
Christian West was established during the last two hundred
years. To the Hindu 'salvation' means *moksha*, and *moksha*,
as usually understood, means salvation or liberation not from
moral guilt but from the human condition as such—it is liberation from space and time, and the felt experience of immortality.

The outstanding characteristic of all the *bhakti* sects is self-
abandonment to a personal God and this tends to be a highly

emotional affair. *Bhakti* is contrasted with *jñāna*, devotion with 'knowledge', and the former is exalted over the latter; but the pantheistic trend which is ever-recurring in Hinduism was not so easily to be eradicated and it is strongly present even in the *bhakti* movement. One is conscious the whole time of an uneasy feeling that because *bhakti* is the easy way to ecstasy, the way of 'knowledge' which in practice means the attainment of *moksha* by rigorous self-discipline, must be superior and more authentic.

In northern and central India the *bhakti* cults flourished from the thirteenth to the eighteenth century. In the Hindī-speaking north the big names are Rāmānand (fourteenth century), Kābir and Nānak (fifteenth to sixteenth century), and Tulsī Dās (seventeenth century); among the Marāthās we have Jñāneśvar (thirteenth century), Nāmdev (fourteenth century), Ekanāth (sixteenth century), and Tukārām (seventeenth century), while in Bengal the most prominent are Caitanya (fifteenth and sixteenth century) and Rāmprāsad Sen (eighteenth century). All these men, with the exception of the last, were worshippers of Vishnu in one or other of his incarnations as Rāma or Krishna.

Rāmānand was brought up in the school of Rāmānuja and was himself a south Indian who emigrated north to Benares. He appears to have been the first teacher outside the Tamil south to have abandoned Sanskrit in favour of the vernacular. Like almost all the great leaders of the *bhakti* movement that followed him he made no distinction of caste among his followers, but this does not mean that either he or they attacked the system as such, for it was only in the religious circle that all men were equal in the sight of God. In the world outside, caste rules were disobeyed at one's peril.

Most distinguished among his followers were Kabīr and Nānak. Kabīr was a Muslim by birth, and though he early abandoned the Muslim faith, he retained the strict monotheism of Islam and a strong aversion to the caste system. It is, then, somewhat strange that he usually calls God 'Rām' (Rāma) despite the fact that he had the strongest dislike of Hindu polytheism. This would seem to indicate that the deification of Rāma had already gone so far that his name had become a synonym for 'God'. For Kabīr he can scarcely have been the mythological hero of the Rāmāyana. It seems to have been Kabīr's intention to found a religion that was inhibited by neither dogma, nor scripture, nor social framework. In spirit he is far more Hindu than Muslim, and this is presumably what led him to reject the rigid and sometimes fierce dogmatism of Islam. Religion was for him a purely personal affair—something between a man, his God, and his Guru. 'Thou shouldst ride on thine own reflection; thou shouldst put thy foot in the stirrup of tranquillity of mind. Kabīr says, "Those are good riders who keep aloof from Veda and Koran." ' His efforts to create a bridge between the two religions, however, failed, and his followers are now split between those who call themselves Muslims and those who call themselves Hindus. There is little communication between them.

Of more lasting importance was the work of Nānak (1469–1538), the founder of the Sikhs. Like Kabīr Nānak was a strict monotheist and a determined opponent of caste. He organized his disciples, the 'Sīkhs', into a close-knit and exclusive community under himself as Guru. The fifth Guru, Arjun (1563–1606) collected together the writings of Nānak and subsequent Gurus as well as the sayings of Kabīr and other Hindu and Muslim saints into what has ever since been the sacred book of the Sikhs, the *Ādi-Granth*. Until Arjun's time the Sikhs had been a pacific community only too anxious to live at peace with their neighbours. Arjun, however, got on the wrong side of the Muslim authorities and was executed. This transformed the Sikhs into an armed brotherhood, violently hostile to Islam but separated from their natural allies, the Hindus. The process of transforming one of many unorthodox Hindu sects into a military brotherhood was completed by the last of the Gurus, Gobind Singh, who instituted an initiation ceremony which consisted of drinking sweetened water out of a communal bowl. This was intended to destroy the last vestige of caste in the community since among the Hindus it was not lawful for men of different castes to drink out of the same bowl without incurring pollution. The Gurus, during their lifetime and after their death, were granted almost divine honours though they strongly discouraged any attempt to elevate them to the dignity of an *avatār*. The tenth Guru, Gobind Singh, had no successor, and supreme authority was thenceforward deemed to reside in the *Ādi-Granth* sometimes known as the *Granth-Sāhib*, the 'Lord Scripture'. The Sikhs are unique among the *bhakti* sects in that they have separated themselves from the main body of Hinduism and do not regard themselves as Hindus. Even in Arjun's time the break between the two communities was complete.

'I have broken with the Hindu and the Muslim,' he writes,
  'I will not worship with the Hindu, nor like the Muslim go to Mecca.
  I shall serve Him and no other.
  I will not pray to idols nor say the Muslim prayer.
  I shall put my heart at the feet of the one Supreme Being,
  For we are neither Hindus nor Musulmans.'

Both Kabīr and Nānak held strong views on what they considered to be the iniquity of the caste system, and they reserved their most savage contempt for the inordinate pretensions of the Brāhmans. 'The Brāhmans of this age', Kabīr wrote, 'are objects of ridicule; . . . they and their families will go to hell, and take with them their employers.' 'They consider themselves polluted by the touch of others: ask them who is lower than they are.' It was due to these extreme views on caste that neither sect could be fully reabsorbed into the Hindu social structure, as the other *bhakti* sects were. The normal process was for the sect itself to become an endogamous and closed social unit, in other words, a new caste. The influence of the *bhakti* reformers was fissiparous on the one hand in that it tended to introduce new divisions in an already sufficiently divided society; on the other hand, the more it insisted on *bhakti* as an alternative to the Brāhmanical ritual, the more it could act as a unifying force. This is particularly true of Tulsī Dās who was himself a Brāhman.

Tulsī Dās is known and loved wherever the Hindī language is spoken, for he is the author of the Hindī version of the Rāmāyana. This is not simply a translation of Valmīki's original, but a refashioning of it in a way that makes it abundantly clear that Rāma is God incarnate. His actions are therefore divine and serve as models for the imitation of the faithful.

According to Tulsī Dās *bhakti* is the only way to approach the
divine in the present degenerate age of the *Kali Yuga*, and
bhakti need mean no more than the recitation of the Holy
Name. Veneration for the Name of God is, of course, not
peculiar to Tulsī Dās within Hinduism, nor to Hinduism among
the great religions of the world. All the *bhakti* reformers stress
the importance of the 'Name', but none give it such prominence
as does he. Like the majority of the great *bhakti* saints, Tulsī
Dās was no theologian: he sometimes exalts the personal God
above the impersonal Absolute, sometimes he considers him
only an aspect of it. His *bhakti*, moreover, is very much more
restrained than that offered to Vishnu's other incarnation,
Krishna, for Rāma is an altogether more conventional and
respectable figure than is the wayward and unpredictable
Krishna. For Tulsī Dās the relationship of the worshipper to his
God is not that of mistress to lover, wife to husband, or even son
to father, but of a servant to his lord or a younger brother to the
elder. Indeed, in one passage (2.123) Rāma's younger brother,
Lakshmana, is compared to the individual soul and Rāma
himself to Brahman, while Sītā, his wife, has to be content with
the role of *māyā*. It is not clear whether Tulsī Dās understood
māyā as God's creative energy as Rāmānuja did or as illusory
appearance as did Śankara and the Advaitins. To all intents and
purposes, however, he accepts the world in which the incarnate
God operates as real, and he accepts the mythological gods as
real but deplorable. Already in the Mahābhārata and the
Sanskrit Rāmāyana the gods other than Vishnu and Śiva
had sunk pretty low, but Tulsī Dās seems to take particular
pleasure in exhibiting them in their worst light. This applies
particularly to Indra who is described as a 'crafty crow' and a
'shameless dog'. Hostile to the gods as he is, however, he shows
no such hostility to those earthly gods, the Brāhmans. 'A
Brāhman', he says, 'is to be reverenced even though he curse
and beat you and use harsh words—so say the saints. A Brāhman must be revered though he be devoid of goodness or
virtue; but a Śūdra never, however virtuous and learned'
(3 C 32). In this respect Tulsī Dās differs from the great
majority of the *bhakti* reformers: he is conservative and at times
even reactionary, particularly in his attitude to women. In

Hinduism, as in other religions, there is a certain ambivalence in the attitude adopted towards women. Tulsī Dās is no exception. Sītā is held up as what a devoted and obedient wife ought to be, and Rāma's mother, Kausalyā, is similarly the paragon of all motherhood. One may perhaps discount passages in which woman is arraigned as 'a most dangerous and tormenting foe; a night impenetrably dark, to bring delight to all the owls of sin; a hook to catch all the fish of sense and strength and goodness and truth' (3 D 43ff.), but it is a little disconcerting to find Rāma, the incarnate God himself, whose devotion to his wife Sītā forms one of the main themes of the book, saying that the loss of a wife is as nothing compared to the loss of a devoted brother (6 C 61). Despite this blind-spot, however, Tulsī Dās's *bhakti* pays far more attention to moral conduct based on natural affection than do the more ecstatic cults of Krishna.

Parallel to the *bhakti* movement in the Hindī-speaking provinces of India a similar renaissance occurred in the Marāthā country between the thirteenth and seventeenth centuries. This was more or less consciously nationalist and anti-Muslim, the hero of the Marāthā defiance of the Moghul power, Śivajī (d. 1680) being himself a pupil and friend of Rāmdās, a prominent holy man of the time. The earliest of the Marāthā saints was Jñāneśvar who wrote a voluminous commentary on the Gītā, the *Jñāneśvarī*, as well as a philosophic poem and numerous *ābhangas* or short devotional hymns which were so characteristic of the whole *bhakti* movement. Philosophically Jñāneśvar stands nearer to Rāmānuja than to Śankara: he is an Advaitin, but with a difference. He does not stress the absolute oneness that, according to Śankara, characterizes Brahman and therefore the state of liberation, but sees it rather as a continuum or perfectly co-ordinated organism, the constitution of which is such that each part is suffused with the full life of the whole. To experience this means that one's own personality has been replaced by God.

We must pass over the two intervening personalities, Nāmdev and Ekanāth, and come straight to Tukārām who fills the place among the Marāthā saints that Tulsī Dās does among the Hindī-speakers. A far more thorough-going representative of *bhakti* than was Jñāneśvar, he claimed that devotion to God

alone sanctifies, not the accident of caste or even the experience
of liberation. 'Holy is the family', he says, 'and holy the
country where the servants of God are born. They have devoted
themselves to God, and by them all the three worlds become
holy. Pride of caste has never made any man holy, says Tukā,
but the untouchables have crossed the ocean of life by devotion
to God' (Ābh, 3241). 'A Brāhman who loves not the Name of
God, is no Brāhman' (Ābh, 706), but 'an outcaste who loves
the Name of God is a Brāhman indeed. In him have tranquillity and forbearance, compassion and courage made their
home. When all the passions have left a man's mind, he is as
good as a Brāhman, says Tukā' (Ābh, 707).

Tukārām puts the love of God above everything. Without
love, which itself is impossible without duality, there can be
no real fruition of the soul: there can only be sterilization. In
Hinduism 'the fool hath said in his heart' not 'there is no God',
but 'I am God'; and Tukārām had no patience with fools.
'There is no fool on this earth, says Tukā, comparable to him
who calls himself God' (Ābh, 2064). In one important respect
Tukārām reverses the whole scheme of Hindu values; instead
of crying out for release from this 'valley of tears' he prays that
he may be incarnated ever again in order that he may continue
to experience the love of God which is infinitely delectable.
Beauty and value depend on individual things being in their
proper place, on their fulfilling their function in an eternal
setting. And so 'thou shouldst be my Lord, and I thy servant.
Thy place should be high, and my place low. . . . Water does not
swallow water. A tree does not swallow its fruits. A diamond
appears beautiful on account of its setting. Gold looks beautiful
when it is transformed into ornaments. Shade gives pleasure
when there is the sun outside. A mother gives out milk when
there is a child to partake of it. What happiness can there be
when one meets oneself? I am happy, says Tukā, in the belief
that I am not liberated' (Ābh, 595).

Tulsī Dās and Tukārām are perhaps the finest as well as the
latest flowers in the anthology of *bhakti*. More exotic, perhaps,
was the Bengālī Caitanya who flourished in the sixteenth
century and is alleged to have met his death by leaping into the
Jumna in a state of uncontrollable ecstasy. Caitanya was a

passionate devotee of the loves of Krishna and Rādhā, Krishna's favourite among the *gopīs* and not his wedded wife. For him the highest bliss was to identify himself with Rādhā and thereby submit himself to the passionate embraces of his Lord. As for the Tamil Śaivites, so for him the soul must play the woman in its dealings with God: all souls are female, God the universal male. It is true that the love of Krishna automatically destroys the cycle of rebirth, but this is but a by-product: 'its highest aim is the enjoyment of love's felicity'. The Tamil saints had regarded *sāyujya*, 'being closely yoked to or linked with God' as the consummation of liberation, but the followers of Caitanya would not even go so far as this, so emphatic were they on the distinction between the soul and God.

'At the sound of *sāyujya*', one of them says, 'the *bhākta* feels hatred and fear. He prefers hell to it.

At the utterance of the word *mukti* (*moksha*) hatred and fear arise in the mind; at the utterance of the word *bhakti* the mind is filled with joy.'

The *bhakti* movement reached its peak in the seventeenth century and it was almost exclusively Vaishnavite, finding its most satisfying symbols in Krishna, the wayward lover, and the more solidly virtuous Rāma. Pure Śaivism produced little that was comparable, though Śāktism in which Śiva's consort who is his energy takes the place of Śiva as the object of worship, produced a *bhakti* of its own especially in Bengal. Rāmprasād Sen, who lived in the eighteenth century, was the most notable figure in the movement.

The Mother-Goddess, called in her terrible aspect Durgā or Kālī and in her more auspicious aspect Umā or Parvatī, has for long been notorious, for it is in her temple in Calcutta that, contrary to the canons of *ahiṁsā*, animals continue to be sacrificed in great numbers even now. Iconographically she is represented as dancing on the body of her prostrate Lord, festooned with skulls, her tongue lolling out and dripping with blood. Such a figure, one would have thought, was more likely to inspire terror than loving adoration, but she fascinated not only Rāmprasād but the far more significant figure who lived a century after him, Rāmakrishna Paramahaṁsa. The ecstasies of sentiment expended on Krishna are scarcely suitable to Śiva's fearful spouse, for she is terrifying in her beauty, and her loveliness lies precisely in her frightfulness. One quotation must suffice to show how Kālī, the universal murderess of all she has brought forth, can yet inspire rapt devotion in the Indian soul.

Ever art thou dancing in battle, Mother. Never was beauty like thine, as, with thy hair flowing about thee, thou dost ever dance, a naked warrior on the breast of Śiva.

Heads of thy sons, daily freshly killed, hang as a garland around thy neck. How is thy waist adorned with human hands! Little children are thy ear-rings. Faultless are thy lovely lips; thy teeth are fair as the jasmin in full bloom. Thy face is bright as the lotus-flower, and terrible is its constant smiling. Beautiful as the rain-clouds is thy form; all blood-stained are thy feet.

Prasād says: My mind is as one that dances. No longer can my eyes behold such beauty.

Rāmprasād Sen marks the end of an epoch—the epoch of *bhakti*. In the course of this epoch Hinduism had undergone a profound change: neither ritualism nor the pursuit of a solitary *moksha* had proved adequate to a people avid for religious experience. Mysticism itself which is so often identical with religion in India turned its gaze away from the deep centre of the soul to the God outside who is the lover of the soul, and it was found that a whole new dimension had been added to the spiritual life. This was the inner experience. Outwardly the *bhakti* reformers looked at the social structure of Hindu society and found it not good. The caste system which may have served a useful purpose once was now manifestly unjust and set intolerable divisions between man and man, so in their own fraternities they abolished it because they believed that God had an equal love for all his creatures. Despite them, however, the evil, if evil it was, continued, and it needed the impact of an alien civilization with values derived from a very different source to jostle the conscience of a nation that seemed liable to forget that it could claim if it would, the King of Righteousness, Yudhishthira, as perhaps the most noble and not the least typical of its sons.

7
Encounter

WHEN THE BRITISH made their appearance on the Indian scene in the eighteenth century, they found a sub-continent politically disunited and religiously split in two. The religious split, however, did not altogether follow territorial lines. The north-west, it is true, had in the course of centuries become predominantly Muslim, but Muslims were also scattered throughout the rest of India, being thinnest in the south. As a reaction against Muslim predominance and Muslim proselytism Hinduism turned in upon itself. Despite the affirmation of the *bhakti* reformers that salvation was open to all, irrespective of creed or caste, and despite their efforts to break down the barriers in their own communities, caste not only persisted but grew more rigid. But caste in the eighteenth century was something very different from the *varṇāśrama-dharma* we outlined in Chapter V. At the beginning of this century there were 2,378 castes in India, and these castes formed closed communities which had no social contact with each other. It was not permissible to marry outside one's own caste or for members of one caste to eat, drink, or smoke with members of another. Each caste was governed by a caste council which jealously guarded the caste rules and punished those who infringed them. In extreme cases a man could be outcasted permanently, which meant that not only were all ties with his own caste severed, but that he would be treated as a pariah by other castes too, for it was in the interest of all the castes that caste rule should be observed.

Of the four ancient *varnas* probably only the Brāhmans who

had a monopoly of the priestly function were the lineal descend-
ants of the ancient class bearing their name, but even they were
divided into sub-castes, those willing to administer to the
religious needs of Śūdras being considered inferior and unclean.
All castes affiliated to the four ancient *varnas* depended on
the Brāhmans for the administration of the numerous sacraments (*samskāras*) that accompany the Hindu from his conception to the burning-ghat. Only the untouchables, that is,
those not included in any of the *varnas* and therefore outcaste,
could not benefit from the administration of the Brāhmans
and had to create priests of their own. They were not admitted
into Hindu temples nor were their gods recognized in the
Hindu pantheon as were the gods of tribes who had been
received into the Hindu fold. These tribes would be incorpor-
ated into a separate caste and their gods would be identified
with one or other of the Hindu gods. Not so with the gods of the
untouchables: with these the Brāhmans would have nothing
to do.

To all caste Hindus the untouchables were a source of
pollution; their touch defiled, and the infection had to be
removed by purificatory rites which usually included ceremonial
washing. In south India their mere propinquity was considered
to cause defilement and they had therefore to be settled some
way outside a village inhabited by caste Hindus. Yet so strong
was the hold of caste on the people that when at last a vigorous
onslaught was made against it, it was from the lower castes and
the untouchables themselves that the most vigorous opposition
proceeded, not from the higher. Those Brāhmans who still
performed priestly functions—and many of them no longer
did—naturally resisted too, but on the whole the lower the
caste the more conservative it would be. The reason would
appear to be that caste discipline was far stricter among the
lower castes and the fear of being outcasted was therefore the
more intense. The whole system, moreover, was considered to
be hallowed by *dharma*, divinely instituted and therefore unalterable.

Apart from the caste system, however, and the inhuman
abuses it had given rise to, there were many other Hindu
practices equally hallowed by *dharma* that would have been

considered inhuman in most other parts of the globe, the encouragement of widows to sacrifice themselves on their husband's funeral pyre, the marriage of children long before they reached the age of puberty, enforced widowhood, and temple prostitution. Less inhuman but quite as cramping was the fact that travel overseas involved loss of caste. These were some of the things that the British found in India in the eighteenth century.

The Muslim domination of India scarcely affected the Hindu way of life at all. There was intermittent persecution and a constant stream of conversions, both forced and voluntary, but on the whole, though the Muslims disliked and despised the Hindus, they did not interfere with their customs nor did they wish to reform them. The British presence in India, however, though on a diminutive scale compared to the Muslim irruptions, threw open to the Hindus totally new perspectives wholly foreign to their own way of life. The Government, it is true, at first intervened as little as possible in the domestic affairs of the Hindu community, they were not primarily interested in the morals of Hinduism, but in restoring order out of the chaos that eighteenth-century India had become. There were, however, the Christian missionaries who, in the nature of the case, could not remain silent in the face of practices and conditions which, according to their *dharma*, were morally wrong, and in fairness it must be said that it was thanks to the often tactless and aggressive denunciation by the Christian missionaries of what are now generally considered to have been inhuman practices that the Hindus, like Yudhishthira of old, looked beyond a *dharma* that had been degraded and corrupted in the course of time, to the *dharma* which they discovered in their own consciences.

The impetus for reform came, as might be expected, from the social *élite* which was most in contact with the new ideas that had been imported from Europe, and it was these ideas that created a desire for reform. The *bhakti* movement had indeed thrown open its doors to all castes and outcastes, but its driving power was religious not social: it was not interested in 'good works' in the Christian sense. The reform movements of the nineteenth century, on the other hand, were animated

primarily by a social conscience and determination to rid
Hinduism of what they were not afraid to call evils, however
hallowed they might be by a supposedly divine sanction.

The first of the reform movements to take the field was the
Brāhmo Samāj, and its inspiration was Western. As in other
parts of the world, Western civilization brought with it two
distinct elements, the 'philosophy' of progress based on the
scientific revolution which looked for its philosophical justi-
fication to the eighteenth-century Enlightenment, and the
Christian religion. The two were not necessarily or even
naturally connected, but Christianity none the less was considered to be the religion of the white man, the religion which
had brought him such astonishing power and success. In the
early stages, then, when Hinduism was going through a period
of stagnation and decline, Christianity received a favourable
hearing. Even so the Christian missions did not make the large
number of converts they had hoped for except among the untouchables, some of whom they were successful in converting
en masse. The educated classes, on the other hand, ashamed
though they may have been of the abuses that disfigured their
religion, were none the less reluctant to exchange it for another
since that would be equivalent to dissociating themselves from
their own nation. While railing at the institution of caste, they
were themselves in some measure in bondage to it. After all,
they were Hindus, and 'Hindu' is simply the Persian word
for 'Indian', and to repudiate Hinduism therefore seemed to
many to amount to repudiating India itself.

Rām Mohan Roy (1772–1833), the founder of the Brāhmo
Samāj, was scarcely a typical Hindu. His family were followers
of Caitanya, and he himself was brought up in Patna, the centre
of Muslim learning. This early schooling developed in him a
deep distaste for image-worship and when he came to draw up
the trust deed of the Brāhmo Samāj he decreed that 'no graven
image, statue or sculpture, carving, painting, picture, portrait,
or the likeness of anything, shall be admitted within the said
building'. His dislike of images, however, did not make him an
iconoclast, his respect for the sincerely held beliefs of others
was too strong for that, and so in the same document he laid
down that 'no object, animate or inanimate, that has been or is

or shall hereafter become or be recognized as an object of worship of any man or set of men, shall be reviled or slightingly or contemptuously spoken of or alluded to'. In 1814 he settled in Calcutta where, after making a thorough study of the Upanishads and *Brahma-sūtras*, he decided that these taught a pure theism and gave no sanction to image-worship. In Calcutta too he met the Serampore missionaries, studied the Bible and concluded that the doctrines contained therein were 'more conducive to moral principles and better adapted for the use of rational beings than any other' that had come his way. His attitude towards Christ was later to become typical of enlightened Hindus in general: he wholeheartedly accepted the ethical teaching of the Gospels, particularly the Sermon on the Mount, but rejected the whole theological superstructure that had been built up around the Person of Christ as Son of God. Among the basic tenets of Hinduism he rejected the doctrine of the transmigration of souls. This, apart from the Lingāyats, was a totally new departure in Hinduism.

Rām Mohan was more interested in the reform of abuses within Hinduism than in the actual practice of religion, and it was largely due to his efforts that the burning of widows was made illegal in 1829. D. S. Sharma is right when he says that Rām Mohan was 'a far greater man than [his successors] Debendranāth Tagore or Keshab Chandra Sen, but not an essentially religious soul'. His rather cold and rationalist temper left its stamp on the Brāhmo Samāj which made its appeal mainly to the intellectuals, not to the mass of the people.

In 1830 the first 'church' of the Brāhmo Samāj was opened, and services were held in it which consisted of reading passages from the Upanishads, a sermon, and the singing of theistic hymns composed by Rām Mohan and his friends. It is noteworthy that the service gave no place to prayer or contemplation. Direct communion with the divine was not encouraged. Rām Mohan died in 1833.

For some years the Brāhmo Samāj languished for lack of proper leadership or organization. In 1842, however, Debendranāth Tagore, the son of one of Rām Mohan's closest collaborators, joined the Samāj, amalgamating with it his own *Tattvabodhinī Sabhā*, an association which met for religious discussion and prayer. Debendranāth was a very different man from Rām Mohan. He was of a deeply religious temperament and throughout his life he was the subject of spontaneous mystical experiences. The first of these occurred after his grandmother's death when he was eighteen. 'A strange sense of the unreality of all things suddenly entered my mind,' he writes. 'A strong aversion to wealth arose within me. . . . In my mind was awakened a joy unfelt before.' From this moment prayer and adoration came naturally to him. Thus when he became the acknowledged leader of the Samāj he added prayer to the service designed by Rām Mohan.

Since Rām Mohan had claimed that his religion was simply a return to the 'pure' religion of the Vedas, Tagore sent four students to Benares to find out what the orthodox interpretation of the Vedas and Upanishads in fact was. On the students' return it became clear that there was much in these venerable texts that did not agree with the principles of the Samāj. It was therefore agreed that the Vedas, the Upanishads, and other sacred writings were not to be accepted as infallible guides. Reason and conscience were henceforth to be regarded as the highest authority, and the teachings of scripture were to be accepted only in so far as they harmonized 'with the light within us'. Among the things that did not so harmonize were the very sentences that Śankara had singled out as being the quintessence of the Vedānta, 'I am Brahman', 'That art thou', and the rest. This attitude towards Holy Writ was not entirely new: what was new was the public denial of the inerrancy of the Vedas. In the past it had been customary simply to ignore the Saṁhitās and the Brāhmanas and to interpret the Upanishads in whatever way one thought fit. Debendranāth rejected whatever did not agree with his own views, and compiled a selection of suitable passages from the Upanishads, the Epic, and elsewhere which he entitled *Brāhma Dharma*, and this was to rank as the sacred book of the sect. This method of selecting only those parts of scripture which fit in with one's own ideas was to be typical of the modern reformers and is particularly noticeable in the case of Gandhi.

In 1857 the Brāhmo Samāj received a new recruit. This was Keshab Chandra Sen who was then only nineteen and full of reformist zeal. Debendranāth became deeply attached to this ardent young man and allowed himself to be carried away on a flood-tide of change that went far beyond what was natural to him.

Saṁskāras or sacraments play an important part throughout the life of a Hindu, but these ceremonies involve the veneration of religious symbols which in the eyes of the Brāhmos amounted to idolatry. It was therefore ruled that no Brāhmo could take part in these ceremonies, and new ones were drawn up on strictly monotheistic lines. Next came the vital question of caste: this too was repudiated and members of the 'twice-born' castes were required to throw away the sacred thread which was the mark of their initiation. All this alarmed the more conservative wing of the Samāj who began to exercise pressure on Tagore. The crisis came when the Samāj building was so badly damaged by a cyclone that meetings had to be held in his house. Since he was indisputably master in his own house, Debendranāth insisted that ministers of the cult should wear the thread when officiating there. At this Keshab and his followers, who were in a majority, walked out and proceeded to call their own party the 'Brāhmo Samāj of India'. Debendranāth's rump, now called the *Ādi Samāj* or 'Original Samāj', became increasingly conservative and pietistic.

After the secession in 1865 Keshab immersed himself in Christian literature and in the sacred books of the other world religions. The result of this eclecticism was yet another collection of texts which this time included much matter that was not Hindu at all. To make the services more lively Keshab introduced the *kīrtan* of Caitanya with its accompaniment of song and dance, while a visit to England aroused in him an enthusiasm for the emancipation of women and the education of girls. On his return he campaigned against child marriage and persuaded the Samāj to celebrate the remarriage of widows and marriages between different castes. Thanks largely to the untiring efforts of the Brāhmos the Government passed an act not only making Brāhmo marriages legal, but also abolishing child-marriage and permitting intercaste marriages and the remarriage of widows.

As we have seen, Keshab's radicalism had been responsible

for the abolition of the Hindu *saṁskāras* within the Samāj. It came, then, as rather a surprise when he allowed his own daughter to be married to a young prince according to the orthodox Hindu ritual, not the Brāhmo variety; and this surprise turned into resentment when Keshab announced that he had only consented to this because he had received a revelation to that effect. This resulted in yet another schism, the majority again seceding to form the *Sādhāran* ('universal') Brāhmo Samāj. Keshab himself named his party the 'Church of the New Dispensation', and a very peculiar 'Church' it was.

In his later life he was strongly influenced by the ideas of Rāmakrishna Paramahaṁsa who considered all religions to be equally true. Keshab thus conceived the idea that it was the mission of the New Dispensation to harmonize all these religions and revelations, and to facilitate this he enriched his ritual not only by bringing back some of the ceremonies of orthodox Hinduism but also by introducing Baptism and the Lord's Supper from Christianity. At the same time he became an increasingly fervent admirer of Christ, even accepting his divinity and the doctrine of the Holy Trinity.

According to him 'the Old Testament was the First Dispensation; the New Testament the Second; unto us in these days has been vouchsafed the Third Dispensation'. This 'Third Dispensation', however, was not to last, for Keshab died in 1884 and the flock was left without a shepherd. Those still loyal to him considered him a god and would not admit of any other leader. The majority group, however, who had seceded after the affair of Keshab's daughter, pulled themselves together and for a time continued to make unspectacular progress. Rejecting utterly the cult of personality which had been offered to Keshab, they delegated authority to a General Committee of a hundred members who in turn elected a small Executive to run the affairs of the Samāj both in Calcutta and in the mission centres. Their creed was anodyne and vaguely Christian in flavour: there is only one God who is to be worshipped in spirit and in truth. No book must be considered infallible, 'but truth is to be reverently accepted from all scriptures and from the teaching of all persons without distinction of creed and country. The Fatherhood of God and

Brotherhood of man and kindness to all living beings are the essence of true religion.'

The Brāhmo Samāj, though plagued with schism, none the less injected into Hinduism a social conscience it had never had before. From the Christian missionaries it eagerly accepted the teachings of Christ as preserved in the synoptic Gospels, but rejected Christ's divinity and was deeply suspicious of missionary Christianity itself which it saw as a menace to Hinduism in its most literal sense: it saw it as disruptive of the Indian nation. The Brāhmos were the first to realize that the coming of Western civilization to India spelled the ruin of the Hindu *dharma* as it had existed for centuries. Their aim was to reform their religion from top to bottom and to force it into the mould of nineteenth-century humanitarianism. They were, however, not of the people, and though they were to disturb the conscience of the upper stratum of society, their effect on the broad masses of the Indian peasantry was nil.

Akin but not affiliated to the Brāhmo Samāj was the Prārthana Samāj of Bombay whose platform was purely social and directed against the well-known evils of child-marriage and the prohibition of the remarriage of widows. Unlike the Brāhmos the Prārthana Samāj did not regard their movement as being a complete break with the past but as a continuation of the *bhakti* tradition of the Marāthā saints who were also monotheistic and opposed to the caste system. The leader of the movement, Mahadev Govind Ranade, saw himself as a Hindu Protestant bent on destroying all the later accretions that, in his opinion, had come to obscure the ancient faith. He differed from the Protestants, however, in that he did his best not to antagonize the orthodox; he did not demand that the members of his Samāj should give up caste or the worship of images or the traditional sacraments of their religion. He saw the Samāj as a ferment that might in the course of time leaven the whole Hindu lump, though he admitted that neither it nor the Brāhmo Samāj had reached the heart of the nation as a whole; but he believed passionately in the greatness and destiny of India, not for any crude nationalistic reasons but because he realized that India's contribution to the religious life of the world was immense and of abiding value. Hinduism was at the

time under heavy fire from the Christian missions, but the best
of India's sons, despite the intemperance of some of the
Christian propagandists, realized the truth of some of the
charges levelled against them. The old abuses could not be
forever tolerated because they were contrary to what an unconditioned human conscience could accept. But all this was
ancillary to and parasitic on a noble religion which was every
bit as worth while as what was being offered by the Christian
missionaries. India, he thought, was as much the chosen people
as was Israel: 'I profess implicit faith in two articles of my
creed. This country of ours is the true land of promise. This
race of ours is the chosen race. . . . If the miraculous preservation
of a few thousand Jews had a purpose, this more miraculous
preservation of one fifth of the human race is not due to mere
chance.' The Christian offensive, backed as it was by the para-
mount power, had severely shaken the Hindu's self-respect.
Ranade, by writing off practices that could no longer be
defended as being peripheral to the Hindu *dharma*, did much
to restore this self-respect and thus paved the way for the
more self-confident reformulations of that *dharma* that were to
follow.

Quite different from the Brāhmo and Prārthana Samājes
was and is the Ārya Samāj. Its founder, Swami Dayānanda
Sarasvatī, differed from his predecessors in that his upbringing
was wholly orthodox; he was a proficient Sanskrit scholar and
his earlier works were written in Sanskrit rather than the
vernacular. His father was a fervent devotee of Śiva and completely orthodox. At the age of fourteen he was taken to the
local temple of Śiva to keep vigil throughout the night, but the
effect of the vigil was the opposite of what his father had
expected and hoped for; for as the boy sat gazing at the idol, he
wondered what conceivable relationship this could have with
the God Śiva who, he had been told, was the omnipotent,
omniscient creator, sustainer, and destroyer of the universe.
'I feel it impossible', he blurted out, 'to reconcile the idea of an
omnipotent, living God with this idol, which allows the mice to
run upon its body, and thus suffers its image to be polluted
without the slightest protest.' In 1846, when he was twenty-
one or twenty-two, his parents decided that the time had

come to marry him off. At this he ran away and wandered throughout India in search of a Guru. After various vicissitudes he found, in 1860, the Guru he had been seeking, and this Guru counselled him to study and interpret the Vedas since these, in his opinion, had been grossly misrepresented throughout the ages. From this time dates his public mission.

At first he wore the dress of a *sannyāsin* and preached in Sanskrit, but later he switched to more conventional dress and the Hindī language. His personal success was tremendous and in 1875 he founded the Ārya Samāj in Bombay; but it was in Lahore in the Punjab that he had his most startling success, and the Samāj he formed there in 1877 very soon eclipsed the mother-house in Bombay and became the headquarters of the movement.

Dayānanda yielded to none in his onslaughts against the corruptions that defaced the Hinduism of his day. This he did not in imitation of the Christians, but because he claimed that it was all clean contrary to the pure teaching of the Vedas. By the Vedas he understood not the complete corpus of Vedic scripture which included the Brāhmanas and Upanishads as well as the Saṁhitās, but the Saṁhitās only. Hitherto, commentators on the Vedas, both Indian and European, had taught that the Saṁhitās were polytheistic since the gods, Agni, Indra, Varuna, and so on, were distinct and had distinct personalities. This Dayānanda violently denied. It might be true if the Vedas were interpreted in a 'worldly' manner, it was not true of them if they were interpreted in a 'yogic' manner which, he maintained, was alone valid. The Veda was not, according to the orthodox, merely a book which had taken shape in the course of history, it was *sanātana dharma*, 'eternal law', and as such it exists in its own right outside and independently of time. It is eternal truth and contains all that is necessary to salvation; but it needs to be correctly interpreted, and it was Dayānanda alone who held the key to this true interpretation.

In his rejection of later accretions on the original Vedic deposit Dayānanda was on fairly safe ground; for it is quite true that there is no image-worship in the Vedas, no caste system, no *avatārs*, no pilgrimages to holy rivers and other holy places, nothing about child-marriage or the prohibition of the

remarriage of widows. It is on the positive side that Dayānanda's claim that his doctrines derive directly from the Saṁhitās is so shaky that it can only be accepted if we are prepared
to accept his further claim to be the sole divinely inspired
interpreter of the Vedas. Most of the doctrines he accepts,
indeed, are post-Vedic. The doctrine of *karma* and rebirth,
for instance, on which he insists, does not appear in the
Saṁhitās; it makes its first appearance in the Upanishads. Just
why he should have chosen to insist against the whole tradition
of Indian Sanskrit scholarship that doctrines which, by common
consent, first appear in the Upanishads or later are really
present in germ in the Saṁhitās is not at all clear, for it brought
him into needless conflict with the orthodox whom it would
have been natural to placate since his principal battle was with
the proselytizing faiths of Christianity and Islam.

Ranade had seen himself as a Hindu Luther, but the com-
parison is inexact, for Luther, partly against his will, split
Western Christendom in two, while Ranade was careful to do
nothing that would impair the unity of Hinduism. The Ārya
Samāj, on the other hand, with its assumption of extreme posi-
tions, its zeal to bring back to the fold those who had succumbed to the attractions of Christianity or Islam, its passion
for reform, its concern for the preservation of Hindu unity in
the face of more aggressive faiths, its vigour, aggressiveness,
and occasional unscrupulousness, was not unlike the Society of
Jesus in Counter-Reformation Europe.

Dayānanda died in 1883. Shortly after his death a controversy
arose between the progressives and the conservatives in the
Samāj. The progressives not only stood for modern education
and freedom of diet, they also regarded the Samāj as a nucleus
of a world religion not confined to India. The conservatives had
no such universalist pretensions, were vegetarian, and favoured
the ancient Hindu method of education. The progressives won.
Their beliefs may be summarized as follows: they 'insist not
only on the infallibility of the Veda, but also on *karma* and
rebirth, the sanctity of the cow, the efficacy of *homa* (Vedic
offering of clarified butter) and the importance of *Saṁskāras*,
and condemn in unequivocal terms idolatry, animal sacrifices,
ancestor-worship, pilgrimages, priestcraft, offerings in temples,

the caste system, untouchability and child-marriages as lacking Vedic sanction. They aim at a universal church without distinctions of caste or race—a church based on the authority of the Veda.'

The Ārya Samāj thus became intolerant, dogmatic, and aggressive. By the institution of a ceremony called *Śuddhi* it made it possible for untouchables to be invested with the sacred thread and thereby to become (in the eyes of the Samāj but not of orthodoxy) the equals of caste Hindus; and the same ceremony was used to re-admit apostate Hindus into their ancestral faith. The Samāj cultivates a militant spirit among its members, conducting a vigorous propaganda against both Christianity and Islam in which practically no holds are barred. In British India the work of the Samāj was not made easy for it, and the Muslims on their side were not slow to meet violence with violence; but the greatest blow they suffered was when India was partitioned and their headquarters at Lahore fell to the Pakistanis. The Ārya Samāj was shown no mercy by its Muslim enemies; its property was confiscated, and all the Samājists the Muslims could lay hands on were put to the sword. In independent India, however, they continue their work of preventing further secessions to Christianity and Islam and of re-converting the lapsed.

Dayānanda's aim had been to inject into Hinduism a self-confidence and an aggressive spirit that it had lacked before. A further boost for Hindu morale was to come from a very different quarter—the Theosophical Society.

The Theosophical Society was the creation of Madame Helena Petrovna Blavatsky (H.P.B. to her followers) and Colonel Olcott. It was opened in New York in 1875 with Olcott as President and Madame Blavatsky as Corresponding Secretary. Madame Blavatsky claimed occult powers and alleged that she was in direct communication with mysterious persons whom she referred to as the 'Masters' or 'Mahātmas' who were, she declared, resident in Tibet. Two of these were exotically named Koot Hoomi and Morya. In New York she had little success; so, for reasons that are not wholly clear, she decided to go to India taking Colonel Olcott with her. There she was more fortunate. From the very moment of landing on

Indian soil she and the Colonel professed themselves fervid
admirers of all things Indian and the sworn enemies of the
Christian missionaries; for them Hinduism was not only the
earliest of the world religions but the fountainhead from which
all true religion flowed. In 1885, however, the prestige of the
Theosophical Society suffered a severe blow. Madame Blavatsky
had achieved her reputation partly by the production of psychic
'phenomena' to which she attached inordinate importance. Her
enemies, however, of whom she had many, suspected her of
fraud and persuaded the Society for Psychical Research in
London to send out a representative to investigate the 'phenomena' on the spot. After a long and patient inquiry he came to
the conclusion that all the 'phenomena' were fraudulent. This
exposure did the Society much harm in the eyes of the outside
world, though its staunchest members did not flinch in their
devotion to the foundress nor did they waver in their belief in
the authenticity of her powers or in the reality of the guidance
she was supposed to receive from the mysterious 'Masters' in
Tibet.

The doctrines of the Theosophists are found in Madame
Blavatsky's two great works *Isis Unveiled* and *The Secret
Doctrine*. To the uninitiated they make wearisome reading and
opponents of the Society have alleged that much of the matter
found in them is plagiarized from other works. This was far
from being the impression they made on Mrs. Annie Besant
who was given *The Secret Doctrine* to review for the *Review
of Reviews*. Hitherto Mrs. Besant had been a free-thinker and a
Socialist, a member of the Fabian Society and associate of the
Webbs and Bernard Shaw. Her reading of *The Secret Doctrine*
was to change all that. Immediately she renounced her former
views and became an ardent Theosophist. Even before she
went there she had grown to love India and all things Indian,
for she believed that she had been a Hindu in a former incarnation. From the moment she set foot on Indian soil she gave
herself entirely to the Hindu people and far exceeded the
indigenous reformers in her zeal to defend all things Hindu,
even those that many of the reformers would have preferred to
forget. Her energy was boundless, and it would be no exaggera-
tion to say that no single person did so much to revive the

Hindu's pride in his religious heritage as did she. She lifted the Hindus out of the deep feeling of inferiority that had been induced in them by the subjugation of their land to an alien yoke and the attacks made on their religion by the self-confident zealots of another faith. It is indeed largely due to the Theosophical Society and its uncritical adulation of all things Hindu that Hinduism has been able not only to shake off its previous inferiority complex but to face the other great religions of the world at least as an equal.

The reform movements within Hinduism had up to this point been entirely sectarian. Neither the Brāhmo Samāj nor the Ārya Samāj, let alone the Theosophical Society, had any real roots in Hindu society. The last was of alien origin, whereas the two Samājes were exclusive in that they required their members to abjure certain practices, like the veneration of images, that had become inseparable from the practice of Hinduism. They lacked the wide tolerance in matters of belief and religious practice that has ever been characteristic of Hinduism.

This could certainly not be said of Rāmakrishna Paramahaṁsa. Gadhādhar Chatterji—for such was his name before he became a *sannyāsin*—was born in 1834 of a poor but orthodox Brāhman family in the Hooghly district of Bengal. At the age of eighteen he was appointed assistant priest at the newly-opened temple of Kālī at Dakshineśvar four miles north of Calcutta. From this moment he fell violently in love with the goddess: there seems no other word for it, though his love was a filial, not a sexual, passion, yet such was its intensity that it left him no peace. He hungered and thirsted after God, his Mother, but his thirst for long remained unsatisfied. He would fall into trances in which all signs of life seemed to have left his body, and so grave did these visitations become that he had to leave the temple. For some twelve years he lived in the woods nearby, tormented by his unsatisfied craving for the divine. At long last he was rewarded by a flash of illumination which he has twice described.

'I was then suffering from excruciating pain', he said, 'because I had not been blessed with a vision of the Mother. I felt as if my heart were being squeezed like a wet towel. I was overpowered by a great restlessness and a fear that it might not be my lot to realize her in this life. I could not bear the separation any longer; life did not seem worth living. Suddenly my eyes fell on the sword that was kept in the Mother's temple. Determined to put an end to my life, I jumped up like a mad man and seized it, when, suddenly, the blessed Mother revealed herself to me and I fell unconscious on the floor. What happened after that externally, or how that day or the next passed, I do not know, but within me there was a steady flow of undiluted bliss altogether new, and I felt the presence of the Divine Mother.'

Or again:

The buildings with their different parts, the temple and all, vanished from my sight, leaving no trace whatsoever, and in their stead was a limitless, infinite, effulgent ocean of consciousness or spirit. As far as the eye could reach, its shining billows were madly rushing towards me from all sides with a terrific noise, to swallow me up! In the twinkling of an eye they were on me and engulfed me completely. I was panting for breath. I was caught up in the billows and fell down senseless.

Sometime during this period he fell in with a female ascetic who instructed him in the *Tantras*, as the least orthodox and most recondite of the Hindu scriptures are called, and these apparently helped to bring under control the visitations that had formerly overwhelmed him. Later he was approached by an Advaitin monk who instructed him in the mysteries of the purist monism and initiated him into his order under the name of Rāmakrishna. On the very first day of their encounter, it is related, he experienced what is called *nirvikalpa-samādhi*, considered by Yogi practitioners to be the highest stage of 'super-consciousness' it is possible to reach. In it all trace of duality vanishes away and the conscious and thinking ego is totally obliterated. Rāmakrishna's spiritual experiences were rich and varied. He continually had visions of the Divine Mother to whom he remained passionately devoted, or again, imagining himself to be Rādhā, the *gopī* most beloved of the youthful Krishna, he would experience the presence of Krishna too; or he would experience the married bliss of Sītā, Rāma's devoted wife. When among Muslim mystics he had a vision of Muhammad, and a study of the New Testament is said to have brought on a vision of Christ. The great variety of his spiritual experience convinced him that all religions must be true, all being but different paths leading to the one goal which is to realize the absolute oneness of all things in the One Brahman.

At the age of twenty-five he had married a little girl of six. The girl, however, stayed on with her parents for thirteen years, after which she joined her husband at Dakshineśvar, there to minister to his needs until he died. Their marriage was never consummated as Rāmakrishna was now a *sannyāsin* and vowed to perpetual chastity. He abhorred sexuality and schooled himself to see in all women the 'Holy Mother' herself, and his disciples, following his example, would refer to his wife as the 'Holy Mother'. 'Women and gold' he considered were the arch-enemies of all spirituality—women, that is, regarded not as human persons but as the objects of male desire. In this there was nothing new, for, contrary to the general impression, there is a strong streak of puritanism in Hinduism, and chastity and voluntary poverty have always been among its most prized virtues.

Of Rāmakrishna D. S. Sharma writes: 'In the teachings of Sri Ramakrishna during the creative period of his life, one may say there is nothing new. For he came neither to destroy nor to fulfil. . . . "He was the embodiment of all the past religious thought of India." He is a branch of the true vine. He does not speak as one of the scribes, but with authority' (*Hinduism through the Ages*, p. 137).

'He came neither to destroy nor to fulfil. . . . He is a branch of the true vine. He does not speak as one of the scribes, but with authority.' The words are familiar, and that they should come so naturally to Hindu lips is a tribute to the success of the British missionaries in spreading the Gospel in its English translation so thoroughly that it has almost become a part of the Hindu *dharma*, but it is also a monument of their failure to persuade the Hindu that he has anything to gain by changing his allegiance. So infinitely capable of assimilation is Hinduism that Rāmakrishna saw no difficulty in accepting Christ as *a* son of God, an *avatār* of Vishnu, if you will, but any unique claim on his behalf he would have regarded as divisive and therefore evil. Christianity, like other religions, was one way among many, and in its proper place a very good one, but it

was very questionable whether its proper place was the holy
land of India.

Rāmakrishna's strength lay in his personality and the
extraordinary power he had to attract others. It is true that he
said nothing new (for it is difficult to say anything new in
Hinduism) but everything he said *sounded* new since he was a
master of the homely phrase and had an unerring touch when
it came to driving a point home to simple and not so simple
minds in words they could readily understand. Many members
of the Brāhmo Samāj came to visit him and among them Keshab
Chandra Sen, and through them he came into contact with the
phenomenon of the Westernized Indian, uprooted from his own
Hindu *dharma* of which he was perhaps secretly ashamed, yet
not integrated into the Christian *dharma* of India's new masters.
These men claimed to be religious, but they did not seem so to
him, for they had had no experience of what Hindus now
habitually call 'God-realization'; they knew nothing of *samādhi*
and *moksha*. They had learnt their monotheism from the lips of
the missionaries and they had accepted what of it seemed good
to them on trust; he had had the living experience of the
presence of his Holy Mother and the wholly ineffable experience of *nirvikalpa-samādhi* in which there is consciousness
of nothing except timeless consciousness itself. The nice
formulations of theology could therefore have no interest for
him; without experience religion was a dead thing. His sole aim
was to transmit some of his own experience to others. Unlike
the Brāhmos he did not seek to reform Hindu society, he sought
to make others realize the divine potentialities in themselves.

Hinduism has often been accused of blurring the distinction
between good and evil; and the charge is not without some
foundation. Yet Yudhishthira's passion for righteousness and
truth and Rāma's perfect devotion to duty are as typical of
Hinduism at its best as is Krishna, the morally rather ambivalent
God or the seeming immorality of some of the Śakti cults.
For Rāmakrishna, however, good and evil cease to have any
meaning once *moksha* has been achieved, for whatever IS is
good because it is God, and just as the poison in the snake does
the snake no harm, so what appears evil to men who are still in
bondage to their egos, is in itself not evil but good.

Many years ago [he is quoted as saying], Vaishnavacharan told me that one attains perfect knowledge only when one sees God in man. Now I see that it is he who is moving about in different forms, now as an honest man, now as a cheat and again as a villain. So I say, Nārāyana (Krishna) in the form of an honest man, Nārāyana in the form of a swindler, Nārāyana in the form of a villain, Nārāyana in the form of a lewd person.

The dangers in such an attitude are obvious, and Rāmakrishna was conscious of them. From the experiences he had had, he accepted such Upanishadic dicta as 'I am Brahman' as being literally true, but until you have had the experience you have no right to say 'I am Brahman', because on the relative plane on which such a person still moves, it is not true. *Dharma* is binding on all who have not yet attained liberation, and *dharma* includes doing good to others if for no other reason than that in doing good to others you are helping yourself. 'By these philanthropic activities', he is recorded as saying, 'you are really doing good to yourself. If you can do them disinterestedly, your mind will become pure and you will develop love of God. As soon as you have that love you will realize him.'

Rāmakrishna was by nature a *bhākta*, not a *jñānin*, a worshipper of God rather than an introspective seeking the One within himself. Despite his Advaitin teacher, however, his trances did not reveal a static Monad, One without a second, they showed rather that 'God has become all things'. Intellectually he may deny this on occasion, but Rāmakrishna set no store by the intellect. His followers, however, have developed philosophically in a purely monistic direction, denying all real existence to all except the One. This, however, would seem to falsify Rāmakrishna's actual experience, for, for him, the infinite and the finite are not distinct, but the finite is wholly suffused by the infinite; the world *is* God, and God *is* the world. Of *māyā* he says: 'The universe is created by the great *māyā* of God. The great *māyā* contains both the *māyā* of knowledge and the *māyā* of ignorance. Through the help of the *māyā* of knowledge one cultivates such virtues as the taste for holy company, knowledge, devotion, love, and renunciation. The *māyā* of ignorance consists of the five elements and the objects of the five senses. . . . These make one forget God.' In a word his teaching could be summarized thus: 'Lead a virtuous life that you may realize God.'

Rāmakrishna had the gift of spontaneity: he had no talent for organization nor did he see himself as the head of a movement. He did, however, recognize spiritual talent when he saw it, and such talent he recognized in Narendranāth Datta who, after his initiation by Rāmakrishna, was to take the name of Swami Vivekānanda. Educated in the Mission College in Calcutta he had distinguished himself in European philosophy; he was a typical product of the new Westernized middle class which seemed to have lost its Indian roots and whose spiritual home was in the Brāhmo Samāj. One meeting with Rāmakrishna was enough to change all that; immediately he fell under the master's spell. Of his second meeting he has left an account of how Rāmakrishna transmitted to him his spiritual power:

Muttering something to himself, with his eyes fixed on me, he slowly drew near me. I thought he might do something queer as on the preceding occasion. But in the twinkling of an eye he placed his right foot on my body. The touch at once gave rise to a novel experience within me. With my eyes open I saw that the walls and everything in the room whirled rapidly and vanished into nought, and the whole universe, together with my individuality, was about to merge in an all-encompassing mysterious void! I was terribly frightened and thought that I was facing death, for the loss of individuality meant nothing short of that. Unable to control myself I cried out, 'What is this you are doing to me? I have my parents at home!' He laughed aloud at this and, striking my chest, said, 'All right, let it rest now. Everything will come in time.' The wonder of it was that no sooner had he said this than that strange experience of mine vanished. I was myself again and found everything, within and without the room, as it had been before. All this happened in less time than it takes me to narrate it, but it revolutionized my mind.

In 1886 Rāmakrishna died making Vivekānanda his spiritual heir. He collected a small group of Rāmakrishna's disciples round him who were to form the nucleus of the Rāmakrishna order which now has representatives throughout the world and is particularly strong in the United States. For five years Vivekānanda wandered all over India living on anything that people were prepared to give in the manner of the *sannyāsins* of an earlier time. When he reached Cape Comorin, the southern-most tip of India, he fell into deep meditation, pondering the wretched lot that was India's.

At Cape Comorin [he wrote], sitting in Mother Kumārī's temple, sitting on the last bit of India's rock, I hit upon a plan. We are so many *sannyāsins* wandering about and teaching the people metaphy-sics—it is all madness. Did not our Gurudeva (Rāmakrishna) use to say, 'An empty stomach is no good for religion.' That these poor people are leading the life of brutes is simply due to ignorance. Suppose some disinterested *sannyāsins*, bent on doing good to others, go from village to village disseminating education and seeking in various ways to better the condition of all, down to the *candāla* (untouchable), through oral teaching and by means of maps, cameras, globes, and such other accessories—can't that bring forth good in time? We, as a nation, have lost our individuality, and that is the cause of all the mischief in India. We have to give back to the nation its lost individuality and raise the masses.

This insight was to change the whole orientation of the Rāma-krishna mission in the future. Its corollary was Vivekānanda's visit to the first session of the World Parliament of Religions in Chicago in 1893. Here for the first time he was able to present Hinduism to the world as a universal faith; and Hinduism, so long on the defensive against Muslim and Christian attack, for the first time went over to the offensive. He spoke of himself as belonging to the 'most ancient order of monks in the world' and of his religion as the 'mother of religions'. Thus emphasizing the primacy of the Vedic revelation, he none the less went on to say, echoing the words of his master, 'We accept all religions as true.'

These were to be the main themes of Vivekānanda's preach-ing in America and England, but he was to elaborate and further refine them. Plainly, if all religions are true, there would be no point in exchanging one true religion for another. Conversion, then, must be vigorously resisted since it means the violent uprooting of the convert and unnecessary distress both for him and for those near and dear to him whom he has left behind. 'Do I wish that the Christian would become a Hindu?' he exclaims, 'God forbid. Do I wish that the Hindu or Buddhist would become a Christian? God forbid. . . . The Christian is

not to become a Hindu or a Buddhist, nor a Hindu or a Buddhist
to become a Christian. But each religion must assimilate the
spirit of the others and yet preserve its individuality and grow
according to its own law of growth.' Despite this profession of
principle, however, it is clear from Vivekānanda's writings
that he does not regard all religions as being equally true. His
reading of the Vedānta is that of Śankara, non-duality at its
starkest. Religions are only true on the relative plane in that
they are all paths leading to the One. Let each man follow the
path on which he was born, for each and every path will in the
end lead him to the Absolute Truth in which all things—
subject, object, and the relationship between them—will be
seen to be unfractionably one.

Vivekānanda performed the extraordinary feat of breathing
life into the purely static monism of Śankara. In Europe and
America he proclaimed from the house-tops the absolute
divinity of man and the sinfulness of the Christian preoccupation with sin. This obsession with sin and its corollary, the
helplessness of man and his absolute dependence on the grace of
God, he, like Nietzsche, saw as something debilitating and
degrading. Man is by nature free (*mukta*), his liberation is
permanently with him, and it is he, no other, who binds himself
in illusion: he has within himself the power to cast off his chains,
and it is only his attachment to his miserable, unreal ego that
prevents him from doing so. So 'when we have nobody to
grope towards, no devil to lay our blame upon, no Personal
God to carry our burdens, when we are alone responsible, then
we shall rise to our highest and best. I am responsible for my
fate, I am the bringer of good unto myself, I am the bringer of
evil. I am the Pure and Blessed One. . . . I have neither death
nor fear, I have neither caste nor creed. I have neither father
nor mother nor brother, neither friend nor foe, for I am
Existence, Knowledge, and Bliss Absolute; I am the Blissful
One, I am the Blissful One. I am not bound by either virtue or
vice, by happiness or misery. Pilgrimages and books and ceremonies can never bind me. I have neither hunger nor thirst;
the body is not mine, nor am I subject to the superstitions and
decay that come to the body, I am Existence, Knowledge, and
Bliss Absolute; I am the Blissful One, I am the Blissful One.'

This open challenge to all the values of orthodox Christianity was not without its effect, for he made several devoted English converts, and laid the foundations of Neo-Vedāntism in America which later captivated Aldous Huxley, Gerald Heard, and other well-known literary figures. On his return to India he saw to the foundation of *maths* or monasteries throughout the peninsula, and these continue to thrive and to multiply. He still believed that Hindu spirituality was supreme—for it alone proclaimed the great Advaitin Truth and the means by which it could be realized but since the revelation he had received at Cape Comorin he realized that this must be allied to practical service to the needy and to the Western scientific techniques which make that service possible. Thus in India the Rāmakrishna mission concentrated on the performance of good works —for only through self-forgetfulness can one hope for self-realization—while abroad it concentrated on spreading the gospel of Neo-Vedāntism, publishing the sayings of Rāmakrishna, the works of Vivekānanda, their lives, and a number of classic Advaitin texts with English translation. In this way it has done much to familiarize the West with Hindu monistic thought; it has put India on the intellectual and religious map of the world, and its huge contribution to thought and religion is now universally admitted. Swami Vivekānanda died on 4 July 1902. Through him the seed that his Master had sown was already beginning to yield an abundant harvest.

8
Yudhishthira Returns

BEHOLD, I SEND YOU FORTH as sheep in the midst of wolves: be ye therefore wise as serpents and harmless as doves.

Mahātma Gandhi was no Christian, and the Christians were amazed that this should be so, for never in modern times had they seen any man tread more faithfully in the footsteps of Christ. Whence did he derive his astonishing strength, and how was it that he alone could transform a 'nation of slaves' into one of free, self-confident, and self-sacrificing men? For Gandhi did not see himself primarily as the architect of Indian independence from British rule but as the liberator of the Indian spirit from the fetters of greed and anger, hatred and despair. In his frail person the ancient ideals of renunciation, 'harmlessness' (ahiṁsā, translated by him as 'non-violence'), and truth met. He described himself as a sanātanī Hindu, one who follows the sanātana dharma, the 'eternal law' once embodied in the dharma-rāja, Yudhishthira. And Gandhi's dilemma was the same as Yudhishthira's: what and where was the sanātana dharma he claimed to follow? Was it in his heart or was it in what the Brāhmans proclaimed?

The Christian missionaries had many faults—'I miss receptiveness, humility, willingness on your part to identify yourselves with the masses of India,' he had told them in Calcutta—but they had pointed accusing fingers at abuses that shocked the conscience of the world—and the greatest of these was untouchability. According to the Brāhmans untouchability was part and parcel of the sanātana dharma, and the Laws of

Manu seemed to bear them out. From his childhood, however, Gandhi had found untouchability absurd; in his later life he was to find it revolting and he refused to co-operate with anyone who failed to denounce it. In what, then, did his 'orthodoxy' consist?

It will be remembered that Yudhishthira was tortured by the same agonizing doubts. Was it the *dharma* preached by the Brāhmans that was the 'eternal' *dharma*, or was it the *dharma* that was the well-spring of his being, the *dharma* by virtue of which he was the 'King of *dharma*'—'King of Righteousness' because the conscience of a truthful man cannot lead astray? He hesitated because God himself had driven him into violence and war, and had made him lie, but he nevertheless *knew* that his conscience transcended the 'righteousness' of the Brāhmans and of Krishna himself. Yudhishthira's dilemma was more agonizing, more searching than Gandhi's was ever to be. *His* conscience was the first to protest against a violent and unjust society: there had been no reformers before him. Gandhi was luckier, for he had been preceded by the Brāhmo Samāj which had openly denounced caste, untouchability, and a host of other questionable institutions, and had challenged the infallible authority of the Vedas themselves; he had before his eyes too the Ārya Samāj of Dayānanda whose interpretation of the Veda was so utterly at variance with that of the orthodox that plainly one could do with the sacred texts almost anything one liked. So it seemed only natural that he could say of the scriptures, 'My belief in the Hindu Scriptures does not require me to accept every word and every verse as divinely inspired. Nor do I claim to have any first-hand knowledge of these wonderful books. But I do claim to know and feel the truths of the essential teaching of the Scriptures. I decline to be bound by any interpretation, however learned it may be, if it is repugnant to reason and moral sense.' The outraged conscience of Yudhishthira speaks through the lips of Mahātma Gandhi. And Gandhi's God too is the God of Yudhishthira, not the God of *bhakti* or of the philosophers. 'To me God is Truth and Love; *God is ethics and morality*; God is fearlessness; God is the source of Light and Life, and yet he is above and beyond all these. *God is conscience.*' God is, in fact, what Gandhi in his heart feels him to be: he is not the God of the law-books or even of the Vedas, should these prove to conflict with the light within him.

Yudhishthira was a Kshatriya in violent revolt against the *dharma* of his class. He was pitted against the usurping power of his cousins, the Kauravas, and he was prepared to go to the limit in making concessions; and it was only when all else had failed and the Kauravas wished to deny him even five villages in which he might reign that, spurred on by Krishna, he plunged into bloody war. From the depths of his soul he hated the war, and after it was over accepted in bitter anguish responsibility for the carnage of which he was in fact innocent. Gandhi was a member of the Vaiśya class, and warfare was therefore in no way part of his duties; but circumstances and his own conscience forced him to declare non-violent war on the Kshatriyas of his time, the British Government in India. Yudhishthira had in the end and against his will to resort to arms because that was the *dharma* of his class; Gandhi was under no such obligation. He had hoped to conduct the struggle entirely by non-violent means, but even he, in the end, could not curb the unreasoning fury of the masses: non-violence gave way to violence, and this for Gandhi spelt spiritual defeat. Just as Yudhishthira, after the conclusion of a triumphant war, could not rid himself of the feeling of guilt and responsibility, so did Gandhi take full responsibility for the eruption of violence that his Civil Disobedience campaign had led to and against which he protested with all his soul.

Yudhishthira who, as *dharma-rāja*, was the embodiment of Hindu orthodoxy, had time and again raised his voice against the injustice of the *kshatriya-dharma*, and when he finally entered into heaven and was acclaimed for his unswerving loyalty to righteousness and truth, he was so sickened by it all that he cursed the specious *dharma* of gods and Brāhmans and asked that he might be allowed to go to hell; for Yudhishthira could not pretend that he did not know the full *dharma* as it was interpreted by men, for every aspect of it had been retailed to him many times over and at enormous length. Gandhi was luckier, for he had no deep knowledge of the sacred texts. Only the Bhagavad-Gītā did he know intimately, and this gave him unfailing spiritual comfort even in his darkest hours. Among more popular works he knew and loved the Rāmāyana of Tulsī Dās, but he had only a nodding acquaintance with the law-books which contained in germ the whole system of caste, untouchability, and the duty of government not only to expand its territories but also to pry into the affairs of its people. And the irony of it was that the British Government, in its scrupulous refusal to interfere in caste law and in its bringing the whole of India under its control, was, according to the standards of the *Laws of Manu*, most admirably fulfilling the duties of its class. The *sanātana dharma*, however, as interpreted by the Brāhmans, had received some very nasty shocks in the course of the nineteenth century, and Gandhi was therefore only following well-established precedent when he declared that he would not 'be bound by any interpretation, however learned it might be, if it is repugnant to reason or moral sense'.

After the massacre at Amritsar in 1919 Gandhi, hitherto a loyal subject of the British Empire, turned against it: it had become 'Satanic'. Yet, so strange was the complex character of this wonderful man that it is fair to say that the struggle for national independence was incidental to the main struggle which, for him, was the struggle for the recovery of India's dignity, self-respect, and soul. For Gandhi the struggle against British imperialism and the struggle against untouchability went hand in hand, for both kept India enslaved, the British politically, untouchability morally, for by treating the untouchables as unclean the caste Hindus made themselves doubly unclean. Whatever the battle Gandhi might be engaged in, his weapons were always *ahimsā* ('non-violence, the refusal to hurt any living thing'), truthfulness, courtesy, and love. It is not easy to love one's enemies, far less easy to make them love you; yet this is the miracle that Gandhi accomplished. Though he might stigmatize British rule in India as 'Satanic', he never confused the system with the British people, let alone with individual Britons among whom he owned many devoted friends. Similarly his campaign against untouchability fired the conscience of India with so hot a flame that there was danger that it might be turned against the Brāhmans who were mainly responsible for the perpetuation of the system. Gandhi would not countenance this; for he knew that just as violence cannot be conquered by violence, but only by its opposite, so could the stubborn opposition of the Brāhmans to what *they* considered wrong only be conquered by convincing them that it was right. And conquer he did: using the weapon that the Hindus have from time immemorial understood, the weapon of fasting, resistance collapsed as if by magic and for the first time in history Hindu temples opened their gates to untouchables, the *Harijans* or 'people of God' as Gandhi had, in his deep compassion, named them. The *dharma* of the Brāhmans had yielded to the *dharma* of conscience and compassion.

Gandhi interpreted the *sanātana dharma* as and how he wished, but he regarded himself as 'orthodox' none the less. Hence he would countenance no move against the Brāhmans as such, particularly at a time when it was plain that the death-knell of the old orthodoxy had already sounded and that the new 'orthodoxy' as preached and lived by the Mahātma was about to take its place. To the non-Brāhmans he said:

Resisting as you are, and as you must, untouchability, do not be guilty of creating a new untouchability in your midst. In your hate, in your blindness, in your anger against the Brāhmans, you are trying to trample under foot the whole of the culture which you have inherited from ages past. With a stroke of the pen, maybe at the point of the sword, you are impatient to rid Hinduism of its bedrock. Being dissatisfied and properly dissatisfied with the husk of Hinduism you are in danger of losing even the kernel, life itself.

Gandhi may have been and indeed was influenced by all kinds of non-Hindu ideas, but he was deeply rooted in, and drew his strength from, the *sanātana dharma* of his native land, not the *dharma* of the law-books and Brāhmans, but the *dharma* that rests on *ahiṁsā*, truth, renunciation, passionlessness, and an equal love for all God's creatures, the *dharma* of Yudhishthira, the King of Righteousness and Truth. But he was wise enough to see that both what was good and of abiding value and what was bad and corrupt had been handed down generation after generation by the Brāhmans and no one else. Destroy the Brāhman class, he thought, and you destroy Hinduism. No one can say whether he was right, but there can be no doubt that if

Hinduism, even in its Gandhian form, is to survive, some directing hand must guide it, and, failing the Brāhmans, what is the alternative? This is the question Gandhi put to the over-zealous reformers, and it has not been answered.

Truth, *ahimsā*, and *brahmacaryā* ('continence') are the three great virtues that presided over Gandhi's life. Unlike the Advaitins he did not claim to know Absolute Truth, but he did claim to know that God is Truth and that Truth is God; and by truth he understood being true to oneself and to the inner light that is our conscience. Thus he did not hesitate to say that atheism sincerely believed in is the atheist's truth. He was, however, not so naïve as to suppose that conscience is necessarily infallible: it can be warped not only by false views but by wrong living. Truth is therefore inseparable from *ahimsā* and *brahmacaryā*—the 'harmlessness' that is yet a positive and universal love, and self-restraint in all things, in eating and drinking as much as in sexual relations.

Gandhi's views on sexuality were quite as strict as were those of Rāmakrishna, for as a young man he had not been a stranger to lust and he knew the vicious dissipation of energy that its unbridled pursuit entails. Of the unmarried he demanded total continence, while for the married he considered that intercourse was allowable for the purpose of procreation only. If one did not want a large family, then one had only to exercise self-restraint. As to contraception it was an abomination. 'He condemns sexual life as inconsistent with the moral progress of man,' Rabindranāth Tagore wrote, 'and has a horror of sex as great as that of the author of *The Kreutzer Sonata*, but, unlike Tolstoy, he betrays no abhorrence of the sex that tempts his kind. In fact, his tenderness for women is one of the noblest and most consistent traits of his character and he counts among the women of his country some of the best and truest comrades in the great movement he is leading.'

To find the truth within oneself one needs to practise the negative virtue of *brahmacaryā*. *Brahmacaryā*, 'faring according to Brahman', in practice means total self-control, and Gandhi saw that the etymology of the word gives the clue to the purpose for which this virtue was ordained: it is the highroad of *dharma* that leads to *moksha*.

The full and proper meaning of *brahmacaryā* [he writes], is search of *Brahman*. *Brahman* pervades every being and can therefore be searched for by diving into and realizing the inner self. This realization is impossible without complete control of the senses. *Brahma-caryā* thus means control in thought, word and action, of all the senses at all times and in all places.

Self-control, however, though indispensable in the quest for the Truth within, must be allied to a self-giving love for all living creatures without. The two balance and complement each other, the one reflecting the *antarātman*, the inmost Self which is the God within us, and the other reaching out towards the all-pervading highest Brahman which is the same Spirit in the objective world.

Gandhi lived by the spirit, not the letter, and it would be futile to try to absolutize his views. It is frequently alleged that he derived his views on *ahiṁsā* from the Jain monks he had known in his youth, or from the Sermon on the Mount, or from Tolstoy. None of this seems necessary, for the doctrine is prominent in the Gītā which he knew intimately and in the Great Epic in general, and it permeates and suffuses all later Hindu thought. Moreover the *ahiṁsā* practised by Gandhi in no way corresponds to the legalistic absurdity of the Jains, for he knew as well as the righteous fowler of the third book of the Mahābhārata that life cannot be lived without the taking of life. On many occasions he was accused of condoning 'violence' done to the animal kingdom. He had arranged for a calf which was lying in agony in his *āśram* to be put out of its misery, he had allowed destructive monkeys to be driven away from the crops of his little community, and he had condoned the destruction of stray dogs in Bombay. The fanatics, of course, accused him of violating his own principles, but Gandhi stuck to his guns and explained that in the case of the calf to put an end to pain when death is in any case bound to supervene is true *ahiṁsā* while to allow it to languish in agony would be 'violence' indeed. In the other cases he affirmed that the good of human beings must take precedence over the good of the brute creation. This seems obvious and sensible to us, but it is not nearly so obvious to the Hindu who feels that the animal world is far closer to us than we can ever do. This is the natural corollary of his belief in reincarnation, and once this is accepted, then the animals are different from humans in degree only, not in kind. Like us they have souls, and so it is quite natural that many of the lesser deities in the Hindu pantheon should appear in animal form—deities like Hanuman, the monkey king whose devotion to Rāma is held up as a model of what human devotion to God should be, and like the elephant-headed Ganesha, one of Śiva's sons, who should be invoked at the inception of any important undertaking. This accounts for the fact that Gandhi, though he always put the good of human beings above that of animals if there was a clash between the two, could never take animal life or consent thereto without undergoing a real agony of soul.

Among the many things that astonish us about Gandhi is that, though claiming to be an orthodox Hindu, he was yet the greatest reformer Hinduism had ever seen. The reason for this is that he practised what he preached, or rather, in the words of Louis Fischer, 'he did not preach about God or religion; he was a living sermon. He was a good man in a world where few resist the corroding influence of power, wealth, and vanity.' Though the centre and leader of India's massive movement for independence, he never saw himself as such: he saw himself as, and was, a *sannyāsin* for whom 'liberation' meant rather liberation from the bondage of sin—desire, anger, avarice, sloth, and so on—than liberation from the British. The latter, he thought, was not possible without the former, for until the Indians had freed themselves from egoistic passions, they would never free themselves from the British: and he was triumphantly right. Through his fearlessness and through his faith, his fasts and unceasing prayer, not only were the Hindu temples thrown open to the untouchables—'God's people' whom Gandhi had adopted as his own—but in the end the British Rāj too abdicated and India won her political independence. But Gandhi took no part in the celebrations: for him it was the biggest defeat of his life. He alone, by his example of courage, total humility in the face of God and man, and utter disregard of self, had spurred on the Indian people, both Hindu and Muslim, to emulate him. The response had been magnificent, but just when the total victory of *ahiṁsā* over a régime of violence and commercial greed seemed within his grasp, the spirit of self-sacrifice turned once again to hatred and open violence. In his later days Gandhi was no longer the architect of independence but the physician who sought to bind up the wounds inflicted by the inter-communal hatred and violence that had begun to disfigure the land and which resulted in what was for him the final and complete tragedy, the partitioning of India and the inter-communal blood-bath that followed, The spirit of violence had not been exorcised, and his mission had therefore been in vain; for this 'liberation', this *moksha*, was not the *moksha* he had had in mind for India. India's progress towards *moksha* should have matched his own; it should have been a way of perfection and example—a way of Truth—truthfulness with oneself and with others, recognizing the Truth in others however different it might be from one's own, a way of self-discipline and self-denial (for only so can the true self be realized) and a way of gentleness and love and returning good for evil. This had been his way; and he was the microcosm of which India was the macrocosm. When India could not rise to the heights he summoned her to, his whole effort was concentrated on healing the wounds that she was madly inflicting on herself. In his own estimation he had failed as Yudhishthira had failed before him. But both were yet triumphant, for both had been true to themselves, to conscience, to Truth, to the *sanātana dharma* as they saw it in themselves, and therefore to God.

Yudhishthira was 'steadfast, self-restrained, chaste, patient, ever devoted to *dharma*, high-mettled; he honoured and gave hospitality to guests, relatives, servants, and all who had resort to him; truthful, generous, ascetic, brave, he was at peace with himself, wise, and imperturbable; himself the soul of *dharma*, he never committed an injustice out of desire or yielding to impetuosity, out of fear, or to promote his own interests'. The same was true of Mahātma Gandhi, the Yudhishthira of his age.

The equation of the mythical hero with the modern saint may sound forced particularly in view of the acknowledged fact that Gandhi underwent many influences that were not Hindu. He made his first acquaintance with his beloved Gītā not in India, but in London where he studied as a young man; his

views on non-violence grew to maturity under the influence
of the ageing Tolstoy with whom he corresponded when he
was making his first experiment in non-violent resistance to an
unjust government on behalf of the Indian community in
South Africa. Add to this his introduction to the Sermon on the
Mount which went straight to his heart, again in London, and
the close and abiding friendships he formed with devout
Christians both in South Africa and after he had returned to
India, and what remains of his much-vaunted Hindu orthodoxy?

It is true that in those early days away from India Gandhi
imbibed a variety of religious ideas drawn from many sources,
but his readings from the Rāmāyana of Tulsī Dās was the soil in
which these new ideas were sown; and his discovery of the Gītā
happened to coincide with a reading of Madame Blavatsky's
Key to Theosophy which directed his gaze once again to his
native faith and 'disabused him of the notion fostered by the
missionaries that Hinduism was rife with superstition'. His
wide religious reading persuaded him that all religions were
true, but that all were imperfect. It was, then, the duty of
men of good will to reform what was imperfect in their own
religions, not to try to uproot individuals from their own
tradition and graft them on to something that was alien and
strange. It had always been the genius of Hinduism to absorb
into itself whatever in other religions was at all absorbable, and
in the Great Epic itself this living process of absorption and
rejection can be seen at work. There Yudhishthira obeys the
ancient *dharma* but with a heavy heart, but, even when he is
near despair, a better and a nobler *dharma* is then put before
him as likely as not by an outcaste or an animal; and it is in this
way that he learns that *ahimsā* is Truth and that the most
sumptuous animal sacrifice is not worth the humblest *self-
sacrifice* even in an unworthy cause. These lessons Hinduism
in fact learned from Buddhism but it was through the personality of the *Dharma-rāja*, Yudhishthira, that they came to
permeate the more ancient creed.

This is exactly what Gandhi did: he absorbed the ethical
teaching of the Sermon on the Mount and the transcendent
monotheism of Islam into his own Hindu life, and through
himself he transmitted it to the whole of India. He could not

have done this if he had continued to 'play the English gentle-man' as he had done in his early days in London; and it was not just good showmanship that led him to forsake European clothes for his *sannyāsin's* loincloth and the spinning-wheel. It was an intuitive understanding of the kind of religious symbolism that would go straight to the heart of his people, for the *sannyāsin's* loincloth represented the total abnegation of self ('a man of devotion reduces himself to zero'), and the humble spinning-wheel represented the dedication of himself and of all who were less than destitute to 'the poorest, the lowliest, and the lost'. By putting aside the trappings of an alien civilization he attuned himself to the lowliest among his people, and through his people to their religion which was his too—more his indeed than the frame of flesh and bone that housed his indomitable spirit. But in him this religion was transmuted into something more noble, more compassionate, and more pure than it had ever been before. Enriched with what he found best in the teachings of Jesus and Tolstoy and the Koran, he returned it to the people, changed, but the eternal *dharma* still.

Hinduism is not an exclusive religion like Christianity or Islam, and the fact that Gandhi was never happier than when he settled down in prayer with adherents of many religions, each praying according to his own *dharma* to the One God, does not make him any less a Hindu. He never could understand the exclusiveness claims of Christianity and Islam, and this is why, in the long run, he did not succeed in cementing Hindus and Muslims into a single nation. For him Islam meant Kabīr and the Sūfī mystics whose tolerance and eclectic-ism were as large as his; he never understood the fierce hatred of 'idol-worship' and the 'association of what is other than God with God' that is ingrained in orthodox Islam. He was much too much of a Hindu for that.

In his later years Gandhi was asked what he considered to be the essence of Hinduism, and he replied that the whole of Hinduism was contained in the first verse of the *Iśā* Upanishad which he translated as follows:

All this that we see in this great universe is permeated by God.
Renounce it and enjoy it.
Do not covet anybody's wealth or possession.

God is the Lord who pervades the whole universe and all of it is his. Therefore you must renounce the world because it is not yours and then enjoy and work in it because it is his and he wishes you to co-operate with him in the destruction of evil. As to evil, that is a mystery and none can understand it. Therefore, says Gandhi,

I call God long-suffering and patient precisely because he permits evil in the world. I know that he has no evil. He is the author of it and yet untouched by it.

I know too that I shall never know God if I do not wrestle with and against evil even at the cost of life itself. I am fortified in the belief by my own humble and limited experience. The purer I try to become, the nearer I feel to be to God. How much more should I be, when my faith is not a mere apology as it is today but has become as immovable as the Himalayas and as white and bright as the snows on their peaks?

To reach Truth—one's own truth, the truth of others, and ultimately the Truth that is God, man must crucify his body; for only by mortifying the body can he mortify the deadly sins of lust, attachment, hatred, envy, sloth, and above all egoism and possessiveness (the sense of 'I' and 'mine') from which all that is evil proceeds. This, for Gandhi, is the *sine qua non* of all virtuous action. 'Not until we have reduced ourselves to nothingness can we conquer the evil in us. God demands nothing less than complete self-surrender as the price for the only real freedom that is worth having. And when a man thus loses himself, he immediately finds himself in the service of all that lives. It becomes his delight and recreation. He is a new man never weary of spending himself in the service of God's creation.' Or in the words of the *Iśā* Upanishad, 'Renounce and enjoy'.

The last thing that Gandhi saw himself as was a religious as opposed to a social reformer: he founded no Samāj, no mission. Rather, following an immemorial tradition, he founded an *āśram* or religious community open, in his case, to men, women, and children, and run according to his own monastic rule. Here he would retire whenever the political and religious situation permitted, and here he was at his happiest and most

relaxed. The principles on which the *āśram* was run are typical
of Gandhi's empirical approach to religion. The trinity of
virtues on which all the other virtues depend—truth, *ahiṁsā*,
and *brahmacaryā*—naturally formed the cornerstone on which
the *āśram's* life was based, the two latter being the indispensable
practical pre-condition of the former. *Brahmacaryā* in the
narrow sense means absolute chastity, rigid control of the re-
productive instinct. This instinct, however, is less fundamental
than the instinct of self-preservation, and self-preservation
in turn depends on food: to live man must eat. All this
Gandhi, following the Gītā, admits, but just as sexual activity
must never be indulged simply for the sake of pleasure, so must
the pleasure motive be absent from the partaking of food.
Hence the fourth vow in the *aśram* was the 'vow to control the
palate' which not only forbade the eating of meat and the con-
sumption of alcohol of which Gandhi had an instinctive horror,
but also the indulgence in any foods liable to excite man's
lower, animal nature. For Gandhi it was self-evident that there
could be no fruitful spiritual life so long as the instinctive life
had not been brought under rigorous control: this is what he
consistently preached and as consistently practised. The vow
not to steal was taken to mean that each man is entitled only to
his minimum needs, anything in excess of that being regarded as
being no better than stolen property. Then came the vow of
fearlessness, and this Gandhi regarded as being absolutely
necessary if India were ever to find her soul again. 'I found,
through my wanderings in India, that my country is seized with
a paralyzing fear,' he wrote. 'I suggest to you that there is only
One whom we have to fear, that is God. When we fear God,
then we shall fear no man, however high-placed he may be; if
you want to follow the vow of Truth, then fearlessness is
absolutely necessary.' The miracle of Gandhi was that, through
his own example of courage in face of overwhelming odds, he
showed the Indian people how to face up to arrest, beatings-up,
and imprisonment with the calm courage of men who know that
their cause is just.

Then there was the vow concerning untouchability, and on
this issue Gandhi knew no compromise. To the members of the
āśram he issued the following directive:

There is an ineffaceable blot that Hinduism today carries with it. I have declined to believe that it has been handed down to us from immemorial times. I think that this miserable, wretched, enslaving spirit of 'untouchableness' must have come to us when we were at our lowest ebb. The evil has stuck to us and still remains with us. It is, to my mind, a curse that has come to us; and as long as that curse remains with us, so long I think we are bound to consider that every affliction in this sacred land is a proper punishment for the indelible crime that we are committing.

To show that he meant what he said Gandhi had already in his South African days taken an untouchable into his house and forced his orthodox wife to minister to him. This defiance of orthodox opinion he was to repeat on his return to India. The untouchables whose dignity he affirmed by calling them *Harijans* or 'people of God', became the object of his passionate and compassionate concern, and by the example he set by eating with them and receiving them into his *āśram*, he shamed the caste Hindus into doing the same.

Among the remaining vows taken by members of the *āśram* were *svadeśi* or the support of local industries and the production of cloth on the hand-loom. To the despair of the intellectuals among his followers he attached as much importance to the spinning-wheel as he did to the more universally acclaimed principles he insisted on in the *āśram*. They could not understand this 'mania' because they had lost their Hindu roots: for Gandhi spinning was *karma-yoga* at its best—action performed without regard for its 'fruits', the 'matchless remedy' and 'centre round which the Gītā is woven'. Not only was it *karma-yoga*, the Yoga of work, it was *brahmacaryā* in that it detached the weaver from evil desires, and it was *ahiṁsā*, a labour of love performed, perhaps in atonement for the 'blot' of untouchability, for India's ragged masses.

Gandhi's attitude to Hinduism was that it is the *dharma* of India. It was, therefore, the duty of the enlightened Hindu to preserve in it all that might be preserved, but to root out whatever offended his social conscience. Thus he defended the *varnāśrama-dharma* (p. 108), temple worship, the veneration of 'idols', the domestic rites that orthodox Hindus were expected to perform in their homes, and the veneration of the cow. His defence of *varnāśrama-dharma*, however, did not mean that he supported the caste system as it existed in his time: he merely affirmed that the division of society on hereditary lines into the broad classes of a learned priesthood, a trained ruling class, the mass of the peasantry and artisans, and a manual working class, made for a more ordered society—a society more consistent with *dharma* than any other. Moreover, he saw that the Hindu rites in home and temple, performed in the presence of images representing some aspect of the divine, were the very cement that held Hinduism together. Do away with these, and you do away with Hinduism. Gandhi accepted religions as they are: they were the organizations of finite human beings the purpose of which was, through rites, ceremonies, and symbols, to lift finite man out of his purely temporal dimension into a state of being that transcends time. Religions are *dharmas* orientated towards *moksha*. Each and all of them are true—and imperfect, and, because they are imperfect, they must aim at perfecting themselves rather than at converting individuals from a *dharma* that is theirs to one that is alien to them. To the Christians he might have said, and with justice: 'And why beholdest thou the mote that is in thy brother's eye, but considerest not the beam that is in thine own eye?' Our motes and our beams are our own affair, and only we can remove them; and it was Gandhi, not the Christian missionaries, who removed the beam of untouchability from the eye of Hinduism.

Gandhi claimed to be an orthodox Hindu, and his attachment to his ancestral religion was deep and genuine, but his attachment to conscience was deeper still. It is immaterial whether this conscience was formed under Christian or Tolstoyan influences, or by Ruskin, Thoreau, and John Stuart Mill—and that there was some influence from all of these few would deny—or whether it was cleansed and polished by the practice of the sternest *brahmacaryā* as he himself would claim; the fact remains that he saw himself as an interpreter of the Hindu *dharma* as it really is, not as, in a corrupt age, it had come to be. He was in history what King Yudhishthira was in myth, the conscience of Hinduism that hungers and thirsts after righteousness in defiance of the letter of the law of gods

and men. Because he was a saint, and because he practised what
he preached, he could rally the Hindu masses behind him not
only in the struggle for political independence but also in the
struggle for the 'liberation' of their souls and the soul of the
nation through the eternal *dharma* that had ever been theirs but
which corrupt and wicked customs had come to obscure. He did
all he could to save the structure of Hinduism, defending even
such practices as the veneration of the cow which in fact entirely
lacks the sanction of antiquity, for in the homage paid to this
gentle beast he saw the 'worship of innocence', the 'protection
of the weak and helpless', and 'one of the most wonderful
phenomena in human evolution'. He saw that if Hinduism were
to be deprived of the 'superstitions' that gave it its characteristic
flavour, and if it were to be reduced to a bloodless ethical system,
it would surely die. Annie Besant had sensed this before him,
and Gandhi would have agreed with her when she said:

Make no mistake. Without Hinduism India has no future. Hinduism
is the soil into which India's roots are struck, and torn out of that she
will inevitably wither, as a tree torn out from its place. . . . Let
Hinduism go, Hinduism that was India's cradle, and in that passing
would be India's grave.

Gandhi did not let Hinduism go: but after Gandhi Hinduism
will never be the same again.

It would be untrue to say that Hinduism is a different
religion from what it was before Rām Mohan Roy first challenged many of its basic assumptions, and the fact that at least
its sacramental and liturgical structure has remained intact
is due very largely to the restraining hand of Gandhi. The old
abuses have been done away with: widows no longer mount the
pyre of their departed lord, nor are they forbidden to remarry;
child marriages are increasingly rare, the temples are open to
untouchables, temple prostitution is no more, and in the towns
at least caste Hindus and untouchables jostle each other without
the former having to worry about incurring pollution. The
barriers between castes are slowly breaking down, though inter-
marriage between castes is still the exception rather than the
rule; but this is true not only of India but of any society that
is still conservative and traditional, and Gandhi himself shared

the instinctive antipathy of the Hindu to the mixing of caste.

The crisis through which Hinduism is passing today resembles in many ways the crisis of modern Judaism; for 'Hindu' like 'Jew' is both a racial and a religious term. Both Jews and Hindus may change their religion; in that case they risk being 'outcasted' by the orthodox in whose eyes they will have ceased to belong to the national community. Or, if they stay within the fold of the national religion, they may be 'orthodox', 'liberal', or merely agnostic in that they conform but do not believe. The 'liberal' Hindu, like the liberal Jew, has broken with much of the written law and oral tradition, he has assimilated much from Christianity and probably knows his synoptic Gospels at least as well as the Gītā and certainly better than the Upanishads. At the same time he sees good in all religions and tends, like Gandhi, to regard them all as different paths leading to an identical Truth. If pressed to specify what this Truth might be, he would probably reply that it is the 'Oneness of all being'. He hates the exclusiveness of Christianity and Islam which he rightly regards as being an obstacle to the harmonious co-operation of religions. Often he will deny that he has any use for religious syncretism, and say rather that it is his dearest wish that each religious tradition should develop and grow in accordance with its own native genius, while honouring and respecting the other great religions as being paths converging upon the same central point, the One which is at the same time Truth and Love. This often appears self-evident to him, and he is genuinely bewildered at the zeal displayed by his Christian and Muslim friends for gathering others into their respective folds; and in this he differs little from his forbears of whom Al-Bīrūnī said: 'There is very little disputing about theological topics among themselves; at the utmost, they fight with words, but they will never stake their soul or body or their property on religious controversy.'

An orthodox party, of course, remains and is organized in the Hindu *Mahāsabhā*; but they are fighting a losing battle and they know it, and it is no accident that Mahātma Gandhi, who did more than anyone to rid Hinduism of the time-hallowed 'curse' of untouchability, met his death at the hands of an orthodox fanatic.

In Europe the Reformation gave birth to the Counter-Reformation, and the old Church succeeded in purging itself of the old abuses and in recreating itself in a new image. Hindu orthodoxy at present shows no signs of such a renovation: it has lost its hold on the towns and, in the opinion of many, it is only a question of time before it loses its hold on the villages, for one of the paradoxes of Hinduism has always been the yawning gap that separates its higher manifestations from the frankly superstitious and magical practices that go to make up the religious fare of the rural masses. With the spread of Western education right down to the lowest strata of society and the progressive industrialization of the country the whole religious structure of Hinduism will be subjected to a severe strain; but such has been its genius for absorption and adaptation that it would be foolhardy to prophesy how it will confront this new and unprecedented crisis.

Meanwhile, thanks to the initiative of Vivekānanda and more recently to the tireless activity of a whole series of propagandists ranging from Śri Aurobindo Ghose to Sir Sarvepalli Rādhakrishnan, Hinduism has established itself firmly in world opinion as one of the greatest and most profound of the religions of the world. It is no criticism of these thinkers to say that their service to India has consisted in presenting Hinduism to the Western world in largely Western terms and in a manner that is easily comprehensible to the Western mind. None of them, however, has made the impact on the Indian masses that Mahātma Gandhi did, nor have they distilled and disseminated the sweet essence of Hinduism as did Rabindranath Tagore.

In the days before independence Gandhi and Tagore between them embodied India's new dignity, self-assurance, and passion for Truth, Gandhi was the *Mahātma*, the 'great-souled one', Tagore the *Gurudev*, 'the divine preceptor'. The two men, though they did not always agree, complemented each other, Gandhi the ascetic *sannyāsin* who yet drew no hard and fast line between the life of prayer and the life of action, between religion and politics, and Tagore, the mystic and contemplative and lover of all natural things, who yet proved in his school at Śāntiniketan that contemplation is meaningless unless it is translated into creative action. Between them Gandhi and Tagore represented, as no one else could hope to, the spirit of the new Hinduism which yet retained so much of the sweet flavour of the old that none could say that this was a new religion or that there had been any violent break with the past.

Rabindranath Tagore, though he was city-bred and English-educated, owed much to his father Debendranāth. From him he inherited a mysticism that was neither Advaita nor yet *bhakti*, but a subtle combination of the two—a combination which Debendranāth had thought was most perfectly expressed in the *Iśā* Upanishad and which, though grounded in the infinite, embraced and sanctified all finite things.

All this, whatever moves on earth, is pervaded by the Lord. Renounce it first, and then enjoy. Covet not the goods of any man at all. . . . Into blind darkness enter they who reverence the non-compounded; into a darkness greater yet enter they who rejoice in the com-pounded.

These two verses might serve as the text of which all the writings of Rabindranath Tagore are the commentary: they form the very stuff of his poetry. The message of Tagore is the very opposite of the Advaita Vedānta of Śankara and Vivekānanda, or even of Rāmakrishna in his more extreme moments. Rāma-krishna once said:

With a stern determination I again sat to meditate, and as soon as the gracious form of the Divine Mother appeared before me, I used my discrimination as a sword and with it severed it into two. There remained no more obstruction to my mind, which at once soared beyond the relative plane, and I lost myself in *samādhi*.

To Tagore this would have appeared as either incomprehensible or perverse. For him immersion in the infinite never meant the exclusion of the finite: finite and infinite were not separate but indissolubly interconnected, there was no conflict between the state of 'liberation' and the state of 'bondage', the 'uncom-pounded' and the 'compounded', between *dharma* as moral duty and *moksha*, of which *dharma* is but the reflection in the finite world, for the golden thread that runs through both the infinite and the finite, God and the world, is love and joy; and there can be neither love nor joy unless there is duality and reciprocity.

Even in his childhood he had been vouchsafed mystical experiences the self-authenticating authority of which had made him understand that man and nature are in some way mysteriously one—there is a harmony and a *rapport* between them which fuses them together yet deprives neither of its true individuality.

I still remember the day in my childhood [he writes], when I was made to struggle across my lessons in a first primer, strewn with isolated words smothered under the burden of spelling. The morning hour appeared to me like a once-illumined page, grown dusty and faded, discoloured with irrelevant marks, smudges and gaps, wearisome in its moth-eaten meaninglessness. Suddenly I came to a rhymed sentence of combined words, which may be translated thus— 'It rains, the leaves tremble.' At once I came to a world wherein I recovered my full meaning. My mind touched the creative realm of expression, and at that moment I was no longer a mere student with his mind muffled by spelling lessons, enclosed by classroom. The rhythmic picture of the tremulous leaves beaten by the rain opened before my mind the world which does not merely carry information, but a harmony with my being. The unmeaning fragments lost their individual isolation and my mind revelled in the unity of a vision. In a similar manner, on that morning in the village the facts of my life suddenly appeared to me in a luminous unity of truth. All things that had seemed like vagrant waves were revealed to my mind in relation to a boundless sea. I felt sure that some Being who comprehended me and my world was seeking his best expression in all my experiences, uniting them into an ever-widening individuality which is a spiritual work of art.

This vision of the interconnexion of all things runs through everything Tagore has written: it is his constantly reiterated theme. His experiences confirmed for him not the monistic abstractions of Śankara but the pantheistic insights of the Upanishads which saw the One in the many, not in isolation from it. What Tagore tried to do, and succeeded wonderfully well in doing, was to re-create in terms that everyone could understand the particular 'atmosphere' of the Upanishads which, when all is said and done, is the atmosphere of Hinduism as a whole, the uniform saltiness that pervades the great ocean of the eternal *dharma*, which remains present even in its most extravagant manifestations. Tagore did not see himself as an 'orthodox' Hindu as Gandhi did, nor did he think that the mechanical civilization introduced into India from the West could or ought to be checked. Gandhi thought that the spinning-wheel would be the salvation of Indian village culture, but Tagore realized, and said so with great forthrightness, that this was a purely artificial form of *karma-yoga*, doomed to extinction once the magic personality of the Mahātma was removed from the scene. His own solution was more modest since it extended only to his personal circle, but it was a model which he hoped others would imitate. Even as a boy in Calcutta his soul had yearned for the open country and the mystery of eternal Being that its ever-changing beauty alternately concealed and disclosed—the world of the *tapovana* of the ancients, the quiet forests where sages built their hermitages and by the work of their hands turned the chaos of a pestilential jungle into an orderly garden. What we make and do, our *karma*, if it is good and in accordance with the *dharma* within us, our conscience and our natural disposition (for *dharma* is both), brings us ever nearer to the eternal destiny to which the whole world, through the very necessity of evolution, is forever tending and which in eternity it already is. And this is perfect 'freedom', perfect *moksha*, which 'lies in the harmony of relationship which we realize not through *knowing*, but in *being*. Objects of knowledge maintain an infinite distance from us who are the knowers. For knowledge is not union. We attain the world of freedom only through perfect sympathy.'

In order to arouse and develop this sympathy and fellow-feeling with nature Tagore founded a school at Śāntiniketan in his native Bengal in which the pupils, through being in constant contact with natural things, were to be led to the apprehension of the divine. Under his affectionate care work was made to resemble play and every day was thus a holiday, that is, a holy day. He wished his pupils to be like God whose work is at the same time his play—his *karma* is his *līlā*—effortless effort expended in joy. The material with which he started was unpromising enough, for his original pupils, he tells us, 'brought with them an intolerable mental perversity; the Brāhman was supercilious, the non-Brāhman pitiable in his shrinking self-abasement. They hated to do any work of

common good lest others besides themselves should get the
least advantage. They sulked when they were asked to do for
their own benefit the kind of work that, they thought, should
be done by a paid servant. They were not averse to living on
charity but were ashamed of self-help.'

But Tagore kneaded these selfish individuals into a selfless
society in which each helped the other by being his own self
and his own 'truth', unconsciously drinking in the strength
that comes from living in harmony with the All and joyously
dedicating that strength to developing to the utmost the
potentialities that lie dormant in each of us, and thereby
expanding the personality until it is big enough to sense the
personality of the God who is at the same time macrocosmic
Man. When love once begins its healing work, then even the
most recalcitrant material melts and becomes malleable. 'For
these boys vacation had no meaning. Their studies, though
strenuous, are not a task, being permeated by a holiday spirit
which takes shape in activities in their kitchen, their vegetable
garden, their weaving, their work of small repairs. It is because
their classwork has not been separated from their normal
activities but forms a part of their daily current of life, that it
easily carries itself by its own onward flow.'

For Tagore Śāntiniketan was a microcosm of the world as he
would have wished it to be, a world in which 'the introspective
vision of the universal soul which an eastern devotee experiences
in the solitude of his mind could be united with this [western]
spirit of service'. In Śāntiniketan that is what he had achieved.

For Tagore as well as for Gandhi *moksha* is both individual
and universal: it is the fruition of the *dharma* of every man,
through the sacrifice of that very *dharma* in the *dharma* of the
community, and through the community in the *dharma* of the
whole created world, and this leads to perfect 'liberation' and
freedom of the spirit in which each pours himself unstintingly
into the one ocean of Truth which is both the One and the All.

And what is Truth? 'To realize one's unity with the entire
universe, to merge the individual soul into the universal soul,
[this] is to know Truth.' And sin? 'Sin is not one mere action,
but it is an attitude to life which takes for granted that our goal
is finite, that our self is the ultimate truth, and that we are not

all essentially one but exist each for his own separate individual existence.' The vision of Tagore is the vision of Rāmānuja, and he more than anyone else has captured and expressed in words that even Western man can understand, if he will, the subtle flavour that pervades the whole majestic fabric of Hinduism. The Absolute is within and without, you cannot divide it. It is as present in the ever-perishing world of *samsāra* as it is in the timeless moment of *moksha*, which according to the monists, is alone real. To say that it is present in the latter only is to mutilate both God and man. 'If we say that we would realize him in introspection alone and leave him out of our external activity, that we would enjoy him by the love in our heart, but not worship him by outward ministrations; or if we say the opposite, and overweight ourselves on one side of the journey of our life's quest, we shall alike totter to our downfall.'

What, then, is the message of Hinduism? If it has a message at all, it would seem to be this: to live out your *dharma* which is embedded in the conscience, to do what instinctively you know to be right, and thereby to live in harmony with the *dharma* of all things, so that in the end you may see all things in yourself and yourself in all things and thereby enter into the eternal and timeless peace which is the *dharma* of *moksha*, the 'law' of 'freedom' that has its being outside space and time yet comprises and hallows both.

Bibliography

N.B. Except for a few standard authorities, this bibliography is confined to books published in English.

I. THE PRINCIPAL SACRED BOOKS IN TRANSLATION

The *Vedas* (*Saṁhitās*)

Rig-Veda: K. F. Geldner, *Der Rig-Veda*, 3 vols., Harvard, 1951, and Index, 1957. In German. This is the only up-to-date complete translation. There are copious notes.

Yajur-Veda: A. B. Keith, *The Veda of the Black Yajus School entitled Taittiriya Sanhitā*, 2 vols., Harvard, 1914. Contains an exhaustive introduction on the very complex problem of Vedic sacrifice.

Atharva-Veda: W. D. Whitney and C. R. Lanman, *Atharva-Veda Saṁhitā*, Harvard, 1905. The standard translation.

The *Upanishads*

The best and most easily available of these vitally important texts are:

R. E. Hume, *The Thirteen Principal Upanishads*, Oxford, 1934. At present the standard English translation of the classical Upanishads.

S. Radhakrishnan, *The Principal Upanishads*, London, 1953. In addition to the translation there is a transliterated Sanskrit text and notes. It also contains five non-classical Upanishads not found in Hume.

The *Bhagavad-Gītā*

The Gītā has been repeatedly translated. The two translations first mentioned below are, perhaps, the best modern translations.

W. D. P. Hill, Oxford, 1928 and reprints. Contains a useful commentary and introduction.

F. Edgerton, 2 vols., Harvard, 1952. Edgerton's translation is almost too literal, but the second volume also contains Sir Edwin Arnold's verse translation entitled *The Song Celestial*.

K. T. Telang, in *Sacred Books of the East*, Oxford, 1882. This also
contains the *Anugītā* otherwise available only in complete translations of the *Mahābhārata*.

The *Sāṁkhya-Kārikā*

H. D. Sharma, *The Sāṁkhya-Kārikā*, Poona, 1933. Sanskrit text and
English translation with the commentary of Gaudapādācārya.

The *Yoga-Sūtras*

J. H. Woods, *The Yoga-System of Patanjali*, Harvard, 1914. Also
contains translations of the important commentaries of Vyāsa and
Vacaspati-Miśra.

The *Brahma-Sūtras* also called *Vedānta-Sūtras*

G. Thibaut, *The Vedânta Sûtras with the Commentary of Śankar-
ācārya*, 2 vols., in *Sacred Books of the East*, Oxford, 1890–6.
——— *The Vedânta Sûtras with the Commentary of Râmânuja* in *Sacred
Books of the East*, Oxford, 1904.

These are the basic texts for the philosophy of Śankara and Rāmānuja. Translations of many of Śankara's other works have been published by the Rāmakrishna Mission and are readily available.

The *Laws of Manu*

G. Bühler, in *Sacred Books of the East*, Oxford, 1886. There is a long
introduction on the sources and date of this classic law-book.

The *Mahābhārata*

P. C. Roy, 11 vols., Calcutta, 1884–94. A third edition is at present in
the process of being published.

The *Rāmāyana*

The most recent translation is: H. P. Shastri, 3 vols., London,
1952–9.

The *Bhāgavata Purāna*

J. M. Sanyal, *The Srimad-Bhagabatam*, 5 vols., Calcutta, 2nd ed., 1950.

Tamil Śaivite Texts

Śiva-Nāna-Bōdham, trs. G. Matthews, Oxford, 1948.
Śivajñāna Siddhiyār of Aruṇandi Śivācārya, trs., J. M. Nallaswami
Pillai, Madras, 1913. Contains an introduction on the philosophy of
the *Śaiva Siddhānta* not elsewhere available in English.

The following selections illustrate the development of Indian
thought:

N. Macnicol, *Hindu Scriptures*, London, 1938 and reprints. Contains selected hymns from the Rig-Veda, five Upanishads, and the whole of the Bhagavad-Gītā.

V. Raghavan, *The Indian Heritage*, Bangalore, 2nd ed., 1958. A representative selection from the Sanskrit sources from the Rig-Veda to the *Bhāgavata-Purāna*.

2. GENERAL WORKS

General Surveys

Hinduism is so vast a subject and can be approached from so many angles that it is not surprising that no popular account of it has become authoritative. The nearest approach to this in the English language is probably Sir Charles Eliot's three-volume *Hinduism and Buddhism*, London, 2nd ed., 1948, although only about half the book is devoted to Hinduism. In German there is the recently published *Die Religion Indiens I, Veda und älterer Hinduismus* by Professor J. Gonda, Stuttgart, 1960. Unfortunately this wholly admirable work only takes us up to the beginning of the medieval period, but a companion volume covering the later period is to appear later. Gonda's work is comprehensive, well-documented, and eminently readable, and he is in full sympathy with his subject. Of the works listed below in alphabetical order none is in quite the same class, though none is devoid of merit.

A. L. Basham, *The Wonder that was India*, London, 1954 and reprints. A general survey of Indian civilization before the coming of the Muslims. The section devoted to religion is relatively short.

A. C. Bouquet, *Hinduism*, London, 1948. A short introduction with a slight missionary bias.

J. N. Farquhar, *A Primer of Hinduism*, London, 1912. Contains a mass of information highly condensed and is best used as a reference book.

—— *The Crown of Hinduism*, London, 1913. A missionary's interpretation of what seems best to him in Hinduism.

E. W. Hopkins, *The Religions of India*, Boston, 1895. A solid piece of work.

N. Macnicol, *Indian Theism*, Oxford, 1915. The slightly censorious approach of the missionary to a baffling religion.

M. Monier Williams, *Hinduism*, Calcutta, 1877 and reprints. Despite its early date this is still a useful book. It crams a mass of information into a short compass.

K. W. Morgan (ed.), *The Religion of the Hindus*, 1953. A collection of articles by Hindu scholars and therefore valuable as showing what Hindus themselves regard as essential to their religion.

L. Renou, *Religions of Ancient India*, London, 1953. The most up-to-date introduction to pre-Muslim Hinduism by one of the world's leading Sanskritists.

D. S. Sharma, *A Primer of Hinduism*, Madras, 1929. A good introduction by a believing Hindu.

Pre-Aryan India

E. Mackay, *Early Indus Civilizations*, London, 2nd ed., 1948. A good popular introduction with a useful section on religion.

S. Piggott, *Prehistoric India*, Harmondsworth, 1950. A Pelican book.

Sir Mortimer Wheeler, *The Indus Civilization*, Cambridge, 1953. Rather technical.

Veda, Upanishads, and Gītā

M. Bloomfield, *The Atharva-Veda*, Strassburg, 1899. The best analysis of the contents of the Atharva-Veda.

P. Deussen, *The Philosophy of the Upanishads*, Edinburgh, 1919. A Hegelian's interpretation of the Upanishads.

J. Gonda, *Notes on Brahman*, Utrecht, 1950. The most up-to-date treatment of a thorny problem.

A. B. Keith, *The Religion and Philosophy of the Veda and Upanishads*, 2 vols., Harvard, 1925. The standard work in English on this subject but not easy to read.

A. A. Macdonell, *Vedic Mythology*, Strassburg, 1897. An indispensable guide to the mythology of the Rig-Veda.

P. D. Mehta, *Early Indian Religious Thought*, London, 1956. A Vedāntin's interpretation of the Upanishads and Gītā.

R. C. Zaehner, *Hindu and Muslim Mysticism*, London, 1960. Emphasizes the theistic trend in the Upanishads and Gītā.

Philosophy (*Sāṁkhya, Yoga, Vedānta*)

S. N. Dasgupta, *A History of Indian Philosophy*, 5 vols., Cambridge, 1951–5. The authoritative work on this subject and quite indispensable to any student of Indian philosophy, it contains a mass of information not available in other works on this subject.

—— *Hindu Mysticism*, Chicago, 1927. A brilliant short study of the varieties of Hindu mysticism which should be read by anyone who interests himself in mysticism.

M. Hiriyanna, *The Essentials of Indian Philosophy*, London, 1949. The best short introduction to Indian philosophy and extremely lucidly written.

R. Otto, *Mysticism East and West*, London, 1932 and reprints. A comparative study of Śankara and Meister Eckhart.

S. Radhakrishnan, *Indian Philosophy*, London, revised ed., 1929–31.

H. Zimmer, *Philosophies of India*, New York, 1951. A psychological interpretation of Indian philosophy published after the author's death.

The standard work in English on *Sāṁkhya* is: A. B. Keith, *The Sāmkhya System*, London, 1918.

Among the more serious works on Yoga the following may be recommended: S. N. Dasgupta, *Yoga as Philosophy and Religion*, London, 1924. The standard work in English by the greatest Hindu scholar of his time.

M. Eliade, *Yoga, Immortality, and Freedom*, London, 1958. The author has really got inside his subject and is more subjective than Dasgupta.
—— *Techniques du Yoga*, Paris, 1948. A useful analysis of Yoga techniques.
J. W. Hauer, *Der Yoga*, Stuttgart, 1958. The most exhaustive historical treatment of Yoga that has appeared to date, it contains a full German translation of the *Yoga-Sūtras*. The author, however, tends to confuse Yoga with Vedānta, which is surprising in a work of such massive learning.

The *Vedānta* in all its aspects is exhaustively and objectively treated by S. N. Dasgupta in his monumental *History*. The following works may also be consulted:
P. Deussen, *The System of the Vedānta*, Chicago, 1912. A classic in its day and still useful.
R. Guénon, *Man and his Becoming according to the Vedānta*, London, 1945. A Western Vedāntin's interpretation of the Vedānta.
O. Lacombe, *L'Absolu selon le Vedānta*, Paris, 1937. A Thomist's approach to the Vedānta.

The *Epics*

G. J. Held, *The Mahābhārata*, Amsterdam, 1935. An ethnological approach to the Great Epic.
E. W. Hopkins, *Epic Mythology*, Strassburg, 1915. Indispensable book of reference.
—— *The Great Epic of India*, New York, 1901. Contains a useful section on the philosophy of the Epic.

The Rise of Theism.

A. Avallon, *Shakti and Shākta*, Madras, 1929. A warmly sympathetic treatment of an aspect of Hinduism that is usually found repellent.
Sir R. G. Bhandarkar, *Vaiṣnavism, Śaivism and Minor Religious Systems*, Strassburg, 1913. A standard work but insufficiently documented.
J. E. Carpenter, *Theism in Medieval India*, London, 1926. An excellent survey from the beginnings till the times of Tulsī Dās.
J. C. Chatterji, *Kashmir Śaivism*, Srinagar, 1914.
J. Gonda, *Aspects of Early Viṣṇuism*, Utrecht, 1954. An exhaustive treatment of Vishnu as he appears in the Sanskrit texts.
H. W. Schomerus, *Çaiva Siddhānta*, Leipzig, 1912. The standard work on the Śaiva Siddhānta.

The *Bhakti Cults*

W. D. P. Hill, *The Holy Lake of the Acts of Rāma*, Oxford, 1952. Translation, with introduction, of the *Rāmāyana* of Tulsī Dās.

J. S. M. Hooper, *Hymns of the Āʻvārs*, London, 1929. An anthology with short introduction.

T. Kennedy, *The Caitanya Movement*, Calcutta, 1925. Concerned more with the purely religious side of Caitanya rather than with his philosophy.

F. Kingbury and G. E. Phillips, *Hymns of the Tamil Śaivite Saints*, London, 1921. Verse anthology with a short introduction.

N. Macnicol, *Psalms of Marāṭha Saints*, London, n.d. Verse anthology with short introduction.

G. U. Pope, *The Tiruvacagam*, Oxford, 1900. Translation of the *Tiruvāśagam*, with a copious introduction dealing with south Indian Śaivism.

R. D. Ranade, *Pathway to God*, Allahabad, 1954. Analyses the mysticism of the *Bhakti* movement as it appears in the Hindī language.

—— *Mysticism in Mahārāshtra*, Poona, 1933. A very full analysis of the types of mysticism to be found in the Marāthī writings on *bhakti*. Deserves to be more widely known.

Khushwant Singh, *The Sikhs*, London, 1953. A Sikh's account of his own religion.

E. J. Thompson, *Bengali Religious Lyrics*, *Śākta*, Calcutta, 1923. Prose anthology with short introduction.

W. H. Westcott, *Kabir and the Kabir Panth*, 2nd ed., Calcutta, 1953.

Caste, Cults, and Customs

Abbé J. A. Dubois, *Hindu Manners, Customs, and Ceremonies*, 3rd ed., and reprints. Oxford, 1906. Still the most exhaustive treatment of a subject scarcely touched on in this book.

J. H. Hutton, *Caste in India*, Cambridge, 1946, reprinted Oxford, 1951. An up-to-date study from a social anthropologist's point of view.

L. S. S. O'Malley, *Indian Caste Customs*, Cambridge, 1932. A short introduction to the caste system.

—— *Popular Hinduism*, Cambridge, 1935. A good brief account of the religion and superstitions of the masses.

The Modern Period

Sri Aurobindo, *The Life Divine*, Pondicherry, 1955. Aurobindo's *magnum opus*.

J. N. Farquhar, *Modern Religious Movements in India*, New York, 1919. A standard work with a strong missionary bias, it contains a full bibliography on the individual sects and personalities.

Swami Nikhilananda (translator), *The Gospel of Sri Ramakrishna*, 2nd ed., Madras, 1947. The sayings of Rāmakrishna taken down by an anonymous disciple.

Sayings of Sri Ramakrishna. Madras, 1949. A short selection.

S. Radhakrishnan, *Eastern Religions and Western Thought*, Oxford, 1939. Perhaps the most typical expression of the author's eclectic views.

D. S. Sharma, *The Renaissance of Hinduism*, Benares, 1944. Probably the best account of the reform movements of the nineteenth and twentieth centuries.

—— *Hinduism through the Ages*, Bombay, 1956. An abridgement of the above with introductory matter dealing with the earlier phases of Hinduism.

Swami Vivekananda, *Collected Works*, 2 vols., Almora, 1915.

Gandhi

C. F. Andrews, *Mahatma Gandhi's Ideas*, London, 1929. Gandhi's ideas as seen by a close Christian friend.

L. Fischer, *The Life of Mahatma Gandhi*, London, 1951. A complete and balanced biography.

M. K. Gandhi, *Autobiography—The Story of My Experiments with Truth*, 2nd ed. and reprints, Ahmedabad, 1940. Stops short at 1920, but is an invaluable guide to Gandhi's spiritual development.

—— *Hindu Dharma*, Ahmedabad, 1950. A selection from Gandhi's religious writings.

Rabindranath Tagore

R. Tagore, *The Religion of Man*, London, 1931. Tagore's Hibbert Lectures for 1930.

—— *Sadhanā*, London, 1915. The most succinct statement of Tagore's views.

—— *Towards Universal Man*, London, 1961. A selection of his most typical writings.

K. Kripalani, *Rabindranath Tagore: A Biography*, London, 1962.

Index

Ābhangas, 143
Absolute, the, 51, 55, 77; and
   God, 142; as God, 83–84;
   identified with soul, 7, 21, 39,
   52, 54, 74, 80; paths to, 125;
   Śiva as, 87. *See* Brahman,
   Brahman-Ātman identification
Adhyātma-Rāmāyana, 92
Ādi-Granth, 140, 141
Ādi Samāj, 153
Aditi, 27
Ādityas, 26
Advaita Vedānta, 73, **75–78**, 80,
   89, 90, 135, 188; Advaitins,
   129, 142, 143, 162, 175
Āgamas, 87, 130
Agni, 18, **19, 20**, 22, 26, 28, 39,
   44, 45, 49, 57, 157
Ahiṁsā ('non-violence'), 71, 111,
   113, 127, 128, 129, 135, 145,
   170, 173, 174, 175, 176, 177,
   179, 182, 183
Ahura Mazdāh, 26
Akbar, 137
Al-Birūnī, 4, 6, 186
All, the, 22, 41, 43, 49, 54, 80, 91,
   191; being and knowing —, 72, 73
Ālvārs, **127–9**, 132
Amritsar, massacre at, 173

Ānava, 88–90
Antarātman, 74, 78, 84, 176
Anugitā, 77
Appar, 131
Āranyakas, 9, 38
Arjun, 140–1
Arjuna, 65, 77, 92, 93–95, 97,
   103–4, 107, 115, 128, 129, 130
Artabhāga, 60
Artha ('property'), 63, 114
Arulananti (Arunandi), 87
Ārya Samāj, **156–9**, 161, 171
Aryans, 14–16, 22–24, 108, 132;
   social classes among, 38, 49
Āśramas, *see* stages of life
Asuras, **26–29**, 30, 105
Aśvatthāman, 114, 117
Atharva-Veda, 16, 27, 34, 36,
   37–38, 43–44, 45, 46, 47, 48,
   49, 52, 57, 83, 86, 88; hell in,
   57–58
Ātman, 49–50, 56, 60, 80, 113;
   'eternal self', 9, 49–50, 53, 59;
   'Great Self', 53, 78, 125; in all
   things, 67, 69–70, 72, 95, 192;
   'little self', 78, 125; 'soul of the
   All', 49, 77, 78; variety of, 51.
   See also Soul
Aurangzeb, 136

Avatārs, 91, 141, 157, 163

Babar, 136
Bāsava, 134
Bees, parable of, 53
Being, 40, 41, 49, 51, 53, 54, 55, 63, 67, 74, 76, 77, 190; timeless, 61
Benares, 130, 139, 152
Bengal, 16, 139, 145, 161, 190
Besant, Annie, 160, 185
Beyond good and evil, 52, 61, 64, 164, 168
Bhagavad-Gītā, 10, 65–66, 67, 72, 77, 84, 92–100, 102–3, 120, 125, 127, 128, 131, 134, 143; Gandhi and, 172, 176, 178–9, 182, 183, 186; paths to the Absolute in, 125–6
Bhāgavata Purāna, 126–7
Bhakti, 7, 12, 66, 73, 84, 87, 93, 95, 98–100, 101, 109, 125–46, 147, 149, 155, 171, 188
Bhīma, 115, 117, 122
Bhīshma, 64, 65, 116, 119–20
Blavatsky, H. P., 159–60, 179
Boghaz Köy, 14
Bombay, 134, 155, 157, 176
Brahmā, 52, 86, 104; day and night of, 61–62, 90, 104
Brāhma Dharma, 152
Brahmabhūta ('become Brahman'), 93, 96, 97, 103, 126
Brahmacārin, 48, 111
Brahmacaryā, 175–6, 182, 183, 184
Brahman, 5, 6, 37, 46–56, 62, 74, 80, 89, 111, 113, 152; and soul, 54–56, 58, 60, 61; as breath, 50–51; as food, 51; attainment of, 54, 71, 78, 81, 83, 93, 95, 96, 97–98, 103, 109, 114, 126, 165; city of, 48, 54, 81; consciousness, 74; eternal ground of universe, 5, 10, 47, 48, 49, 54, 55, 60, 68–69, 93; eternal life, 54; eternal state, 6, 10, 93, 120, 126; first

cause, 55, 56, 94; Gandhi on, 175–6; in man, 47–48, 67; inherent in Brāhmans, 5–6, 49, 50, 109–10; Krishna as, 64; *nirguna*, 99; One and many, 49; primal matter, 69; Rāma as, 142; the Absolute (q.v.), 51; the All, 49–50; the One, 53, 143, 163; 'the sacred', 6, 37, 46, 51; the Veda, 46, 47, 51; two forms of, 55–56, 93
Brāhman class, 5–6, 12, 46–47, 104, 105–6, 111, 114, 119, 121, 122, 123, 125, 131, 135, 170–1, 173–4, 190; duties of, 59, 110, 138, 147–8; embody Brahman, 37, 47–48, 109, 119; gods on earth, 6, 47, 109, 142; hostility to, 138, 142; Kabīr on, 141; pretensions of, 109–10, 141; priests, 18, 22, 24, 148; 'real'—, 119, 144; slaying of, 123, 131; Tukārām on, 143–4; Tulsī Dās on, 142–3; Varuna as, 19
Brāhmanas, 9, 21, 33, 37, 38–39, 42, 44, 45, 46, 49, 50, 52, 57, 152, 157; Hell in, 58
Brahmanaspati, 40, 47
Brahman–Ātman identification, 39, 49, 50, 55, 56, 60, 67, 70, 73–74, 76, 80
Brahma-sūtras, 73, 76, 151
Brāhmo Samāj, 150–5, 161, 166, 171
Bṛhadāranyaka Upanishad, 39, 54, 58
British, India and, 12, 147, 149, 170, 172–3, 177
Buddha, Vishnu incarnate as, 91
Buddhism, 8, 42, 57, 63, 67, 70, 87, 121, 129, 131, 135, 167–8, 179; and *ahimsā*, 135

Caitanya, 100, 139, 144–5, 150, 153
Calcutta, 85, 145, 151, 154, 161, 166, 170, 190; temple of Kālī at, 85, 145

Caste system, (a) the four great 'classes', 17–19, 38, 59, 108, 125–6, 147–8; disruption of — in *Kali Yuga*, 104, 106; divinely sanctioned, 49, 102, 148; duties of, 97, 106, **109–11**; mixture of, 108–9, 186; origin of, 44, 108; (b) the developed system, 7, 8, 9, 12, **147–8**, 157; Ārya Samāj and, 158–9, *bhakti* and, 127; Brāhmo Samāj and, 153, 171; British and, 173; development of, 108–9; Gandhi and, 184; Kabīr and, 139–41; Kāpālikas and, 130; Lingāyats and, 134; Nānak and, 140–1; opposition to, 12, 130, 131, 134, 139–41, 144, 146, 148, 150, 153, 185; Prārthana Samāj and, 155; Tukārām and, 143–4; Vrātyas and, 130

Chāndogya Upanishad, 39, **50**, **52–55**, 80

Chatterji, Gadādhar, *see* Rāmakrishna Paramahaṁsa

Chicago, 167

Childlessness, 58

Child-marriage, 111, 134, 155, 157, 159; abolished, 153

Christ, 170; Brāhmo Samāj and, 151, 155; Keshab Chandra Sen and, 154; Rāmakrishna and, 162, 163

Christianity, 138, 186; Ārya Samāj and, 158, 159; converts to Hinduism from, 169; Gandhi and, 170–1, 176, **179–80**; 184; Hindu mysticism and, 129; Hinduism influenced by, **150–1**, 153, **154–6**, 186; Islam and, 135–6; its doctrine of hell, 101; its missions, 12, **149–51**, 155, 156, 160, 163–4, 166, 170, 179, 184; *Śaiva Siddhānta* and, 88; Vivekānanda and, 167–8

Civil Disobedience campaign, **172–4**, 177

Classes, Four, *see* Caste system

Cows, sanctity of, 117, 131–2, 158; Gandhi on, 185

Creation, 28, **38–44**, 56, **61–62**, 77, 104

Creation hymns, 41–42, 43, 81–82

Cremation, 57, 138

Dakshineśvar, 161, 163

Dāsas, 23, 24, 27

Dasgupta, S., 128

Dasyus, 23

Datta Narendranāth, *see* Vivekānanda

Dayānanda Sarasvatī, Swami, **156–9**, 171

De Nobili, 112

Delhi, Sultanate of, 136

Devārām, 130

Devas, 26–27

Dharma, the god, 11, 108, 119, 121–2, 124

Dharma, 4, 5, 6, 8, 13, 29, 30, 35, 44, 62, 66, 78, 88, 91, 94, 97, **102–24**, 148, 165, 178, 179, 180, 189–90; absolute moral order, 8; and *moksha*, 6, 7, 12, 64, 96, 175, 184, 188, 190, 191–2; conscience, 9, 64, 121, 124, 149, 171, 190, 192; duty, 11, 66, 102; etymology of, 2; fetters of, 32, 118; *habitus* of cosmos, 41; Hindu —, 42, 109, 112, 135, 137, 155, 156, 163, 183, 184; *Kshatriya* —, 110, 116, 118, 121–2, 124, 172; law, 2, 6, 7–8, 9, 10, 27, 41, 65; of caste, 98, 103; of the Brāhmans, 47, 64, 110, 126, 171, 172, 173, 174; religion, 2, 184; right order, 18; righteousness, 11, 63–64, 81, 131, 171, 184; transcending of, 52, 64, 65, 98; Yudhishthira and, 115–24

Dhṛtarāshtra, 107, 108, 118

Draupadī, 111, 118, 122, 124

Dravidians, 127

Dreamless sleep, 56, 74
Drona, 114, 117, 120
Dualism, 100
Dumézil, 18
Durgā, 16, 85, 145
Duryodhana, 107–8, 118, 124
Dvāpara age, 62
Dyaus, 19

Education, 158
Ekanāth, 139, 143
Existence, categories of, 67–69

Faith, 96, 122
Fate, 103, 105, 106–7, 116
'Fathers', 45, 58
Fig-tree, parable of, 54
Fischer, Louis, 177
Food, as Brahman, 51–52
Forgiveness, 32, 96

Gandhāra, 54
Gandhi, Mahātma, 170–86, 190,
    191; and Brāhmans, 173–5; and
    Christianity, 170, 179, 180, 184;
    and Hinduism, 183–5; and
    Islam, 179–80; and untouch-
    ability, 171, 173–4, 182–3, 184,
    186; his āśram, 176, 181–3; his
    God, 171–2, 180–2; on Scrip-
    ture, 171
Ganesha, 177
Ganges, 124, 132
Gaudapāda, 73
Ghose, Śrī Aurobindo, 187
Ghūrids, 136
Gobind Singh, 140–1
God, 1, 2, 7, 11, 40, 42, 43, 47, 55,
    80–101, 103, 104, 106, 107, 136,
    139, 140, 171, 176, 177, 178,
    180, 188, 191, 192; and Brah-
    man, 77, 78, 81–82, 83, 93–94,
    95–96, 103, 141–2; as father, 90,
    134, 154; as love, 88, 171; as
    Truth, 13, 171, 174–5, 181;
    contemplation of, 71–72, 126;
    deified by Draupadī, 118; devo-

tion to, 66, 93, 95, 96, 98, 109,
    127, 138, 144, 177; faith in, 96;
    Gandhi's, 171, 180–2; grace of,
    see Grace; his activity, 102–3,
    106; his will, 107–8, 126; in
    Advaita Vedānta, 75–77; in
    Bhagavad-Gītā, 92–99; in
    Śaiva Siddhānta, 88–91; in
    Śvetāśvatara Upanishad, 80–84;
    in Yoga system, 71–73; incar-
    nate, 65, 91–93, 99, 116–18, 122,
    126–7, 139, 141, 143, 154; Inner
    Self, 81, 83; love of, 10, 12, 65,
    87, 88–91, 92–93, 97–100, 127–
    34, 138–9, 144–6, 165; Madhva
    on, 100; Rāmakrishna on, 164–
    6; Rāmānuja on, 98–101; union
    with, 78, 79, 90–91, 98, 107,
    126, 143; worship of, 73, 81, 84,
    96, 98, 127, 138, 165, 192
'God-realization', 164
Golden Seed, 41, 46
Gopis, 127, 129, 145, 162
Grace, 66, 84, 88, 89, 92, 96,
    129–34, 168
Granth-Sāhib, 141
Great Epic, see Mahābhārata
Gross elements, 68
Gunas, 69–70, 111
Guru, 72, 74, 90, 111, 138, 140–1;
    God as, 71

Hanuman, 177
Harappā, 15; seals, 16, 34, 84
Hari-hara, 84
Harijans, see Untouchables
Harivaṁśa, 126
Heard, Gerald, 169
Heaven, 57, 60, 62, 94, 105, 107,
    172
Hell, 57, 60, 62, 101, 104–5, 124,
    141, 172
Hindī, 137, 141
Hinduism, passim; definition of,
    1, 3–4
Hinduism through the Ages, 163
'House of Worship', 137

Huxley, Aldous, 169

Image-worship, 134, 136, 150–1,
  153, 155, 156, 157, 158, 161,
  180, 183–4
India, British and, 12, 147, 149,
  159, 170, 172–3, 177; Muslim
  invasion of, 135–7; partition of,
  159, 178; pre-Aryan civilization
  of, 15; vernacular languages of,
  12
Indra, 14, 18, 19, 22–29, 30, 32,
  34–35, 36, 39, 44, 45, 49, 74–75,
  94, 121, 123, 125, 132, 142, 157
Iśā Upanishad, 180, 181, 188
Isis Unveiled, 160
Islam, 3, 4, 6, 135, 136–7, 141,
  147, 158, 179–80, 186; influence
  on Hinduism, 149; propaganda
  against, 158, 159
Iśvara-pranidhāna, 71–72

Jainism, 63, 66–67, 70, 87, 121,
  129, 131, 176; ahiṁsā and, 135
Jātis, 108
Jesus, 180
Jñāna, 125, 128, 139
Jñāneśvar, 139, 143
Judaism, 1, 156, 186; Islam and,
  136

Kabīr, 131, 137, 139–41, 180
Kaivalyam, 89
Kālī, 16, 85, 145–6, 161–2
Kali age, 62, 104–6
Kalkin, 91, 106
Kalyān, 134
Kāmu ('desire'), 42, 63, 115, 121
Kaṁsa, 127
Kāpālikas, 130
Kapila, 67
Karma, 4, 6, 35, 59–61, 62, 64,
  65, 66, 71, 78, 79, 81, 88, 90, 96,
  102–3, 106–7, 109, 118, 125–6,
  158–9; rajas and, 69; Tagore
  and, 190
Karma-yoga, 183, 190

Kashmir, 87, 130
Kauravas, 91, 94, 107, 114, 117,
  118, 172
Kausalyā, 143
Kaushītaki Upanishad, 51, 60–61
Keshab Chandra Sen, 152–4, 164
Key to Theosophy, 179
Kīrtan, 138, 153
Koot Hoomi, 159
Koran, 136, 140, 180
Krishna, 23–24, 25, 35, 64–65,
  77, 84, 91–99, 102–4, 107, 116–
  17, 121, 122, 126–7, 129–30,
  139, 142, 143, 145–6, 162, 164–5,
  171, 172; Rādhā and, 145
Kṛta age, 62
Kshatra, 45, 46, 49
Kshatriyas, 18, 22, 24, 38, 44, 46,
  47, 49, 91, 94, 107, 108–11, 118,
  121, 122, 124, 125, 172; duties
  of, 59, 110

Lahore, 157, 159
Lakshmī, 101, 130
Laws of Manu, 109, 112, 113,
  170–1, 173
Līlā, 99, 190
Lingam, 82, 85, 134
Lingāyats, 134, 151
London, 178–9, 180

Macrocosm, 4, 5, 18, 20, 31, 39,
  44, 47, 48, 49, 56, 68–69, 74,
  77, 178, 191
Madhva, 100
Mahābhārata ('Great Epic'), 8,
  10, 11, 23, 25, 63, 64–65, 82, 92,
  106–8, 114, 126, 142, 152, 176,
  179; moksha in, 77–79; Krishna
  in, 91, 107, 116–22; Śiva in,
  84–87
Mahāsabhā, 186
Mahmūd of Ghazni, 136
Maitrī Upanishad, 55, 63, 67, 73
Māndūkya Upanishad, 55, 56,
  73–75
Mānikka Vāśagar, 87, 130, 132–4

Marāthās, 137, 139, 143, 155
Mārkāndeya, 104–5, 121
Marriage, 111–12
Maruts, 25–27, 30, 33, 45
Mātariśvan, 19, 39
Mattiwaza, 14
Māyā, 90, 95; appearance, 75,
    142; creative power, 83, 142;
    guile, 28, 29, 31; illusion, 75,
    142; in Advaita, 75–77; in
    Kashmir Śaivism, 87–88; in
    Śaiva Siddhānta, 88; Rāma-
    krishna on, 165; Rāmānuja on,
    98; Śankara on, 75–76; uncanny
    power, 29, 30, 32, 104
Maykandar Karulturai, 87
Mecca, 141
Mesopotamia, 15, 16
Microcosm, 4, 5, 18, 20, 39, 44,
    48, 49, 55, 56, 63, 68, 74, 77,
    178, 191
Mill, John Stuart, 184
Mitanni, 14–15
Mitra, 14, 29, 30, 31, 39
Moghuls, 136–7, 143
Mohenjo-Dāro, 15
Moksha ('liberation'), 7, 42, 57–
    79, 84, 87, 90, 96, 98, 114, 124,
    128, 164, 178, 190, 192; and
    dharma, see Dharma; Bhakti
    and, 145, 146; meaning of, 5–7,
    12, 35, 55, 80, 83, 93, 138; Rāmā-
    nuja on, 99
Monism, 12, 38, 52, 53, 55, 73,
    74, 75, 162, 165
Monotheism, 153, 155, 164, 179
Morya, 159
Mother-goddess, 16, 146, 161–2,
    164, 167, 188
Motor organs, 68
Muhammad, 162
Muhammadanism, *see* Islam,
    Muslims
Muslims, 136–7, 147, 159, 162,
    177

Naciketas, 64

Nāmdev, 139, 143
Nāmm'ālvār, 128–9
Nānak, 137, 139, 140–1
Nandin, 86
Nara, 65
Nārāyana, 65, 91, 165
Nāsatyas, 14
Natarāja, 85
'Navel of the earth', 20, 44
Neo-Vedāntism, 73, 169
Nietzsche, 168
Nimbārka, 100
Nirvāna, 67, 95, 116; of Brah-
    man, 95
Nirvikalpa-samādhi, 162, 164
Not-being, 40, 41, 53, 67
Number three, 19–20, 63–64, 114

Olcott, Colonel, 159
One, the, 7, 40, 41, 43, 49, 53,
    55–56, 63, 75–76, 79, 100, 165,
    168, 186, 189, 191; God as, 81
Outcastes, 59, 122, 127, 132, 148;
    see also Untouchables
Ox, hymn to, 45

Pāndavas, 91, 94, 107, 111, 114,
    117
Pāndu, 107
Pantheism, 39, 52, 67, 127, 139
Pantheistic monism, 10, 38, 40
Paraśu-Rāma, 91
Parvatī, 85, 133, 145
Paśupati, 16, 34, 86, 88
Pāśupatyas, 86
Patañjali, 73
Phallus-worship, 16, 85
Pilgrimage, 157, 158
Prajāpati, 40–42, 45, 46, 48, 74–
    75
Prakṛti ('Nature'), 67–69, 76–77,
    82, 83, 87, 95, 111
Prārthana Samāj, 155–6
Praśna Upanishad, 67
Primal matter, 43, 55, 69, 81
Purānas, 10, 12, 126–7

Purusha, (a) 'primal man', 40,
43–45, 46, 47–48, 49, 50, 52, 73,
74, 78, 82, 83, 87, 108; (b)
'individual soul', 47–48, 49, 50,
68–69, 78, 82
Purusha-sūkta, 43–45, 47, 91, 108

Rādhā, 145, 162
Radhakrishnan, Sir Sarvepalli, 1,
187
Rajas, 69, 111
Rākshasas, 105
Rām Mohan Roy, 150–2, 185
Rāma, 11, 91–92, 112, 139,
141–3, 145, 162, 164; Hanuman
and, 177
Rāmakrishna mission, 73, 167,
169; order, 166
Rāmakrishna Paramahaṁsa, 145,
154, 161–6, 169, 175, 188
Rāmānand, 139
Rāmānuja, 98–101, 129, 135,
139, 142, 143, 192
Rāmāyana, 10, 11, 91–92, 112,
140, 173, 179; Hindi version,
141; Sanskrit version, 142
Rāmdās, 143
Ranade, Mahadev Govind,
155–6, 158
Reincarnation, *see*
Transmigration of souls
Renou, Professor, 18
Review of Reviews, 160
Rig-Veda, 6, 9, 10, 15, 16–17,
22–35, 36, 37, 39, 40, 46, 52,
57, 58, 82, 84, 96, 108; creation
hymns in, 82; Primal Man in,
68, 69; souls of the dead in,
57–59
Rope–snake simile, 76
Rshis, 9, 18, 45
Rudra-Śiva, 16, 19, 29, 32–35,
80–82, 83–84, 130; *see also* Śiva
Ruskin, J., 184

Sac-cid-ānanda ('Being,

consciousness and bliss'), 63,
74, 76, 90, 114, 168
Sacrifice, 18, 19–21, 28–29, 31,
36, 38–46, 58, 118, 121–2, 138,
145
Sādhāran Brāhmo Samāj, 154
St. John of the Cross, 129
St. Paul, 133
St. Teresa of Avila, 129
Śaiva Siddhānta, 83, 88–91, 93,
98–99, 130
Śaivite hymns, 130–4
Śaivites, 87, 92, 130–4, 138, 145
Śāktas, 85, 86, 130, 145
Śakti, 81, 82, 83, 86–87, 88, 89,
130, 132, 145, 164
Sāma-Veda, 17, 36–37
Samādhi, 72, 164, 188
Sambandhar, 87
Saṁhitās, 9, 36, 37, 38, 57, 152,
157, 158
Sāṁkhya, 67–70, 73, 80, 82, 89
Sāṁkhya-Kārikā, 67
Sāṁkhya-Yoga, 70, 73–75, 78,
80, 83, 90, 100
Saṁsāra, 34, 35, 42, 61–63,
66–67, 74, 82, 87, 93, 95, 96,
109, 110, 192; definition of,
4–6, 93
Saṁskāras, 148, 153, 154, 158
Sanātana dharma, 2, 3, 8, 157,
170, 173–4, 178
Śankara, 12, 73–78, 87, 100, 101,
135, 142, 143, 152, 168, 188,
189
Sannyāsa, 102
Sannyāsin, 113, 114, 157, 161,
163, 166, 167, 177, 180, 187
Sanskrit, 6, 12, 14, 137, 139, 156
Śānti, 128
Śāntiniketan, 187, 190–1
Śatapatha Brāhmana, 37, 50
Sati, 112
Sattva, 69, 111
Secret Doctrine, 160
Sen, Rāmprasād, 139, 145–6
Sensory organs, 68

Sermon on the Mount, 151, 176, 179
Serampore mission, 151
Sex, 85, 86–87, 132, 163, 182; Gandhi on, 175
Sharma, D. S., 151, 163
Shuppiluliumash, 14
Sikhs, 137, **140–1**
Sin, 28, 30, 31–32, 44, 96, 117, 132, 134, 138, 168, 177, 181; Śaivites and, 132; Tagore on, 191
Sind, 136
Sītā, 112, 142–3, 162
Śiva, 7, 11, 16, 32, 34, 35, 104, 114, 126, 142, 145, 146, 156, 177; and Śakti, **85–88**, 89, 132; and Vishnu, 84, 86; attributes of, **84–85**; *bhakti* and, **130–4**; fetters of, 32, 88; his dance, 85, 133; his *lingam*, *see lingam*; in *Śaiva Siddhānta*, **88–91**; ithyphallic, 15, 82, 84, 85, 86; male and female, 82, 85; *paśupati*, q.v.; Yogin, 16, 84, 85. *See also* Rudra-Śiva
Śivācārya, 87
Śivajī, 137, 143
Śiva-jñāna-bodham, 87
Śiva-jñāna-siddhiyār, 87
Smārtas, 127
Smṛti, 9–10, 12, 110, 126, 127
Society of Psychical Research, 160
Soma, 19, **20–22**, 24, 26, 44, 45, 57
Somānanda, 87
Soul, 43, 52, 63, 82, 83; and Brahman, **54–56**, 59, 60–61, 76–77, 93, 95, 96, 97; and *dharma*, 113–14; and God, *see* God; at death, **57–59**, 60–61, 94; at *moksha*, **67–79**, 95, 99; female, 127, 128, 145; identified with Absolute, 7, 39, 50, *see also* Brahman-Ātman identification; immortal, 50,

60, 61, **74**, 94, 95, 128; in Advaita Vedānta, **75–77**; in *Śaiva Siddhānta*, **88–91**; in Sāṁkhya-Yoga, **68–73**; Nāmm'ālvār on, 128; Rāmānuja on, 98–99; three classes of, 59, 101; universal, 191. *See also* Ātman
South India, 31, 87, **127–35**, 148
Spinning-wheel, 180, 183, 190
Śruti, 9–10, 92
Stages of life, **111–14**
Subtle elements, 68
Śuddhi, 159
Śūdras, 12, 18, 38, 44, 49, 95, 104, 106, 108, 110, 111, 119, 121, 125, 127, 142, 148; duties of, 59; in *Kali* age, 104
Sūfi mystics, 180
Suttee, *see Satī*
Svadeśi, 183
Śvetāśvatara Upanishad, 67, 73–74, **80–82**, 83–84, 92–93, 96, 130

Tagore, Debendranāth, **151–3**, 188
Tagore, Rabindranath, 175, **187–92**
Taittirīya Upanishad, 51–52, 54–55
Tamas, 69, 111
Tamil Saints, 31, **87, 127–34**
'Tamil Veda', 130
Tapas ('austerity'), 42, 48, 58, 71, 78, 113, 115
Tattvabodhinī, 151
Tattvas, 68, 70
Temple prostitution, 149, 185
Theism, 10, 15, 41, 73–74, 77, 80, 151
Theosophical Society, 159–61
Thieme, 17
'Third Dispensation', Church of, 154
Thoreau, H. D., 184

Three goals of life, 63–64,
114–15
Tibet, 159, 160
Time, 104, 106; cyclic, 4–5, 34;
fetters of, 4, 5, 32, 52; wheel of,
5; with and without parts, 55,
73
Tiruvācakam, 130
Tolstoy, Leo, 175, 176, 179, 180
Transmigration of souls, 4–5, 8,
57, 58–62, 101, 134, 151, 158,
177
Tretā age, 62
Trimūrti, 86
Trivarga, 114–15
Truth, Gandhi on, 174–5, 178,
181; Tagore on, 192
Tukārām, 139, 143–4
Tulsī Dās, 92, 139, 141–3, 144,
173, 179
Tvashtr, 24
'Twice-born' castes, 12, 38,
110–11, 114, 138, 153

Umā, 85
Untouchability, campaign
against, 173–4, 177, 182–3
Untouchables, 9, 12, 59, 109,
137, 144, 148, 150, 159, 177,
182–3, 185
Upanishads, 9, 10, 15, 21, 29, 38,
39, 40, 41, 42, 44, 46, 49, 50, 52,
53–57, 59, 60, 63, 67, 68, 69, 70,
73, 74, 76, 77, 82, 96, 97, 113,
125, 151, 186; Dayānanda and,
157–8; interpretation of, 152;
pantheism of, 127, 189. *See also*
Bṛhadāranyaka, *Chāndogya*,
Iśā, *Maitrī*, *Māndūkya*, *Praśna*,
Śvetāśvatara

Vāc, 46
Vaishnavacaran, 165
Vaishnavites, 87, 100, 104, 145
Vaiśyas, 18, 38, 44, 108, 111,
125, 172; duties of, 59
Vallabha, 100

Valmīki, 91, 141
Varnāśrama-dharma, 108–14,
147, 184
Varuna, 14, 19, 22, 24, 26–33,
35, 36, 39, 96, 157; his fetters,
31–32, 88
Vasugupta, 87
Vasudeva, 91
Vāyu, 44, 101
Veda, 8, 9–10, 12, 14–35, 110,
113, 115, 131, 134, 140, 152,
157–9, 171, 172; the four,
36–38
Vedāngas, 131
Vedānta, 7, 12, 63, 129, 152,
168; 'end of Veda', 38, 73. *See
also Advaita*, *Viśishtādvaita*
Vedānta-sūtras, 73
Vedāntins, 100, 128
Vidura, 114–15
Vijayanagar, 136
Vīra-Śaivas, *see* Lingāyats
Vishnu, 7, 11, 19, 34, 35, 78, 84,
85, 86, 91–92, 101, 104, 129–30,
142; incarnations of, 11, 91,
126, 142. *See also* Krishna,
Rāma
Viśishtādvaita, 73, 100
Viśvakarman, 40
Viśvāmitra, 122
Vivekānanda, Swami, 166–9,
187, 188
Vrātyas, 130
Vṛtra, 22–24, 25, 26, 28, 29

'Way of the Fathers', 58–59
'Way of the gods', 58–59, 60
Western civilization, 150, 155
Widows, burning of, 112, 118,
149, 185; abolished, 151;
remarriage of, 134, 149, 153,
155, 158, 185
Women, position of, 12, 111–13,
134, 149, 157–8; *bhakti* open to,
95; emancipation of, 153;
Gandhi and, 175; in *Kali* age,
104; Rāmakrishna and, 163;

Women, position of—*cont.*
Tulsī Dās and, 142–3; veiling
of, 137
World Parliament of Religions,
167
World-Soul, 52, 53, 70

Yādavas, 91
Yājñavalkya, 59
Yajur-veda, 17, 36–37
Yakshas, 105
Yoga, 51, 67, **70–74**, 82, 84, 114,

162, 183; Nāmm'ālvār and,
128; *Yoga-darśana*, 70
Yoga-sūtras, 71–73, 84, 126, 129
Yogins, 16, 34, 89, 95, 128
Yudhishthira, 11, 13, **64–65**, 78,
94, 107–8, 111, **115–25**, 146,
149, 164, 170–2, 174, 178, 179,
184
Yugas, 62, 104

Zoroastrians, 136

OXFORD

MORE OXFORD PAPERBACKS

Details of a selection of other Oxford Paperbacks follow. A complete list of Oxford Paperbacks, including The World's Classics, Twentieth-Century Classics, OPUS, Past Masters, Oxford Authors, Oxford Shakespeare, and Oxford Paperback Reference, is available in the UK from the General Publicity Department, Oxford University Press (RS), Walton Street, Oxford, OX2 6DP.

In the USA, complete lists are available from the Paperbacks Marketing Manager, Oxford University Press, 200 Madison Avenue, New York, NY 10016.

Oxford Paperbacks are available from all good bookshops. In case of difficulty, customers in the UK can order direct from Oxford University Press Bookshop, 116 High Street, Oxford, Freepost, OX1 4BR, enclosing full payment. Please add 10 per cent of the published price for postage and packing.

OPUS

General Editors: Walter Bodmer, Christopher Butler,
Robert Evans, John Skorupski

A HISTORY OF WESTERN PHILOSOPHY

This series of OPUS books offers a comprehensive and up-to-date survey of the history of philosophical ideas from earliest times. Its aim is not only to set those ideas in their immediate cultural context, but also to focus on their value and relevance to twentieth-century thinking.

CLASSICAL THOUGHT

Terence Irwin

Spanning over a thousand years from Homer to Saint Augustine, *Classical Thought* encompasses a vast range of material, in succinct style, while remaining clear and lucid even to those with no philosophical or Classical background.

The major philosophers and philosophical schools are examined—the Presocratics, Socrates, Plato, Aristotle, Stoicism, Epicureanism, Neoplatonism; but other important thinkers, such as Greek tragedians, historians, medical writers, and early Christian writers, are also discussed. The emphasis is naturally on questions of philosophical interest (although the literary and historical background to Classical philosophy is not ignored), and again the scope is broad—ethics, the theory of knowledge, philosophy of mind, philosophical theology. All this is presented in a fully integrated, highly readable text which covers many of the most important areas of ancient thought and in which stress is laid on the variety and continuity of philosophical thinking after Aristotle.

Also available in the History of Western Philosophy series:

The Rationalists   John Cottingham
Continental Philosophy since 1750   Robert C. Solomon
The Empiricists   R. S. Woolhouse

OPUS

General Editors: Walter Bodmer, Christopher Butler, Robert Evans, John Skorupski

OPUS is a series of accessible introductions to a wide range of studies in the sciences and humanities.

METROPOLIS

Emrys Jones

Past civilizations have always expressed themselves in great cities, immense in size, wealth, and in their contribution to human progress. We are still enthralled by ancient cities like Babylon, Rome, and Constantinople. Today, giant cities abound, but some are pre-eminent. As always, they represent the greatest achievements of different cultures. But increasingly, they have also been drawn into a world economic system as communications have improved.

Metropolis explores the idea of a class of supercities in the past and in the present, and in the western and developing worlds. It analyses the characteristics they share as well as those that make them unique; the effect of technology on their form and function; and the problems that come with size—congestion, poverty and inequality, squalor—that are sobering contrasts to the inherent glamour and attraction of great cities throughout time.

Also available in OPUS:

The Medieval Expansion of Europe   J. R. S. Phillips
Metaphysics: The Logical Approach   José A. Bernadete
The Voice of the Past 2/e   Paul Thompson
Thinking About Peace and War   Martin Ceadel

PHILOSOPHY IN OXFORD PAPERBACKS

Ranging from authoritative introductions in the Past Masters and OPUS series to in-depth studies of classical and modern thought, the Oxford Paperbacks' philosophy list is one of the most provocative and challenging available.

THE GREAT PHILOSOPHERS
Bryan Magee

Beginning with the death of Socrates in 399, and following the story through the centuries to recent figures such as Bertrand Russell and Wittgenstein, Bryan Magee and fifteen contemporary writers and philosophers provide an accessible and exciting introduction to Western philosophy and its greatest thinkers.

Bryan Magee in conversation with:

A. J. Ayer	John Passmore
Michael Ayers	Anthony Quinton
Miles Burnyeat	John Searle
Frederick Copleston	Peter Singer
Hubert Dreyfus	J. P. Stern
Anthony Kenny	Geoffrey Warnock
Sidney Morgenbesser	Bernard Williams
Martha Nussbaum	

'Magee is to be congratulated . . . anyone who sees the programmes or reads the book will be left in no danger of believing philosophical thinking is unpractical and uninteresting.' Ronald Hayman, *Times Educational Supplement*

'one of the liveliest, fast-paced introductions to philosophy, ancient and modern that one could wish for' *Universe*

Also by Bryan Magee in Oxford Paperbacks:

Men of Ideas
Aspects of Wagner 2/e

RELIGION AND THEOLOGY
IN OXFORD PAPERBACKS

Oxford Paperbacks offers incisive studies of the philosophies and ceremonies of the world's major religions, including Christianity, Judaism, Islam, Buddhism, and Hinduism.

A HISTORY OF HERESY

David Christie-Murray

'Heresy, a cynic might say, is the opinion held by a minority of men which the majority declares unacceptable and is strong enough to punish.'

What is heresy? Who were the great heretics and what did they believe? Why might those originally condemned as heretics come to be regarded as martyrs and cherished as saints?

Heretics, those who dissent from orthodox Christian belief, have existed at all times since the Christian Church was founded and the first Christians became themselves heretics within Judaism. From earliest times too, politics, orthodoxy, and heresy have been inextricably entwined—to be a heretic was often to be a traitor and punishable by death at the stake— and heresy deserves to be placed against the background of political and social developments which shaped it.

This book is a vivid combination of narrative and comment which succeeds in both re-creating historical events and elucidating the most important—and most disputed—doctrines and philosophies.

Also in Oxford Paperbacks:

Christianity in the West 1400–1700   John Bossy
John Henry Newman: A Biography   Ian Ker
Islam: The Straight Path   John L. Esposito